The Legend of **RED KLOTZ**

How Basketball's Loss Leader
Won Over the World—14,000 Times

TIM KELLY

COMTEQ
PUBLISHING
MARGATE, NEW JERSEY

Margate, New Jersey

A division of ComteQ Communications, LLC

www.ComteQpublishing.com

Printed in the United States
10 9 8 7 6 5 4 3 2 1

ISBN 978-1-935232-75-9

ComteQ Publishing
101 N. Washington Ave. • Suite 1B
Margate, New Jersey 08402
609-487-9000 • Fax 609-487-9099
Email: publisher@ComteQpublishing.com

Book & cover design by Rob Huberman

This book is dedicated in honor of my wife, Gloria. She made it possible for my success in the world of basketball.

Red Klotz, September, 2013

For James J. Skedzielewski,
who taught me much about
basketball, life, honesty, and integrity.

Tim Kelly, September, 2013

Red Klotz in the early 60s.
Portrait by Wallace Seawell, "Photographer to the stars."

Table of Contents

By Joe Posnanski

As you will see in this wonderful book by Tim Kelly, it is impossible to sum up the amazing Red Klotz in a single story. But I like to think of this one: We were sitting in his office, and all of a sudden he said: "You know, I was almost on the cover of *Sports Illustrated* one time."

To prove this, he pointed to a photograph on his wall – it was a mock-up of a *Sports Illustrated* cover. Red Klotz was on it.

"They never used this?" I asked, already knowing the answer.

"No," he said. "You know what they used instead?"

"What?"

"A beautiful woman in a bathing suit," he said, and he smiled. Then Red looked out the window over the Atlantic Ocean like he had countless times before.

"What chance did I have," he asked, "against a beautiful woman in a bathing suit?"

Isn't that perfect? Red Klotz lost more basketball games than any man who ever lived. He lost games with the New Jersey Reds, with the New York Nationals, and with the Atlantic City Seagulls. He lost games with the Boston Shamrocks and Chicago Demons and Baltimore Rockets. He lost games with the International All-Stars and, most of all, with the ubiquitous Washington Generals.

He lost all these games to the Harlem Globetrotters, or, as he inevitably called them, "the world famous Harlem Globetrotters."

He lost basketball games in all sorts of places in all sorts of countries all over the world. He lost games inside and outside, on dirt and concrete, on sand and ice, on a battleship, and in a jail. He did not just lose games. He had his pants pulled down. He had buckets of water splashed on him. He fell for the hidden ball trick time and again. He chased after Globetrotters and chased after them and never caught them.

He also crossed that ocean outside his window too many times to count.

In the end, you find that winning and losing is what you make of it. There are countless so-called winners who cannot find happiness. Then there's Red Klotz, still with Gloria 75 years after they met on a beach, surrounded by loving family and a million memories, living in that wonderful house in a little beach town by the Atlantic Ocean. He belongs in the Basketball Hall of Fame for all the joy he's brought people and all the long jump shots he has swished around the world, but they haven't voted him in yet. Sometimes people miss what's right in front of them. Red Klotz lost games, but he won everything else.

"Look out there," he said to me, and he pointed out toward the ocean.

"Yes, it's beautiful," I said.

"You know," he told me, "every day it looks different. Every single day."

"Because of the weather?" I asked.

"No," he said. "Because of the ocean."

Joe Posnanski is a senior writer at the new venture, Sports On Earth. Previously he was senior writer at Sports Illustrated, and in 2011 was named National Sportswriter of the year by the National Sportswriters and Sportscasters Hall of Fame. He was a sports writer for the Kansas City Star for sixteen years and was twice named Best Sports Columnist in America by the Associated Press Sports Editors. Joe is the author of four books including The Soul of Baseball, the 2007 winner of the Casey Award, as America's best baseball book.

Red Klotz at age 88 in his Margate, NJ office

Red, (top row, left) with his first organized basketball
team, the Outlaws

"At guard, number three, Red Klotz."

There can be little doubt the most traveled player/coach/team executive in the history of basketball is one Louis Herman "Red" Klotz. "I have run more miles on more courts, in more countries, than any other human being," Red is fond of saying.

This is not some empty boast. As founder, owner, coach, tour manager, and star player, Red Klotz has played or coached, in a conservative estimate, in excess of 14,000 professional ball games in more than 100 countries during a career spanning parts of eight decades. The fact that the overwhelming majority of the games were on the losing end of exhibitions to the legendary Harlem Globetrotters hardly matters. Long before the National Basketball Association (NBA) was bragging about its globalization, Red Klotz was the most prolific foot soldier in actually laying the foundation. The NBA would not be comprised of 20 percent foreign players, nor would it have such strong international appeal, were it not for the groundbreaking work of the Globetrotters and Red's team, the Washington Generals.

"The Globetrotters should get most of the credit for making basketball the second most popular team sport in the world," Klotz maintains. "They couldn't do it alone. We were there too, and we were part of it. We helped pioneer basketball all over the world."

Red Klotz has played basketball in the Egyptian Desert, the Brazilian Rain Forest, and the Australian Outback. He has played on grass surfaces, dirt surfaces, and even the surface of an aircraft carrier's flight deck. Red Klotz has played before popes, peasants, and kings, Christians, Jews, and Muslems, decorated war heroes, and maximum security prisoners. He played behind the Iron Curtain, the Bamboo Curtain, and the curtain of security guarding the classified locations of American troops. Along the way, he conducted hundreds of clinics on the game and left just as many basketballs behind.

"When we got to most of these places for the first time, everybody was kicking soccer balls around. When we returned, we'd see a few (basketball) goals. And now…well, now there are baskets hanging all over the place."

Not only have international player taken over one-fifth of the NBA, so-called American professional "Dream Teams" have been beaten in the Olympics and international competitions by a diverse list of nations, including the former Soviet Union, its breakaway republics, and teams from Europe and South America. It's not a coincidence that all of these places first witnessed professional games involving the Harlem Globetrotters and teams featuring Red Klotz as player, coach, and owner.

"Absolutely, Red Klotz belongs in the Hall of Fame," says longtime friend Chris Ford, who won three NBA championship rings as a player and coach with the Boston Celtics. "People who think of him as the Globetrotters' patsy just don't get it. They don't see the very significant impact he has had on the game. This is a gentleman who has opened the game to millions and millions of people."

Of his 14,000-plus losses, former college and NBA Coach Don Casey said: "He should be in the Hall of Fame for that alone!"

Despite standing just 67 inches from the soles of his Converse All-Stars to the crown of his tangerine-colored locks that led to his nickname, Red Klotz thrived in a game dominated by giants.

He won big at every level of the game before embarking on a career that took him to the losing side of the scoreboard versus the Globetrotters. His most recent win over the Trotters may have come more than 40 years ago on his last-second shot, but his winning passion for basketball and life transcends all. He is a stickler for fundamentals, and for doing the little things correctly. He is prideful of his role as a leading basketball ambassador to the world, and for launching the careers of hundreds of players and coaches.

"I owe him everything," said the late Gene Hudgins, the first well-known black member of the Generals who went on to play for the Globetrotters. "He is an icon," Hudgins told the *Los Angeles Times*. "He's as important to the Globetrotters' tradition as the Globetrotters…"

"Opportunities were scarce for black players in the 1950s," Hudgins went on. "Red gave me the chance to play beyond college and to see the world doing something that I loved to do. He was like a father to me."

Despite such heartfelt accolades, Klotz' devotion to the game always has been overshadowed by his popular image as one of the most famous symbols for losing. He frequently is mentioned in the same grouping with Charlie Brown, perennial presidential candidate Harold Stassen, and the old Brooklyn Dodgers, who almost always came in second best to the cross-town New York Yankees. Pop culture references to Klotz' history of losing have turned up on Monday Night Football, the pages of countless magazines and newspapers, and even on two separate episodes of the hit cartoon series, "The Simpsons." "Ahh, the Luftwaffe," Homer Simpson famously intoned, "the Washington Generals of the History Channel."

But what is "losing?" Though the Trotters and Generals games are mostly about fun, Red has used his popular image to preach a serious message. "Losing's part of life," he said. "You can't lose if you are striving to do your best. They keep score in a game to determine which team scores the most points. They call the team with the most points the winner and the team with fewer points the loser. But if you tried your best and didn't score the most points you still won. Only one team wins the NBA championship. Only one team wins the Super Bowl. You mean to tell me every other team is not successful, just because they didn't win the championship? It just doesn't work that way. What matters is getting up. If you lose a game you can get up and try again the next time. That's a win right there. You learn that lesson and you learn a lot about life. If you can regroup after a loss and keep going, you're going to be okay."

Never one to take himself too seriously, Red shifts easily from the philosophical back into his familiar comedy mode. In December 2011 following four consecutive losses, NBA superstar Kobe Bryant said that he wished his Los Angeles Lakers had the Generals on the schedule. Red, with tongue in cheek, graciously offered to play the game. "We haven't beaten the Globetrotters in 42 years, so I know a little bit about what Kobe is going through," he said.

Red wasn't always a loser. He led his South Philadelphia High School teams to a pair of Public League titles and the city championship in 1939-40. The following year, he sparked the Villanova freshmen to a 32-0 record and starred on the winning varsity team in 1941-42. During World War II, he was a key member of the Army Transport team, along with future Philadelphia Warriors' ace Petey Rosenberg. Red was a member of an American League champion Philadelphia Sphas, a dominant pre-NBA pro team, and he won an NBA championship in 1947-48 with the Baltimore Bullets. He is tied with six other players as the third-shortest player in NBA history, and he is still the shortest ever to win an NBA crown. Hardly a loser's resume.

Klotz began playing against the Globetrotters regularly in 1950, and then with his own organization in 1952. He didn't stop playing professionally for good until the age of 68, making him one of the oldest professional athletes in history. Even then, he still packed a uniform on the road in case of being needed in an emergency. "In fact, I'm still available!" he chirps. He played competitively in half-court pickup games into his 90s, and when he stopped doing that after a series of strokes, he continued to go out on the court and shoot. His famous two-hand set shot, once the game's standard technique, is now a relic from when basketball was played in cages and hotel ballrooms. Red has kept the shot alive, with stunning accuracy.

During an informal conversation about basketball, the author offered that Pete Maravich was the best pure shooter he had ever seen. Following a pause, Klotz said "you mean the best one-handed shooter you ever saw."

Cindy Loffel is a longtime friend and the only female in Red's former group of pickup players. A former Division One college player, Loffel often was matched up against Red.

"He's another player out there I'd be trying to beat," she said, "and it was a real challenge to try to stop him. "He put so much into it every time he stepped on the court. It might be a fun pickup game, but he took it very seriously."

"Sometimes," Loffel said, "I really stop and think about what he has meant to the game of basketball. His contributions are truly remarkable."

Maybe Loffel hit on an explaination as to the reason why Red's Hall of Fame induction is still pending.

The man has one of the great under-appreciated legacies in basketball and until now, one of the last great untold stories in all of sports.

Red guards an unidentified Globetrotter during an early European tour game, 1951.

Chapter 1

Pardon Me, Shah

Where were the basketballs? The unsettling thought came to Red Klotz as he prepared to take the court with his Washington Generals and face the world-famous Harlem Globetrotters.

As owner, coach, and tour manager of the Generals, the Globetrotters' primary opponents, Red had plenty to worry about. Player acquisitions and contracts, hotel arrangements, and transportation were just a few of the major items crowding Red's plate. Locating the balls for pregame warm-ups? That was a detail left to one of his players. On this particular night, Friday July 22, 1955, whoever had been in charge of the task had let Klotz down. The canvass bag of orange leather spheres was nowhere to be found.

This wasn't a routine game among the roughly 300 the Generals and Trotters would play in a typical year. It was the second of two scheduled at the request of the U.S. Department of State in the politically and religiously-charged city of Tehran, Iran. The night before, the teams squared off in front of an audience comprised mainly of peasants. In attendance on this night was none other than His Imperial Royal Majesty himself, Mohammad Reza Pahlavi, the *Shahanshah* or, "king of kings:" The Shah of Iran.

There were no basketball facilities in Iran, as was the case in most parts of the world in 1955. The Trotters and Generals carried their own equipment along for such occasions. Along with the

traveling party went the world's first custom-built portable basketball court – a seven-ton wooden floor – as well as heavy steel
poles anchored by sandbags to support the backboards and goals.
If they couldn't bring Mohammad to the mountain, the Harlem
Globetrotters could bring a basketball court to the Shah of Iran.

Just as they had done previously in the British Isles and
throughout Western Europe, Africa, the Far East, and Australia,
the ballplayers were introducing the American sport to a whole
new audience. Not with intense competition, although that did
occur, but through comedy, music, and what would come to be
known as sports entertainment. This time, their appearance was
the result of a request by their government. They had endured dif-
ficulties and had made their way to the Middle East. The newfound fans of the game were eating it up.

Red scanned his surroundings for the bag of basketballs and
he couldn't help but be impressed by the scene. For a guy who
had faced the Globetrotters in bull rings, ancient Greek am-
phitheatres, and soccer fields, this was something altogether different.

At this relatively early stage of his career, Red Klotz had
coached and played in well over 1,000 games on the way to his
career total in excess of 14,000. He was accustomed to dealing
with the unexpected, but this was a new one. "We were outdoors
in a field surrounded by grandstands, and they were packed," he
remembered. "There was a low fence around the area. Low enough
that hundreds of people could easily climb over it...and they did.
The only boundary that meant anything was a line of armed Iranian military troops."

Red looked on in astonishment as dozens of anxious spectators
jumped the fence at one end of the field until the guards came
over. No sooner had they controlled the area than dozens more
would jump the fence at the other end. "This kept going on, with
the guards running back and forth," Klotz said. "They used long

wooden sticks to lash at the crowd and move people back. They weren't asking anyone to move. They were telling them with solid wood."

At center court, something else caught Red's eye. The Shah was looking on from a specially built royal viewing platform. The stands were divided, with the Shah's perch in the middle. It contained Pahlavi, family members, and an additional compliment of armed guards. "The Shah was isolated and was not mingling among his people," Red recalled. "He couldn't be among the people, because of attempts that had been made on his life."

Just a few years prior, Pahlavi's regime had taken over British refining interests in the oil-rich kingdom and nationalized the industry. The royal family had accumulated spectacular wealth while millions suffered in poverty. The anti-Shah sentiment was growing steadily and would explode in 1979 when Pahlavi left the country for cancer treatment in the U.S. His government would be overthrown while fundamentalists seized the U.S. Embassy and took U.S. citizen hostages.

The Shah's popularity had started to wane decades earlier. At a 1949 public ceremony in Tehran, an assailant somehow breeched security and fired five shots. One of the bullets grazed Pahlavi, and the would-be assassin was shot and killed on the spot by the guards.

Such history resulted in the show of force at the game, and despite the dangers, Pahlavi looked on in the very public setting to observe the American athletes. By his side was the second of his three wives, Malakey (Arabic for Queen) Soraya. More of the rifle-toting military officers guarded the area in front of the box, so positioned to serve as human shields, if need be.

A plush, bright red carpet ran from the edge of the basketball court to the steps of the platform. "Better to hide any blood that might be spilled," Red said, only half-kidding. "Things over there were a little jumpy."

Nevertheless, Red was at an age when dangers and hassles just didn't seem to matter. Why would they? Klotz was being well-paid to play a game he loved against a great team. Together, they were introducing basketball to millions of people.

The Generals were second fiddle to the Globetrotters and always would be, but Red's team was selected from the best talent available in order to push the Trotters to play their best. Through the years, this would mean signing more than two dozen players talented enough to switch locker rooms and sign with the Trotters. Some, like Greg Kohls and Bill Campion, were big name players in the college ranks, and a select few, like Charlie Criss, Med Parks, Sam Pellom, and Ron Sobie, made it to the NBA. One, Nancy Lieberman, became the first woman pro to play with men, and would be enshrined in the Hall of Fame. Red's efforts with the team would stretch over 14,000 games in 100 countries and more than six decades. However, on this night in 1955, Red's and the Generals' impact on the game was not at top of mind. The main objective was to get through the game successfully and without incident.

At the time of the State Department's requested Middle East appearance, the Globetrotters' brilliant entrepreneurial founder and owner-coach, Abe Saperstein, was on the verge of wrapping up his fifth triumphant international tour. Crowds were receptive and enthusiastic in places where Cold War propaganda had painted an ugly picture of America.

The all-black Trotters and integrated Generals dispelled many preconceived notions. Two teams shared the same court, laughs, and good sportsmanship in competition. The laughter and fellowship that was apparent deflated many ideas about racial prejudice and inequality. Some of the Communist nations were holding that African Americans had not advanced much at all since the abolition of slavery. It was true that race relations still needed to come a long way in the U.S., but one never would know that from what was happening on the court in Iran that night.

The tour's appeal also could be traced to Saperstein's intuitive sense of promotion and star power. The London-born, Chicago-raised Abe was the first person truly to understand and exploit the fact that professional sports were entertainment. In contrast, the NBA, spawned a decade earlier by large arena owners, had not yet gotten the hint. The NBA had plenty of basketball talent, but the games were slow and plodding, especially next to the freewheeling style and speed of play displayed by the Trotters and Generals. In an effort to boost attendance, Abe's team also was hired to play in doubleheaders with the NBA squads,

In an interview for a Globetrotters' documentary, Boston Celtics' Hall of Famer Bob Cousy talked about the folly of having the Globies open such twin bills. The owners would sell a lot of tickets, and when the Trotters-Generals' "preliminary game" was through, "half the house would get up and leave," Cousy said. That only happened a few times before the owners wised up and switched the NBA games to the preliminary billing.

At least 30 years before "Showtime" was coined to describe the 1980s' Los Angeles Lakers, Saperstein was dimming the house lights and having his players burst through a giant paper basketball-shaped Globetrotters logo and run onto the court to the strains of "Sweet Georgia Brown." Brother Bones' toe-tapping version of the song was blared over the public address system while the crowd clapped along and the Trotters formed their "magic circle" at midcourt. They performed all kinds of ball tricks and fancy dribbling, spun the balls on their fingers, and rolled them across their backs and down their arms.

Once the game began, the Trotters' usual method was to roll up a big lead and then perform comedy routines, or "reams," during the action. They always had a dribbling specialist and a dead-eye shooter who could convert long hook shots from a distance seldom seen in conventional competition. As if that weren't enough, Abe kept things interesting at halftime and pregame by adding jugglers, acrobats, table tennis champions, singers and dancers, and star athletes from other sports. The Globies weren't just a basketball team. They were a traveling variety show.

The fans responded at the turnstiles, and the Trotters became international sensations. The Generals' talents also were recognized with appreciative applause both at home in the U.S. and on the world stage. The little five-foot-seven flame-haired guard from South Philly proved to be a big crowd favorite. Red Klotz had the uncanny ability to nail his two-handed set shot and his nearly-as-deadly hook from long distances. Klotz also participated in many of the reams. His specialty was to chase the Globetrottters' dribbler in a well-choreographed routine, or he would improvise something on the spot. In between the tricks and comedy, the teams slugged it out in serious hard-nosed basketball played at the highest skill level. It was a winning formula.

"We made people like Americans wherever we went," Klotz said. "Language barriers and social customs did not matter in the slightest. We went into places that hated America, and by the time we left, they were bowing down to us. That's no exaggeration. Laughter has no language."

Said ex-Trotter and NBA star Connie Hawkins: "We were…the Pied Piper. Everywhere we went, people would be walking around, following us."

Basketball-wise, the product Saperstein rolled out was jaw-dropping. Though known as a flamboyant showman and promoter, Abe was a basketball guy first, and the Trotters certainly could play. By 1955, Abe was already in his twenty-eighth season. He had grown the franchise from a ragtag band of barnstormers who sometimes slept in Abe's car to the most recognized name in the game. They were champs of the pre-NBA World Professional Tournament, and consistently beat a traveling troupe of former college All-Americans in what was dubbed the World Series of Basketball.

Another watershed moment occurred in 1948, shortly after Jackie Robinson had broken through baseball's color line. The Trotters challenged and defeated the mighty Minneapolis Lakers and their six-foot-10 superstar center, one George Mikan. Fans wondered if the showboating Trotters belonged on the same court; they did. More than 17,800 witnessed a tense and thrilling 61-59 Trotter win at Chicago Stadium. Ermer Robinson's winning shot burned the net an instant before the buzzer sounded.

Dispelling any idea that the outcome was a fluke, the Trotters beat the Lakers again the next year, 49-45. This time, it was in front of more than 20,000, and they had a comfortable enough lead at the end to perform a few of their reams. Not only did they humble the Lakers on the court, they "put on the show" against them. Millions more saw it the following week on Movietone newsreel footage in theatres across the United States. The Harlem Globetrotters had arrived. They had made it not merely as entertainers, but perhaps as the best team in all of basketball.

The Generals had been the Globetrotters' regular opponent in the U.S. and world tours since the 1952-53 season. Previously, Abe's squad played against whatever opponent was available. As a result, the Trotters often thrashed a squad of overmatched locals. This did not make for great community relations or for ticket sales on a return visit.

Abe knew Red Klotz was the right man with whom to forge a good working relationship. He became acquainted with Red as a man who shared his deep passion for the game, strong sense of responsibility, and the understanding of what made a good Globetrotter show. Initially, he had seen Klotz perform for the Philadelphia Sphas in back-to-back wins over his team in 1942, and an overtime battle when Red was coaching the Cumberland (Maryland) Dukes of the All-American League. Over the years, he also faced Saperstein with the Sphas' touring team and the U.S. All-Stars squad. He knew Klotz always came to play and to press the Trotters to be at their best. At the same time, Red knew why people were buying the tickets, and he never got in the way of a ream. However, that didn't mean the Generals would roll over. "We were going to make them earn every field goal and make them respect us."

The Generals' formation was the start of a very strong professional marriage. "Abe and I understood one another. He knew I would never miss a date and that we would be excellent representatives of the United States overseas. We didn't have guys who got into trouble. If one of my guys did, I sent them home."

The State Department took notice and saw the chance for the group to serve as informal ambassadors. They were asked to play behind the Iron Curtain in Berlin, Germany, and across North Africa. It happened again in 1955 in the political and religious tinderbox of the Middle East.

Abe, always up to the challenge, was a patriot who answered his government's call. He was also an inveterate traveler who loved seeing new places, and experiencing new cultures. The more exotic the locale, the more eager Saperstein was to take his Globetrotters and Red's Generals. For his part, Klotz was excited to grow his organization and to see the world himself.

As he came off the Generals' first trip to Israel that summer, Red wrote to his wife Gloria in Atlantic City: "State Department met us here after the Iranian Air Force picked us up in Bagdad, Iraq in old C-47 paratroop planes," he penned on the stationery of Tehran's Darband Hotel. Six days earlier in Libya, he wrote: "Feel fine although the heat is terrible. The government of the USA asked us to play in Iran and Iraq. It's only 125 degrees there and going up."

The action was hot on the court, also. Among other stars on the '55 squad, the Globetrotters featured Reece "Goose" Tatum. A six-foot-four forward and the original "Clown Prince of Basketball," Tatum was one of the most famous names in the sport, having played a pivotal role in the defeats of Lakers and entertained tens of thousands with his comedy antics. The Trotters also had seven-foot future NBA star Walter Dukes, dribbling ace Leon Hillard, and Robinson, whose long shot proved to be the game winner in the first meeting with the Lakers.

Klotz had a star-packed roster as well. The Generals were an attraction in their own right, with former University of Kentucky All-American Bill Spivey, a seven-foot center who could launch ferocious drives to the basket and shoot with either hand. He led his team to the national title and seemingly was headed to the NBA until his name surfaced in a point-shaving scandal. Despite being cleared of all wrongdoing in a jury trial, Spivey was banned for life from the NBA by Commissioner Maurice Podoloff.

The NBA's loss was the Generals' gain. In Klotz and Spivey, Washington had the best high-low combination in pro basketball at the time. They also had Fred Iehle the six-foot-three forward from LaSalle College, the 1953 MVP of the National Invitation Tournament, and Curt Cuncle, and, a six-foot-three forward from the University of Florida via San Antonio, Texas. Cuncle had been named to the first team Associated Press All American team. Two hard-nosed six-foot-three brothers from Jackson, Tennessee named Tom and Bill Scott rounded out Klotz' formidable top six players.

On the 1955 pro basketball scene, there was the nine-team NBA, and there were the Harlem Globetrotters. There were also the Washington Generals. Despite losing every night and sometimes twice a day, the Generals were one of the 11 best teams on the planet. "People don't think of it that way because we lost, but that was definitely the case," Klotz said. "We could play with pretty much anybody."

Bragging rights and a loaded roster did Klotz no good without the basketballs needed to play. Where were the balls? Klotz thought again and realized the bag was most likely where he last saw it, on the team bus. With a shrug, he headed back toward the vehicle. Knowing time was short, he broke into a jog.

The bright red carpet leading from the court to the Shah of Iran's viewing booth lay in Klotz' path. Red didn't know it, but the carpet represented some kind of demarcation line for the no-man's-land in the eyes of the Shah's elite armed guard.

Red: "I got to the carpet, and the crowd became hushed. It was dead silent. And then there was this ear-piercing scream from someone in the crowd. It was like something out of a horror picture. It was a scream that could've made your blood run cold. The next thing I knew, I found myself staring down the barrels of the guards' rifles. You could say people were a little on edge."

Klotz stopped running, inches short of the guns. "Somebody points a gun like that at you, it gets your attention," he said. "One more step, and they might have turned me into a big piece of Swiss cheese."

If Red was terrified, he may have been the only one among the American delegation. "I looked back at the benches, and the Trotters and all my players were doubled over, laughing! They were hysterical. It was quite an amusing moment, at least for them."

Klotz convinced the guards he was not an assassin and that the balls were necessary if the Shah was going to get the show he came to see. From that point on, everything worked out well for the second game in Iran. "We lost the game, the Trotters were great, the crowd loved it, and the Shah was not harmed. Oh yes… and nobody got killed."

Red (top row, third from left) poses on camelback with members of the Washington Generals and Harlem Globetrotters in Egypt, 1955. Abe Saperstein is in the white captain's hat front and center.

Louis Herman Klotz with basketball, age 2

Chapter 2

Philly Ball

The basketball journey of Red Klotz begins in South Philadelphia, some 6,208 miles from the site of his "almost" international incident in Iran. Asked about his initial encounter with the game, he pokes fun at his longevity: "My first shot was at a peach basket nailed to a wall by Dr. James Naismith."

Though sometimes given to hyperbole to make a point, Red's stock answer isn't that far off. Naismith, the game's inventor, published his *Rules of Basketball* in 1892, less than 30 years before Klotz was born. As a child, peach baskets were still a common sight on makeshift courts all over his neighborhood and many other urban areas of the Northeast. By the time Klotz became a star player at South Philadelphia High School in the late 1930s, Naismith still was active in the sport, helping to found the National Association of Intercollegiate Basketball.

Klotz' actual first shot may not have been aimed at a Naismith-installed goal; however, it was memorable in its own right and would serve as a metaphor for his seemingly charmed life in the game.

Growing up in South Philly during the Great Depression, neighborhood kids played every kind of game imaginable, and some imagined on the spot. If there was a ball, there was a game: step ball, wire ball, wall ball (also known as "chink"), one-bounce, and half ball. Most were variations of baseball modified for the narrow confines of Philly's row-house-lined streets. Kids also played sand-lot football and baseball wherever they could find room.

One day, young "Reds" Klotz – the nickname would be shortened to Red some years later – was chasing an errant football that had bounced onto the basketball court at George J. Thomas Jr. High School at Ninth and Oregon Avenues. A since-forgotten playmate flipped the basketball to Red and invited him to give it a try. Never shy to join in a game of any kind, young Red heaved the round ball toward the hoop. It came down cleanly through the cords, making that distinctive sound he would hear countless times in the future. "This game is easy," thought the then eight-year-old. He soon would learn quite differently. To excel at the game would require countless hours of practice and many scrimmages. Still, basketball intrigued him from the very start.

"I just fell in love with it…the physical nature of the game, but also the mental side," he said. "I liked the fact that you could have a game with your friends, and also that you could work out by yourself and improve. All you needed was a goal and a ball. You know that story about the kid who wanted to play so badly he shoveled snow off the court? That kid was me! There was more than one time I cleared snow from a court. I'd play all day, and when it got dark, I'd go to the end closest to the streetlight until I got used to it. I think that helped me develop an actual feel for the game. Later, when I became very nearsighted, so nearsighted I couldn't read the scoreboard clock, I could always find the basket. I had practiced and played so much under so many crazy conditions that I could feel comfortable around any court, the basket, and of course, the ball."

Basketballs of that era had laces on one of the seams, similar to footballs. "If I was open for a shot, I got to be pretty good at spinning the ball quickly to where the laces would be at my fingertips. It gave me more control when I shot it."

Virtually all players of that era used a two-hand set shot. Klotz shot that way his entire career and as a recreational player into his 90s. He could dominate games with that shot against players 65 years his junior. "The game has changed so much," he says. "It was much more of a passing game as opposed to all the dribbling today. A few things haven't changed, though. The best teams and the best players are masters of the fundamentals."

Though still relatively new, basketball was a solidly established "city game" when Klotz was growing up. Its birthplace is claimed by Springfield, Massachusetts, and the Canadian-born Naismith earned his coaching chops in the Great Plains at Kansas University, but it was the cities, particularly New York City and Philadelphia, which were ground zero for the explosion of the game's popularity. The game was well-suited for the confines of the streets, small clubs and gyms, settlement houses, YMCAs and YMHAs, and the schools of the urban areas. The Jewish sons of immigrants were among the best players, while the Irish, Germans, Polish and Italians also were well-represented on the playgrounds. "In our neighborhood, there were many Jews, and just about every other group, too. There weren't many blacks in that area at the time. They were concentrated in other areas of the city. Still, it was a pretty good example of the 'melting pot,' right within a few blocks of our house."

Professional ball was already in existence and gaining a following in those cities. Many of the best players were Jewish, coming out of pickup games, school teams, and community leagues in predominantly Jewish areas. African Americans had discovered the game as well and became quite proficient, though not in the same numbers as the Jewish players. The New York Renaissance, or "Rens," was the first well-known and accomplished all-black pro squad. Philadelphia's Sphas (an acronym for the South Philadelphia Hebrew Association) were all Jewish and won championships in several pro leagues.

Red Klotz was all of six years old when in Chicago, a Jewish immigrant named Abe Saperstein founded another all-black team he called the New York Harlem Globe Trotters, despite the fact they hadn't set foot very far East of the Windy City, much less Harlem. The Trotters had great players, such as "Runt" Pullins and Inman Jackson. Ultimately, with their name shortened to Harlem Globetrotters, they would achieve great success through Saperstein's sports and entertainment innovations.

However, the team's foundation for that success began with skillful play on the court. They beat almost all of the local teams before Saperstein began barnstorming the far West in his beat-up Model T Ford. When the nation's banks began to fail in 1929, Abe made the decision, "to take the team where there were no banks." It began a lifetime penchant for exploring new and exotic locales.

Pro basketball, though firmly established, was not yet considered a major sport, and the teams' exploits earned little space in the daily newspapers of the day. Baseball was tops (Philadelphia had two major league teams, the Athletics and Phillies). Boxing and horse racing were the other top spectator sports, followed by college football. "Pro" basketball players of that time earned a few extra grocery dollars but not a living. Everyone had a day job, and games were played mostly on weekends. To a star-struck boy growing up playing in the shadow of some of the sport's early pioneers, there was no better place to be. Klotz' Jewish parents had emigrated from Russia to an area with a strong Jewish presence, along with many other ethnic groups.

"Harry Litwak was my idol," Klotz said of the Sphas' star player, Philadelphia Warriors assistant coach, and longtime head coach at Temple University. Litwak was a South Philly native like Klotz and is enshrined in the Hall of Fame. "We thought of the Sphas the way kids today think of the Lakers or the Celtics. They represented the best. We wanted to be just like them."

Though Klotz didn't realize it at the time, he was learning the game in a true cradle of the sport. Not only was South Philly home to Litwak, the schoolyard at Thomas Jr. High where Red sank that first basket was the workplace just a few years earlier of a Russian immigrant gym teacher born Isadore Gottlieb. He would become much better known as "Eddie," cofounder of the Sphas, organizer, coach, and owner of the Philadelphia Warriors, and one of the original executives of the Basketball Association of America, which became today's NBA. He was also an owner of the Philadelphia Stars baseball team of the Negro Leagues, and a promoter of boxing and wrestling matches, semi-pro football games, and even women's baseball. A born promoter, Eddie was associated most closely with basketball and would become known as one of the sport's premier judges of talent. Red had absolutely no clue that one day in the not-too-distant future, Gottlieb would sign him to his first pro contract.

Time only has enhanced Philly's reputation as a basketball Mecca. The foundation laid by the Sphas was built upon by Gottlieb's efforts to found the NBA. He was instrumental in starting up Philly's first NBA franchise and the league's first champions, the Philadelphia Warriors.

Philadelphia was also the birthplace and home of arguably the greatest player ever, Wilton Norman Chamberlain. The "Big Dipper" would bring international attention to the city beginning in his days at Overbrook High School in the mid-50s. At just under seven feet, two inches, with the physical dexterity of a much smaller athlete, Chamberlain not only would revolutionize how the game was played, he would usher in the era of the "big money" athlete and the concept of basketball superstars as major national celebrities.

Philly is also home to six thriving Division One college basketball programs, more than any city in America. In addition to Drexel, which competed in a variety of Middle Atlantic Region leagues over the years, the city series league called the Big Five consisted of LaSalle, Pennsylvania, Temple, St. Joseph's, and Villanova. It would be in this nurturing basketball environment, perhaps the strongest in the world, that Red Klotz would develop his game, learn its many nuances, and ultimately carve out his own niche and contribute to the growth of basketball as much as anyone.

Louis Herman Klotz was thought to have come into the world on October 21, 1921. The birth certificate, located by his son Glenn more than eight decades later, would list a birth date of October 23. The certificate doesn't say exactly where, but the best guess is that the birth took place in the family's row home on Darien Street. A delay in the issuance of paperwork may have been responsible for the disagreement on the precise date.

Robert and Lena Klotz were the parents of two older sons, Joseph and Samuel. A sister had fallen victim to a flu epidemic that swept through the city in 1918. The so-called Spanish flu killed more than 12,000 people in Philadelphia alone, according to *The New York Times*. Officials speculated that large public gatherings such as a World War I loan drive rally may have caused the "bug" to spread so quickly.

In his earliest known baby picture, two-year-old Red is seen clutching a ball. "I was crying until the photographer handed me the ball...I stopped immediately. He kept trying to take it away from me, because he didn't want the ball to be in the picture. Each time he tried that, I began to cry again, until he finally gave up and let me hold onto it. As if on cue, I stopped crying, and he was able to take the picture."

When he wasn't in school, running errands, or doing the occasional odd job, Red's parents knew they either could find him out in the street, playing one of the aforementioned games, or at the Thomas Jr. High playground. Robert was too busy earning a living and serving his community as a volunteer firefighter to scrutinize the play habits of his three boys. Mom was a different story. The tragic loss of her baby girl had made Lena highly protective of Red, the youngest and smallest of the brood.

"My mother was a wonderful woman, kind and caring and thoughtful of all her children and my dad before herself," Klotz recalled. "When it came to me and the idea of playing sports, she didn't like it. She thought I was going to get hurt. She was always trying to put a sweater on me or fussing over the state of my health. She never embraced the idea of me as a ballplayer. She didn't even know I was a real player until my name began showing up in the papers and people would tell her about it."

In 1929, around the time Red sank that first shot, the bank failures that sent Abe Saperstein Westward in his Model T eventually led to an historic stock market crash and a scarcity of jobs. While Red was making his own fun with a variety of ball games, it wasn't much fun to be an adult during the Depression that lasted until World War II. Robert Klotz, a master carpenter and cabinetmaker, was much more fortunate than most. His skills were in demand, even during the lean times. "My dad was always able to keep food on the table," Red recalls. "We were not rich by any means, but my brothers and I never went hungry. We had decent, clean clothes, though mine were mostly handed down."

Like most immigrants who never looked back after taking the bold step of leaving family and friends to forge a new and better life in America, Robert Klotz embraced his new country and impressed his offspring with the importance of patriotism. His willingness to put his life on the line as a firefighter and to help out wherever possible at neighborhood functions backed up his words. Robert and Lena fled the *pogroms*, a ruthless campaign of violence led by the Czar's organized forces against innocent Jews. "My Dad never really spoke about the dangers he faced or all of the horrible things he saw," Red Klotz said. "He did make it very clear it had been a life and death decision. He was a very happy and considerate man with a great sense of humor. He didn't concentrate on a bad situation he left behind. It was about raising his family in a wonderful country that embraced all the groups, and to have settled into a better, peaceful life. He believed in the ideal that America was known as the land of opportunity."

The better life certainly included the very American concept of leisure time and the good old American road trip. "We had a Model T, and Dad always scraped enough together to spend a week or two every summer in Atlantic City. The car would break down, flat tires and the like, and we still always made it there and back (about 130 miles round trip)."

"Dad would stop the car along the way at one of the many roadside farm stands and markets in South Jersey. He would give us delicious fresh fruit to eat. Then we would finally arrive in Atlantic City and there would be the ocean. I thought it was wonderful, and I still do. The ocean gives you a different view every day. To walk along the beach…it clears your mind. When it was time to leave and go back to the city, I wasn't too happy about that. I always liked the seashore a lot better."

Seeing the beach, ocean, and bright lights of the boardwalk and its many entertainment piers, smelling the salt-scented air and feeling the fine white sand between his toes proved exciting. Red's world previously consisted of concrete, tall buildings, row houses, and the smells of Philly's industrial heyday. No disrespect to his biological hometown, Red always insists. It was just that this was the start of a lifelong love of the Jersey Shore. Atlantic City and environs would be where he would meet Gloria, his future wife, where his six children would be born and raised, and the place he considered to be his adopted hometown. For the present, though, Atlantic City was merely a respite. Robert would return and resume practicing his tremendous work ethic. Lena would tend to the kids and Red would return to school, errands, and lots of street games, especially basketball.

His newfound passion translated to more playing and more improvement to his game. Before long, he outgrew the games at Thomas Jr. High. The neighborhood kids were great friends, but

not at the same level basketball-wise. This being South Philadelphia, Red didn't need to travel very far to find the challenge of
stronger competition. One such facility was an indoor "cage" court
at Fifth and Bainbridge. Many such wire mesh courts were still in
use at the time, a throwback to when "cagers" were the norm among
basketball players. The cage itself was in bounds during games, and
bloody injuries were common as players dove after loose balls or
were shoved into the sometimes jagged and rusty metal.

Another place where higher-level games took place was at St.
Thomas Aquinas Catholic Church on Morris Street. Shooters had
to guide the ball at a low trajectory through a maze of wooden
rafters. "You had to adjust your shot to be able to score from the
outside in that place," Klotz said, and he was able to more than
hold his own. Red began to get to know some of the city's better
basketball contemporaries and they got to know and respect him
as well. Among the new acquaintances was a boy named Herman
"Chuck" Drizen, who, like Red, had traveled by public transportation to find games in South Philly. Chuck came from the several-
miles-distant Frankford section.

"Chuck Drizen was a guy I met through basketball, a wonderful player, and we hit it off right away. He really knew about basketball and was a very smart guy in general. We shared the love
of the game and became the best of friends. He was my best friend
for the rest of his life."

Not long after venturing beyond the confines of the Darien
Street area, Klotz joined his first organized team, called the Outlaws. The name of the coach is lost in Red's memory, but a photo
of the squad survives. The lads are portrayed against the backdrop
of a phony jail cell. "That was my first team, and we beat everybody. I was probably no more than 12, and I was one of the bigger
guys on the squad, believe it or not." The team picture bears this
statement out, as Red Klotz, who would grow to all of five-feet,
seven-inches, towers over most of his teammates. It wouldn't be

long before those behind the growth curve caught up and soon left little Red in the dust as far as height was concerned. This mattered little, as Red's basketball growth was light years ahead and would remain that way.

"I was probably one of the fastest guys in that part of the city," Klotz says with pride. "I may have been one of the bigger guys on that team, yet I played the same way I did when I was older and the shortest guy, by far, on the court. I almost always played outside the perimeter and controlled the offense. I wanted the ball in my hands, because I could get the ball to a teammate in good position, or I could score myself."

Nobody knows how or why, but the Outlaws caught the eye of one Eddie Gottlieb. "He found us," Red surmises. "Eddie knew everybody connected with the game in the city. As far as running sports in the city, he was the guy. They called him 'the Mogul' for a reason." Gottlieb's business savvy and promotional genius surpassed a razor-sharp mind for the game.

"Eddie was a businessman first," said Simcha "Sid" Gersh, President of the Philadelphia Jewish Basketball League Alumni. "He would have a preliminary game going on when you showed up to watch the Sphas. There were the Spha Reserves (a kind of farm club for the varsity Sphas) and youth teams." Gottlieb's team offered something else that attracted Gersh to games during his boyhood. "They had, without a doubt, the best hot dogs I ever ate. You had to walk up a flight of steps to get to the court (the Broadwood Hotel at North Broad and Wood Streets in Center City Philly was the Sphas' home). You could smell those hot dogs and the aroma kept getting better the closer you got."

Most famously, the Broadwood, which seated about 3,000 for basketball, was known for its dances after the games. "It was a very social setting," Gersh said. For a long time, the Sphas' games were among the top attractions on the Jewish social calendar. Gersh confirmed the legend that holds many a marriage took place after a meeting at the Sphas' game or the postgame dance. "Absolutely, that was the case. It was a place where people could come together and have a great time for not much money."

The Outlaws were called upon to play in several of the preliminary games. Red remembers watching the crowd slowly fill the seats while he and the Outlaws dispatched a hapless group of opposing kids. "We were a good team, and Eddie knew it was entertaining to watch a bunch of little guys out there who knew what they were doing."

For the youngster, it wasn't so much the game as it was the honor of playing at the home of his pro idols, the Sphas. "The Broadwood was the best. The Sphas were our heroes, and we loved playing there. Here we were, playing on the same court! There was nothing else like that place. It was a great atmosphere to watch a game or to play in one. Right away, I began dreaming about playing for them." Although the dream indeed would come true, it wouldn't come before achieving a different measure of basketball glory, right in his own stomping grounds.

Red's parents, Robert and Lena

Red, age 10

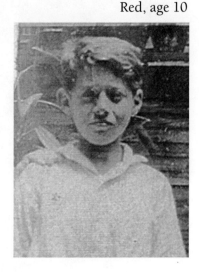

Red is carried off the floor by South Philadelphia High School teammates following a Public League victory over West Philadelphia.

Chapter Three

Southern Comfort Zone

Sharing the same Broadwood Hotel basketball court with his idols, the Philadelphia Sphas, did little to sate Reds' appetite for the game. Just the opposite, young Red couldn't get enough hoops. He played for community teams and participated in pickup games whenever and wherever he could. When he was walking around the city, he wasn't exactly walking. "I'd dribble around the trash cans and fire hydrants," he said.

With newfound buddy Chuck Drizen often in tow, Red always seemed to be in search of a game. He learned the intricacies of Philly's extensive public transit system at an early age. He knew what trolley car to hop to get to the right subway or elevated train to find that game. Chuck Drizen did the same thing from his house in the Frankford section. They would meet up at regular haunts, such as Moose Hall in South Philly and the cage gym at Fifth and Bainbridge. They also were likely to jump into games in lesser-known places.

If Red couldn't raise 10 players for a full run, he would play four-on-four, three-on-three, or two-on-two. If it was just Chuck or another playmate available, there were a myriad of shooting games to be played, such as "H-O-R-S-E" or "Around the World." If faced with inclement weather, or if nobody was around, he would work out by himself, shooting, rebounding his missed shots, and working on his floor game.

Other times, the bodies were there but the competition wasn't enough of a challenge. In a case like that, Red would dream up a "handicap match," in which he would size up the other players and spot them points. He always still figured out a way to win. "I would play '21' and let the other guys start out with 10 points. I would still outshoot everybody."

When he wasn't playing basketball, young Red Klotz likely was thinking about it or watching it. South Philadelphia High School was a dominating force in the city's highly competitive basketball scene, and Red knew that one day he would don the red and black of the fabled Rams. The esteem Red held for the local high school team was just slightly less than that of the Sphas. Located at Broad Street and Tasker Avenue, "Southern" High was segregated by gender, with the girls' high school housed in an adjacent building. It was unified by the student body's support of their powerhouse basketball team.

"Southern High was *it* as far as basketball was concerned," remembered Frank Raible, a classmate who resided on Oregon Avenue. "We got the biggest crowds and the most interest of any team in the city. I saw them play many times. They were great. They hardly ever lost."

Southern was the alma mater of Eddie Gottlieb and Harry Litwak, as well as Eddie's cofounders of the Sphas, Hughie Black and Chickie Passon. Petey Rosenberg, a future teammate of Reds' on the Sphas and a champion with the Philadelphia Warriors, would precede Klotz at Southern by two years. He didn't realize it at the time, but Red Klotz was assimilating into one of the strongest basketball cultures in the world, and it happened to be located in his own neighborhood.

"It was a very warm relationship between the players and the school," said Warren Jordan, one of Klotz' high school teammates.

Like Klotz, Jordan went by the nickname "Reds." "Everybody loved Southern High. If you loved basketball, you loved Southern High. And if you played ball for Southern, you were a star."

Howard "Ziddie" Trautwein was the Rams' legendary coach. He won 73 games and lost just 13 from 1929 through 1938. Trautwein's clubs would take seven Public League championships in the decade leading up to Red's graduation.

"I was fortunate to go there. Southern was the place to be as a basketball player," Klotz proclaimed. "Just making the varsity team and wearing that uniform was an accomplishment for any aspiring player in that part of the city."

By the time he had reached Thomas Jr. High, Red already was poised to add his own chapter to the local legend. Red would climb the fire escape ladder and sneak into the gym to watch the older kids go through Trautwein's strict marching orders and he would daydream about playing for Philadelphia's greatest high school coach.

Sometimes dreaming wasn't good enough. The precocious Red would surreptitiously make his way onto the court and jump right into drills and scrimmages. Trautwein couldn't help but notice the relatively tiny, flame-haired youngster who just didn't belong. Not only was he younger and smaller than the high school guys, he was far ahead of the older kids' development. "I couldn't just sit there and watch," Red recalled many decades later. "This was a real basketball court, not some goal nailed to a pole on a rough concrete floor. I couldn't resist. I had to go down there and play."

After slipping onto the smooth hardwood, Red provided Ziddie Trautwein with a preview of what he could expect in a few years. The little redhead was faster, a better shooter, and protected the ball. The coach would make his way toward Red, and before he could admonish him, the lad was gone. "I would sneak out the same way I came in, through the fire escape. I did that a few times and he never caught me."

Maybe Ziddie didn't want to catch him. By the time Red en-
rolled at the school as a freshman student and could enter Southern's gym through the front door, no introduction was needed.
"Ziddie might not have known my name, but he knew me. And
he knew he had a player," Klotz said. It was as if Ziddie was saying
to himself, "THAT kid! He finally got here."

It wasn't simply pure talent and the chutzpah of jumping into
practices that set Red apart. His mastery of the fundamentals was
a process learned over time and hours of practice. It was during
the junior high school years that Red met a teacher and coach who
would forever set the tone for his basketball career. Sam Cozen
would go on to mentor Wilt Chamberlain at Overbrook High before he became the winningest coach in the history of Drexel University (then Drexel Institute of Technology.) In 1934, Cozen was
cutting his teeth as an educator at Thomas Jr. High. Although junior high schools in Philly did not have formal basketball teams in
those days, Cozen, a gym teacher, found a willing pupil in one
Louis H. Klotz.

Sam Cozen was yet another Southern High basketball alum.
He possessed a keen ability to communicate the game's finer
points. "Sam Cozen was the guy who taught me what basketball
was really all about," Red would say. "If you are a great shooter
and dribbler, you still aren't going to amount to much if you don't
know how to play the game."

Cozen was very firm and a disciplinarian, yet at the same time
patient, Klotz said. "He was the first coach I had who taught me
that basketball was a thinking game and a game of decisions. He
taught me that if you do the right things it didn't matter if you
were the smallest guy out there. As a matter of fact, I could have
quite an advantage over the big guys."

Cozen invested his coaching talents in the eager and hardworking Reds, a true student of the game. Talent was evident in
Reds' speed and his uncanny ability to sink the two-hander. Al-

ready addicted to practice, Red now embraced the cerebral elements of the game. In addition to defense, boxing out, and distributing the ball to teammates in the most advantageous position to score, Klotz learned about faking, running off picks, reading the opposing defense, and making the proper on-court adjustments. Most importantly, Red was learning how to take charge of a game and make his teammates better. He still hadn't reached high school, and Red was learning at a level not just ahead of his peers, but also in some cases ahead of adult coaches of the era.

"There were so many little things to learn about, like waving a hand in the field of vision of the guy you are guarding. Everything I learned made me a better player. Situations would come up in a game and I knew exactly what to do. Sam Cozen was a great communicator. He took the understanding I already had and heightened it."

After leaving Thomas Jr. High, Cozen would fashion a dazzling 52-12 record in his first head coaching job at Overbrook in West Philly. He would guide many of the great Overbrook players of the 1950s, including Hal Lear, who would go to the Final Four with Temple and play in the NBA, and of course Chamberlain, perhaps the second-most famous Philadelphian ever, behind Benjamin Franklin. Cozen led Overbrook to several city and Public League titles before taking over the program at Drexel, where he stayed until 1968 and compiled a 213-93 mark. His teams won seven Middle Atlantic Conference championships, and he took four squads to the NCAA tourney. The basketball court at Drexel is named in his honor.

In the 1930s, basketball wasn't quite so serious for Cozen or for Red Klotz. As hard as Red would work on his game, he never lost sight of the fact it was just that, a game meant to be fun. "I kept coming back to basketball because I enjoyed it so much. The better I developed as a player, the more enjoyable basketball became. And of course, that was incentive to keep getting even better."

Klotz finally entered Southern for real in September of 1936. He was an intelligent kid and a decent student; however,. there was no doubt as to where his priorities were centered. Reds' yearbook entry lists one activity, basketball; one interest, sports; and one ambition: "to make the All American team in college."

The previous experience of sneaking in the gym as an elementary and junior high schooler had given Red an edge, yet Ziddie Trautwein was clearly in charge. Early on, the legendary coach took Red aside when he saw the youngster shooting fouls overhand. "We shoot fouls underhanded," Trautwein told Reds. "It gives you better control and you will shoot for a higher percentage."

"I don't shoot them that way," the normally obedient Red replied. "I have to shoot overhand."

"Well, you're going to learn to shoot them underhanded," Trautwein said, in a stern voice.

"I can't," Red persisted.

Trautwein knew how to break the impasse with the competitive boy. He challenged Red to a contest and the coach made eight of 10 shots underhanded. He flipped the ball over and looked on as Red sank 15 in a row. The coach stopped the "contest."

"You'll be shooting your fouls overhand," Trautwein said. The matter never was discussed again, despite Ziddie's insistence the rest of the squad use his preferred method.

As a sophomore, Klotz was the playmaker as the Rams went 8-1 and won the Public League Championship. The City Championship would not be inaugurated until the following year, but Red was still a big shot in the hallways of Southern High. He received the coveted varsity letter on the red and black wool varsity sweater. He wore it everywhere, even to the beach when the family went on their annual Atlantic City vacation.

Gloria Stein, who resided in the Inlet section of Atlantic City, took in the sight of the handsome tangerine-haired boy with a mixture of interest, curiosity, and incredulity.

The first thing I noticed were these muscular white legs sticking out from the bottom of that sweater," she recalled more than seven decades later. "Then I thought, 'Who wears a sweater on the beach in August?'"

Red has a vivid memory of the moment, too. "She was wearing a yellow bathing suit. I took one look, and that was it for me." He was 14. Gloria was 12.

Neither remembers who made the first move, although both agree the attraction was mutual. Gloria soon would attend Atlantic City High School, where she would be chosen drum majorette at the football games. The Vikings' basketball team was one of South Jersey's best. Wanting desperately to see Gloria during the school year, Red somehow managed to persuade Trautwein to schedule a non-league game at the resort. "It was really all about seeing Gloria, even though we beat her high school pretty good," he said.

"He was a basketball promoter, even back then," is Gloria's take.

In addition to his trips down the shore, Red would spend time in the summer in the Pocono Mountains. Cozen enlisted Red as a camp counselor and put him in charge of an area known as the "Nature Den," which housed indigenous wild animals, including a wide assortment of snakes. Red loved handling and caring for the animals. The summers at the camp developed and nurtured what would become a lifelong love of animals. He also learned how to fish, and he coached the young campers at basketball.

In Red's junior year, Southern's dynasty hit a bump in the road. Simon Gratz High won the Public League and defeated Southeast Catholic 23-13 at Convention Hall in the first Philadelphia City Championship game. The end of the season also brought to conclusion the remarkable tenure of Ziddie Trautwein at Southern. The popular coach moved on at the start of the following school year to accept an administrative position at a different school.

"Ziddie moved on to a better job. Remember, this was the Great Depression, and people had to do what was best for their families," Klotz said. "What it meant, though, we were left without a coach."

With insufficient time available to the school to hire an established basketball coach, the reins for the 1939-40 season were left to Dr. Richard "Doc" Ker, the head of the school's athletic department. Ker was a very popular teacher at the school and worked well with the young people. However, he was not much of a basketball coach.

"Before the season, Doc Ker took me aside and asked me what we could do to regain the Public League championship and to win the city championship," Klotz said. "We had uniforms that were rags. I told him, 'You get us new uniforms, and we'll win the city championship.'"

The coach held up his end of the bargain. By the time the Rams took the court for their first regular season game, Red's old jersey with the number three separating from the garment would be replaced with a snazzy new outfit.

Prior to the first game, Reds Jordan sensed 1939-40 was going to be a special season. In addition to the "all Reds" backcourt of Klotz and Jordan, the Rams had a strong rebounder and scorer in Irv Reichman, who would go on to play at LaSalle College. Len Weiner and Gene Dongiven also knew how to put the ball in the basket.

Reds Jordan: "We were invited to play a scrimmage at Lower Merion High School (a suburban school just outside of Philly). They were a privileged school district, and to us they represented serious money. We were from way down in South Philly and we had nothing. It was a practice scrimmage, so we just took our old clothes. We walked in the gym, they had a band playing, and everything was hustle and bustle. Their kids came out and they had these beautiful uniforms. They were tossing the ball around and the stands were filled with fans and everybody was going crazy cheering for them. We just sat there and watched. And then the game started. The first five times we had the ball, Red Klotz took the shot. We were up, 10-0 just like that. That was just the start of it. We blew them so far out of their gym they wondered what hit them."

The regular season played out much the same way. The Rams opened with a 37-29 win over Frankford High, Chuck Drizen's old school. Drizen had graduated in 1938, spent a year at Brown Prep School, and was a standout on the freshman team at Villanova. After the dispatch of Frankford, Red directed the offense as Northeast, Ben Franklin, Central, and Germantown all fell victim to the Rams' juggernaut.

With the exception of a six-point win over Ben Franklin, all were by lopsided margins. The Rams posted a 30-22 triumph over the reigning city champions, Gratz. They appeared headed for an undefeated year, but the hopes for perfection evaporated the next game when Southern had an uncharacteristic off-night and lost, 20-12, to Overbrook. In the previous games, Southern had averaged 36 points, a high number for the era, and enjoyed an average margin of victory of 14 points.

"When they took the court, they expected to win, and as a fan, you expected them to win," Frank Raible said. "It was the same with Red Klotz' shooting. When he shot it, you naturally expected the ball to go in, and most of the time it did."

Southern's success made the Overbrook game all the more shocking. "We rarely lost, and when we did, nobody was happy about it," Reds Jordan recalled. He said Southern's practices were businesslike, and one person was in charge.

"Doc Ker would walk into the gym and everybody would cheer. Here Doc would come, waving his hat, and everyone would greet him and say, 'Doc's the greatest,' and Doc would say his hellos to us. Then he would go over and take his seat. At that point, Red would take over. Red *was* the coach. No question about it, and Doc accepted that. We had a very good team, but Red was exceptional. He was the best player, by far, and he was our coach."

"I was the assistant coach," Klotz allows. "You have to understand, we all respected Doc and loved him. He was taking the team under tough circumstances of Ziddie leaving for the new job. All we were doing was helping him."

Following the Overbook loss, the Rams seemed to play with an even heightened sense of purpose. They blew out West Philadelphia and Olney by the respective scores of 30-16 and 44-22. Then Roxborough tried a stall on the Rams and held them to 15 points, but scored just eight. The close win set the stage for the Public League championship game on Tuesday, March 5, 1940, at LaSalle College in the Olney section. The Rams made Overbook pay for inflicting the only blemish on their record with a 33-17 destruction.

At that point, only Southeast Catholic, also referred to as South Catholic, stood between the Rams and high school basketball supremacy in the basketball-mad city of Philadelphia. Southeast Catholic (which became St. John Neumann before merging with St. Maria Goretti to become Neumann-Goretti) was in the midst of a run of three straight Catholic League titles and five over a seven-year stretch. They did so on the strength of a sticky man-to-man defense and the scoring prowess of their star forward, Mickey Hannon. It was also a natural rivalry, as the Pirates were the closest Catholic high school geographically to South Philadelphia High.

Game night, Saturday, March 9, 1940, saw more than 7,500 fans crowd into Convention Hall for the only the second city championship contest in history. They saw a battle that inspired *Philadelphia Daily News'* Bill Shefski to write about it 21 years later. "Over 10,000 enthusiasts attended a fox hunt (in Fairmount Park, the nation's largest such municipal park, on the day of the game)," Shefski wrote. "It's improbable they saw anything as foxy as the performance of Louis 'Red' Klotz."

Southeast Catholic took the game right to the favored Rams and initially confused them with a zone defense. "They hadn't shown a zone all season," Klotz said. "When they came out in one, we had to adjust to it."

South Catholic worked the ball around, patiently looking for high percentage shots before taking them. After scoring, their zone kicked in and collapsed around the Southern frontcourt. The Rams were hitting their shots, but they had to earn every point. The parochial champs had scouted Southern and prepared well.

Klotz took matters quite literally into his own hands. He went on a dribbling spree and read the floor to find creases in the zone. He would penetrate and dish off or stalk the perimeter and hit a cutter. "My job in that game," Reds Jordan said, "was to get the ball to Red Klotz. We had supreme confidence in his ability to put us in a position to succeed."

It was a tense game in the passing style of the day, in which possessions could last several minutes and low percentage shots simply were not taken. Klotz dished almost equally to his teammates. Whoever was open got the ball.

"I could outshoot anyone on the floor, but that's not the kind of game this was," Klotz said. "In order for us to win, we had to take advantage of the openings we found and spread the scoring around." Running off hard picks set by his teammates, Klotz made the Pirates work even harder on the defensive end.

"Red was just so fast and clever with the ball," Reds Jordan said. "He was a whirlwind and nobody could keep up with him. In trying, you were going to get tired."

Tired or not, Southeast stayed right with the Rams, holding a 19-18 edge in the second half before Klotz took over completely. "He had the strongest will and wouldn't be denied," Jordan said.

"We worked hard to get open and the first guy who did better be ready because the ball was going to wind up in his hands."

"Klotz dominated the game (despite scoring only) one field goal," Shefski wrote. Red was, "the spark plug of the Southern team," according to Jack Ryan, veteran *Evening Bulletin* reporter who covered the game. "In fact, (Klotz) was the difference between victory and defeat. His brilliant ball-handling kept Southern in motion and…it was not long before the Public High five mastered (the Pirates' zone defense). Klotz was on the front end of almost every scoring play with Irving Reichman, Warren Jordan, Gene Dongiven and Leonard Weiner doing the shooting."

Weiner and Jordan each hit key shots off assists from Klotz late in the game to seal the hard-earned 33-26 victory. The four starters other than Klotz accounted for 11 of Southern's 12 field goals. Hannon led all scorers with seven points but four Rams had six each. Their balance was just too much for South Catholic to handle. Reichman and Jordan Dongiven each had three field goals, and Weiner had two.

Klotz' box score line read one field goal and a perfect four for four from the foul line, shot overhand. "It was a true team victory, but let me be clear about something," Red Jordan said. "We don't win that game without the performance of Red Klotz. He directed the whole show."

Ryan, who was in the fifteenth year of a 40-year run covering Philadelphia high school sports, saw it the same way. "If there is such a thing as perfection in basketball, Southern High School reached that point on Saturday night at Convention Hall," Ryan gushed. "Led by the clever passing of Captain Herman (Reds) Klotz, the public high school champions defeated South Catholic, the Catholic title holders…and captured the Temple University Cup. The newly crowned champions hardly made a mistake and the fans who saw the game marveled at the smoothness with which the Southern five performed."

When the clock finally reached all zeros, the Rams hoisted Red on their shoulders and carried him off the court. Klotz shared a hug with Doc Ker, nonverbal acknowledgement that he had upheld his promise in the deal for the new playing togs. When he took the red and black silks off for the final time, which college uniform he would exchange them for became the burning question of basketball fans citywide. For his year-long excellence and performance in the championship game, Red was named Philadelphia's Player of the Year. Someone wrote in the school yearbook's sports section that Red would be attending Temple University on a basketball scholarship. First, Red would savor the moment.

"Looking back at things, winning the City Championship in a city like Philadelphia ranks near the very top of my list of thrills in the game," Red said. "When you are that age playing for your neighborhood, your friends and your high school, there is something pure about that. Today, knowing what I was fortunate enough to accomplish in the game after high school, I look back on that season and that team, and feel great about what we achieved. Winning a City Championship is something every player in Philadelphia wanted, and very few actually did it."

1939-40 Philadelphia city champions.
Red, kneeling, bottom left.

Coach Al Severance is surrounded by his Villanova Wildcats of 1941-42. Red Klotz (center, second row from the top) has arms around his best friend, Chuck Drizen (left of Klotz) and Joe Lord. Klotz, Drizen and Lord all started as sophomores. Former Philadelphia Phillies pitcher Maje McDonnell is second from far left, holding ball.

Chapter 4

Little Big Man on Campus

By the time he graduated from South Philadelphia High School, Red Klotz was an established sports celebrity in what was then the nation's third largest city. Among his fans was Temple University basketball coach James Usilton.

Temple, the city's public university located on North Broad Street just a few blocks from the Broadwood Hotel, was a major college sports power in the 1930s. While Glenn Scobey "Pop" Warner was guiding the Owls football program to major bowl games, "Jimmy" Usilton was pushing Temple to the very top of the nation's basketball pecking order. Usilton's teams were 195-67 in 12 seasons, including a glittering 23-2 regular season in 1938-39. They then went on to defeat Bradley, Oklahoma A&M, and Colorado to win the National Invitation Tournament. This was before the formation of the NCAA Tourney, and Temple was regarded as the national champion of college basketball.

Usilton was a shrewd a recruiter who always seemed to keep his program infused with fresh talent and Jimmy was salivating at the chance to turn the keys of his offense over to Red. What was not to like? Not only was the kid a winner, he was a coach on the floor. Here was a homegrown talent who could become a future cog in the Temple basketball machine's continued dominance.

49

In his own house, Red's parents were too busy earning a living and running a household to understand the significance of their youngest child's burgeoning reputation as an athlete. Neighbors began to comment, newspaper reporters came calling, and younger kids would elbow each other and say, "There he is!" when Red walked down the street. The Philadelphia *Public Ledger, Bulletin,* and *Inquirer* all carried stories detailing Southern's dominance and the little redheaded playmaker who made the Rams go. Despite all this, Robert and Lena thought their son was excelling at a mere childhood pastime. Lena continued to fuss over the possibility that Red could be hurt in the pursuit of the activity. When Usilton came calling, attitudes shifted on the Klotz home front. "When it looked like basketball was going to be my ticket to a free college education, her attitude changed a little bit."

There was clear justification for all the excitement about Klotz' ability. "In high school, he was master of the ball and the court," said Eddie Lerner, a former Southern High great who came along two years behind Red. "He was the best at finding open teammates for high percentage shots. He was ahead of his time and doing things nobody had seen before. Before Red came along, passing was mechanical and slow. He was the first guy I ever saw who threw a no-look pass. No defense could contain him. He was too fast with the ball and could find the smallest opening."

Red just approached his game as the way it was meant to be played. "Somebody works hard to get open, you reward him with a nice pass," he said. "That's how you make guys believe in you and believe in themselves and make a great team. It's just playing smart."

Usilton loved Klotz' brainy approach and wasted no time contacting him. There were no real college recruiting guidelines in those days, and it's likely Jimmy and Red had a handshake agreement. The Southern High yearbook and school paper both carried references that the school's star player would take his talents up

Broad Street to North Philly. Red says he was receptive and probably would have donned the Owls' cherry and white had a complication not arisen.

Nobody talked about it, and certainly no one spelled it out to Red. However, a quota system on Jewish ballplayers existed at many colleges and universities of the day. It was thought that Temple might have been among those. The incumbent backcourt star on the 1940-41 Temple varsity was a Jewish player named Mendy Snyder. Snyder was a very good player, good enough to play professionally, and he would indeed suit up for a number of seasons with the Sphas. "I can't exactly recall how they contacted me but it was made clear that Temple wanted me to play for a year at Brown Prep before they would admit me," Klotz said.

The common belief was that Temple wanted Snyder to graduate before the Owls unveiled a five-foot-seven guard who would dominate possession of the basketball. "Temple knew that if (Red) were to be admitted immediately after high school, he would have been eligible to play as a sophomore (freshman eligibility did not exist then) when Snyder would be a senior," one insider said. "Red would have had the ball most of the time, and Snyder would have done most of the scoring. That would mean the two most visible guys on the court for Temple would be Jews. Some people didn't want that."

Temple's alleged position didn't bother Klotz at the time, and it does not to this day. However, he was not about to accede to the Owls' wishes. Brown Prep was a basketball power, and future teammates were there during the 1939-40 season, including his best friend Chuck Drizen of Frankford, and North Catholic's Robert "Major" McDonnell. Still, prep school was not on Reds' radar. "I was ready for college ball," he said. "My grades were good. It wasn't an issue about the books. I didn't mind it; that's just the way it was. Other groups such as African Americans would be the victims of quota systems too. All I wanted to do was to play college ball, and Brown Prep was not for me. I wasn't going to wait for (Snyder) or for anybody."

After his own year at Brown Prep, Chuck Drizen arrived on Villanova College's leafy campus in suburban Radnor Township and immediately liked what he saw in the Wildcats' blueprint for basketball success. Villanova placed an emphasis on results, not quotas. The players, regardless of religious or ethnic backgrounds, felt at ease, at home, and welcomed on campus. This attitude was true of Coach Al Severance and the Augustinian Brothers who founded the school. It should be noted, that Villanova's roster, like virtually every other major team of the era, was still all-white.

"We were treated like royalty," said McDonnell, who, like Chuck and Red, was a former all-city high school player. McDonnell was from the Kensington section of Philly and would be a two-sport star at 'Nova. He would eventually choose baseball as his main game. McDonnell derived his nickname from the widely-held opinion the lad would one day play major league baseball. He was seen with a glove in his hand so often the neighborhood wags knew what destiny held for McDonnell. "People would say, 'There goes the little major leaguer,'" he said. The nickname "Major" stuck and eventually was shortened to "Maje" before McDonnell would go on to a 64-year career as player, coach, scout, and community ambassador with his hometown Philadelphia Phillies.

Despite his known baseball talent, it was basketball that opened the doors of Villanova for McDonnell. There was no doubt young Maje would be a baseball star for the Wildcats. "Everyone knew that was my best sport, but college basketball was already very big in Philadelphia. Villanova people wanted to make a name for the school, and they knew having a winner in basketball was the way to go. I was given a basketball scholarship. If I remember correctly, nine guys on our freshman team were given scholarships."

After Drizen became aware of Reds' Temple dilemma, Chuck immediately told Severance that his friend might be available to bolster the Cats' roster. Severance sensed an opening to steal Philly's Player of the Year from the larger, more established program. He invited Red in for a meeting right away.

Red: "Chuck called and said he told Al Severance about the situation, and that Al would be happy to have me. I went out there and met with the coach, who told me the same thing. I wanted to play college basketball. It was good to be wanted, and Villanova said they'd be happy to give me a scholarship, and that was it."

The young coach, who would build the program and go on to a 413-201 record over a Villanova career spanning 25 seasons, also taught business courses at the college. Severance was well-heeled in the business of basketball and how it enhanced the college's bottom line. For Severance, offering a free ride to the best scholastic player in perhaps the best basketball city on earth wasn't too tough of a call. "Just that simple, I was coming to Villanova," said Red.

The South Philly guy almost was overwhelmed by the Villanova campus upon his arrival. The lover of the mountains and the shore was blown away by Villanova's pastoral beauty, and it was just a couple of public transit connections away from home. It was a great escape, and it was almost local.

Red: "The campus was and still is beautiful. To me, Villanova was very appealing. It was also a very good school, even though that didn't matter much to me. I was going to class, but I was there to play ball. They wanted me to start on the freshman team right away, which also meant a great deal. Nobody said the words 'prep school' to me. They were happy to have me and were great to me, and I was very happy to be there."

Located along suburban Philly's "Main Line" towns, so-named for the direct trains in and out of the city, Villanova is nestled among some of the most exclusive communities in the area. The oldest and largest Catholic institution of higher education in the state, Villanova College (now University) was founded in 1842 by the Augustinians. The monastic order bought a 200-acre estate on which the campus was built. The school's roots go back to 1796 and St. Augustine's Catholic Church in Philly, which burned to the ground in the anti-Catholic rioting of 1844. The current church at Fourth and New Streets opened four years later and still operates as a parish.

Despite such tradition, Villanova's attitudes toward basketball were decidedly modern in 1940. Coached by Severance since 1936, the Wildcats had a beautiful home court in the Field House on Lancaster Avenue. Built in 1932 with seating for 1,500 fans, what would come to be known as the "Cat House," and renamed decades later as the Jake Nevin Fieldhouse, was state-of-the-art at that time. In the Depression years, the administrators realized the positive impact sports could have on keeping the institution solvent. In the sports-crazed Philadelphia region, with its large Catholic population, it just made good economic and survival sense to field a powerhouse basketball squad.

During Red's junior year at Southern, Villanova participated in the very first NCAA men's basketball tournament, winning its first game and securing a berth in the first-ever Final Four. Severance used his recruiting skills to mine the rich Philly talent pool. The fact that many of the best players of the era were Jewish did not impact Villanova's recruiting even a little bit. What mattered to Villanova was winning.

Though he was not a scholar, Red slipped comfortably onto the campus scene. It didn't matter to him that the school was all male at the time. He was in love with Gloria. As for classes, he attended, paid attention, and did the academic work that was asked of him. He doesn't remember what his actual grades were. "They couldn't have been too bad, because I was never in any academic difficulty," he said.

A family photo of Red as a Villanova student gave the impression the young man did give serious weight to academics. He is pictured in glasses, a suit jacket, and slacks, holding a book. He is almost professorial in appearance, save the ice cream cone he is holding in the other hand. "That's a great photo of him and quite telling," said Red's eldest daughter Ronee Groff. "The ice cream says more about my dad than the book."

Campus life consisted of basketball practice, recreational basketball, socializing, and studying, in that order. "It's not that I was a bad student, or that I didn't care. I was grateful to be getting a free college education. It was just that we loved the game so much and we really wanted to win."

Win they did. The freshman squad, not eligible for varsity play, appeared to be on par with the Wildcat varsity. In a published account, sportswriter Bill McBride hinted at what was to come: "Before the varsity staged its usual stretch drive only to find itself on the short in a 38-32 game played strictly on the scientific side, the freshmen polished off an intramural rival and looked as good as the varsity. With such standout youngsters as Red Klotz, Southern High's All Scholastic; Herman (sic) Drissen, Brown prep ace; Ted Rapella, Paterson (N.J.) star and Joe Lord, all-Suburban from Norristown, the material seemed deep enough to give Al Severance another fine year."

In actuality, the frosh proved better than the varsity, as the schedule showed them handing the big squad a loss. No article or box score was found from the game, however. The students caught on and freshman games sometimes out-drew the varsity. "We didn't just beat the varsity once in a game," Maje McDonnell said, "we beat them every day in practice."

In the days before college basketball conferences gained in popularity, Villanova played all comers including armed services teams, and one representing Philadelphia's Central YMCA mostly comprised of older players. "We probably had the best freshman team in the country," Klotz said. We took on everybody and we beat everybody." The Wildcat yearlings went on to post a perfect

32-0 record. Just as he had been at Southern, Klotz was the engine that powered the Villanova freshman basketball machine.

McDonnell: "He was just a wonderful player, so intelligent about the game, smooth and extremely fast. Red did everything well and made it look easy. Nobody could touch him as a dribbler. He was one of the best passers I ever saw, and of course, just a great, great shooter. The thing was, he didn't shoot much. What he did best was get the other guys going. He could size up what was happening. If the other team left him alone, he punished them with his shot. His shot seemed effortless, even when he was shooting from far outside. He was always in motion, but there was still a sense of calmness, especially when he shot. He would let the ball fly, and you just knew it was going in." McDonnell said both Hermans on the team, Louis Herman Red Klotz and Herman Chuck Drizen, were the standouts.

McDonnell: "We didn't have a good team, we had a great one. The two Jewish boys on the freshmen could have both played in the NBA. Of course, Red did before he went on to work with Abe Saperstein, and Chuck Drizen certainly could have. Drizen had a great all-around game. He could score and rebound and play well defensively. His best attribute was his toughness. He wasn't going to back down for any reason, under any circumstances. That is something you really admire as a teammate, especially when you're in a close ball game. You knew you could always depend on those guys. They were always going to come through for us. Knowing that helped the other guys. It built up our confidence and we knew we could play with anybody and beat them."

In the season's finale, the Villanova frosh went into Center City Philadelphia to play the Central YMCA at the Y at 1421 Arch St. "Coach Ben Emory's charges are all expected to be on hand and will seek to halt the collegians' streak," an advance newspaper article proclaimed. "The 'Y' has lost only two games at home all season, both by a single point." The game did not live up to the hype, as the Wildcats blew Central out, 53-29. Klotz (15 points) and Drizen (12) combined to score just two points less than the entire Central Y squad. The next morning's *Ledger* reported the extent of the carnage: "Villanova Freshmen crushed Central YMCA…on the 'Y' court," the non-bylined story began. "Led by Red Klotz, former Southern High star, Villanova took the lead a half minute after the opening tapoff and ran up a commanding lead. Klotz's backhand passes, brilliant dribbling and sizzling long shots featured the game."

It was the 32nd consecutive win for the Wildcats. Although war was raging overseas, all seemed right in Reds' world. Just one year removed from leading his high school team to the pinnacle of success, he had directed the best freshman team in the country to an undefeated season. Red, seemingly headed to Temple via Brown Prep, certainly made the correct decision to forgo North Broad Street for the Main Line.

When summer came, Red again was spending extended time with his beloved Gloria, working as a camp counselor in the Poconos, and of course, playing lots and lots of basketball. Despite the war, which still seemed very far away, Red was leading a happy, idyllic life. It was made even more perfect by Reds' proposal of marriage to Gloria, her acceptance and their elopement.

"You were young and nothing bothered you," he said. "Little things that might bother you when you were older just didn't seem to matter. If things got rough for a while, you just didn't care. You were young and you thought you could accomplish anything."

Red as a Villanova freshman, 1940.

Chapter 5

A Changing World

By 1941, the basketball world of Red Klotz was coming together nicely while the real world was tearing violently apart.

In December, Red was starting for the Villanova varsity when a surprise attack by Japanese forces on the United States fleet docked at Peal Harbor plunged America into World War II. Suddenly, basketball didn't seem like such a big deal anymore.

Red, then 20, and his 18-year-old sweetheart Gloria were watching a long-since-forgotten movie at the Landis Theater in Vineland, New Jersey when the feature was interrupted to inform the audience of what had happened far out in the Pacific Ocean. The large crowd attending the Sunday matinee was stunned and eventually filed out of the theater and onto the street, where word was already spreading.

Red: "We were sitting there watching the movie when they stopped it and a guy walked out on stage and announced the attack had taken place. It sent chills up our backs. It was a shock to the entire country. Everyone knew what that attack meant the moment we heard about it. We didn't need to wait for President (Franklin D.) Roosevelt to announce it. We were in the war."

A prelude to American involvement had been building for years. At the start of Red's senior year in high school, Germany had launched the infamous *Blitzkrieg* offensive in Poland. The U.S.

had tried to remain officially neutral while the Nazis rampaged their way through much of Western Europe.

Gloria immediately thought ahead to the possible impact for the young couple. "I wouldn't say we were scared," she said. "Most people knew the day was coming when we would enter the war. We were resigned to the fact that our boys would be called and our lives would have to be put on hold. I knew this was going to affect us for a long, long time."

The affection between Red and Gloria had grown steadily ever since that first chance meeting on the Atlantic City beach. Red couldn't wait for the winter holidays and summers to see Gloria, and he would dream up any excuse possible to travel to Vineland, where Gloria's parents had moved. While not together, they were exchanging long love letters which today Gloria still keeps in a decorated box. "It was a happy and innocent time for us. But the war was always in the back of everyone's mind. Pearl Harbor changed everything. Innocence was now out the window."

Basketball became an afterthought. Like most able-bodied men, the members of the Villanova team wanted to fight and signed on for active military service.

"We joined different branches of the service and we were called up at different times, but we signed up together, as a team," Red remembers. "Chuck Drizen joined the Marines. My poor eyesight was a problem and only the Army would take me. It was a patriotic war and people got behind the effort. Everyone wanted to do their part. The war effort was much more important than anything else in the big picture. We knew most of us would not be back at Villanova the following year."

As the 1941-42 season wore on, players were inducted into the service, completed their basic training and were eventually shipped off to the European and Pacific theaters. Toward the end of the season, the Wildcats were traveling to road games with as few as five players. "We would get tired to the point of exhaustion and we had to make sure not to foul out of games. With only five players there's no margin for error."

The season had begun on a brighter and more upbeat note. There was much hope and promise, built largely on the strength of the previous year's undefeated frosh unit. Red, Chuck and Joe Lord, a Norristown, Pennsylvania native were installed in the starting five and eight of the 13 members of the squad were sophs.

"At first glance this smacks of inexperience, of a lack of smoothness. But the set-up is misleading," wrote the Philadelphia *Ledger*'s Tommy Lovett in an article previewing the season. "For three of the sophs are slick enough to hold starting positions and they're as satiny as seniors."

Lovett was particularly high on Red and Chuck. "Philadelphia scholastic ranks have produced few players as smooth at Red Klotz, of Southern High, and Chuck Drizen, of Frankford and later of Brown Prep."

That left the lone senior Dick Gray and Billy Woods, a junior from Philly's South Catholic as the upperclassmen in the starting lineup from the previous year's 13-3 squad. Very good players such as Fred Gerland from New York City, and Bob Kelty, a former high school teammate of Gray's from Trenton Catholic in New Jersey, were relegated to the bench, where they seethed. Additional talented sophs also seeking playing time were sprinkled among them, such as McDonnell and Ernie Melofchik, which further complicated the situation. Melofchick, from North Jersey, heard the griping. "It was not the ideal situation," he remembered. These were good players who were used to playing, and who wanted to play. I couldn't blame them. Good players don't want to sit."

In the early part of the schedule, Villanova lost a few games, which led to additional grumbling from the bench. Red, who had done nothing but win with the Outlaws, Southern High and the freshman team, got his first taste of .500 basketball. "It takes time to get used to your new teammates," Klotz said. "It also took some getting used to when we didn't win as much as I would have liked. We lost a few games and the upperclassmen didn't like it very much, either."

Severance had the unenviable task of meting out playing time on a roster loaded with stars. Each individual had an ego, according to McDonnell: "The upperclassmen didn't have many good things to say about the sophomores, even though they knew we were better than them. We showed them how good we were every day in practice. And we didn't give in to them. We didn't take too kindly to their attitudes toward us. We just wanted to play and win."

Red put the drama aside and concentrated on his work on the court. Before long he, Drizen and Lord melded their talents with those of Gray and Woods and Villanova began winning more consistently.

"Chuck and Red were the difference," McDonnell said. "They were clearly the stars of the team. Red didn't make any bad decisions or take bad shots. He got a lot of steals for us because his hands and feet were quick. If a big guy was dumb enough to try to dribble anywhere near him, well Red would find a way to take it from him. Then he would turn it into an easy basket at the other end of the court. Drizen did everything: shoot, rebound, play defense. He had the talent to play professionally. We were really playing a college schedule with two pros on our team."

Typical of Reds' sophomore year was a hard-fought 47-43 win over Westminster College at the Villanova Field House. Red was playing one of his better games in his customary passing mode and Villanova still trailed 24-21 at the half. This was mainly due to Westminster's Dale Dunmire getting the best of the Villanova interior defense. Dunmire's 10-point first half was equivalent to twice that point output in today's game. The 'Cats still managed to keep it close.

In the second half, Red realized he would have to take matters into his own hands and unleashed his two-hander to turn the game around. A reporter for the student newspaper put it this way: "Dynamic Red Klotz paced the 'Cats to victory by tallying 14 points (to lead all scorers in the game). Tired by Reds' second half pace, Dunmire scored just two points the rest of the way, as the 2,000 fans at the Field House roared their approval.

Klotz and Gray teamed together in grand fashion, each taking the limelight at moments when Villanova was as much as seven points behind," according to the newspaper report. Drizen, too, made his presence felt when he sank a field goal and two foul shots during a surge that would see 'Nova gain its largest lead of the night.

"Red and Chuck Drizen grew up together and were very friendly off the court," said Melofchik. "When they were on the court together they had a special chemistry. Each one knew where the other one was at all times. Better still, they both had the ability to get each other the ball." Whether the upperclassmen liked it or not, it was Red's and Chuck's team.

VILLANOVA BEATS GENEVA AS KLOTZ STARS blared the headline of another article in the student newspaper from later in the season. "Two set shots by 'Reds' Klotz in the last minute of play gave Villanova College a 43-40 victory at the Villanova Field House," the student reporter chronicled. "Klotz looped in a sensational shot from outside the foul circle to give the Wildcats a 41-38 lead." Red hit another long two-hander in the closing seconds to preserve the outcome.

In another contest, this one on the road at the favored University of Scranton, the sophs bailed out Villanova once again. Depleted by injuries and the wartime call-ups of players, only seven members of the roster made the trip to Northeastern Pennsylvania. Nova played almost the entire game with all sophs. Drizen and Klotz were the stalwarts, with Red connecting on five buckets before he crumpled to the floor in exhaustion with three minutes left. Drizen, who poured in 17, was "good enough last night to be a club all by himself," waxed Scranton scribe Chic Feldman. "Fact is, he practically was. With the score tied at 14 all, Drizen picked up the niftiest occasion to bunch another pair and Klotz showed his appreciation by winging in another from a neighboring county and the Wildcats were ahead to stay."

Villanova's iron man lineup withstood a late charge after Red left the game. "Second year sensations Herman Drizen and Lou Klotz…profited by every error of the Tomcats," Feldman wrote. "Klotz, a ballhandler of the old school and speedier than a radio signal, virtually collapsed with three minutes and 25 seconds to go and the redhead seemed to take most of the flaming determination with him at the time, for the Villanovans, ahead 45-29 at the time, never scored a point thereafter. A lionhearted Villanova Wildcat traveled further on raw courage than any basketball troupe to grace the Armory court in this or any other year," Feldman wrote.

More than 2,500 fans showed up for the game. In a bit of foreshadowing of his pro career, Klotz met up for the first time with Hall of Fame referee and future social friend, Pat Kennedy. The demonstrative Irishman was one of the first basketball referees to be known by name and became a star attraction in his own right. His trademark cry of "No! No! No! No! NO! You can't DO THAT!" entertained the fans and kept the game under control. Although always smiling and bantering with players and fans, Kennedy was an excellent official first and foremost. He rarely missed a call and was the model of consistency, something players appreciate in an official. Kennedy would later tour with the Grobetrotters and Washington Generals and would hang out on off days and nights with Red and Gloria.

In didn't matter if a seasoned pro like Kennedy was officiating or if some high school ref had been pressed into action because of the wartime manpower shortage. Severance never really found the right combination to use during the 1941-42 season. Maje McDonnell felt that trying to appease the few veterans on the roster may have been the team's undoing. "(Severance) probably should have just gone ahead and used the sophomores exclusively and taken his lumps from the older guys," he said. "We were just better than they were. There were times we had a game well in hand until he put the veteran guys back in there. He had a lot of loyalty to the guys that had gone through the program ahead of us. But it was to a fault as far as success of the team went. A couple of times Severance actually cost us games that should have been locked up because he felt that he had to get the older guys in there."

Going into the final game at Washington and Jefferson College, an institution located about 30 miles south of Pittsburgh, Villanova's record stood at 14-14. A winning or losing season hung in the balance.

Villanova came out quite flat in the game and Severance did something he had not done all season long. He benched Red Klotz. "I was sitting there fuming, burning mad," Red said, his face showing anger 70 years after the fact. "There was no way I should have been taken out of the game at that point. The upperclassmen weren't playing well and if anybody should have been pulled it should have been them."

The shake-up failed to work as Villanova's struggles continued. McDonnell likened the move to removing "the rudder from a sailboat and expecting it to win a race."

Despite this, Washington & Jefferson wilted offensively late in the game and Villanova managed to draw to within a point. The Wildcats then regained the ball with 20 seconds to go. A timeout was called and Severance decided he would insert Red back into the contest.

"That only made me even madder," Klotz said. "He had me sitting when we could have put them away easily. Then he gets a chance at the end and decides it's time to use me? I wasn't very happy about it at all."

During the timeout, Chuck took Red aside. "What should we do?" Drizen asked his childhood buddy. Red looked at him and replied "Just give me the ball."

Drizen was open at midcourt and received the inbound at half court. Instantly, he whipped a crisp pass to Reds. Klotz dribbled to the right side of the court and saw an opening. He was at least a step behind today's NBA three-point line. Red looked up and measured the shot, then fired. He turned around and ran for the locker room.

I knew it was in the moment it left my hands," he said. "I never saw it go in, but I heard the buzzer go off and heard the groan of the crowd. I was so mad about sitting on the bench that I never stopped running. I just ran straight to my locker. I didn't want to talk to anybody."

The old news clipping without a byline understated the significance of the moment: "A field goal from the side court in the last 20 seconds by Red Klotz, his only goal of the game, gave Villanova a 51-50 basketball victory over Washington & Jefferson College before 2,000 last night," the dispatch said.

The very spare press notice also distinguished itself for being the first print reference to Klotz' nickname being shortened from "Reds" to "Red."

"It seemed like Reds was my Philly name and Red was my nickname later on from people outside of Philly. Red became the more famous name but plenty of people still call me Reds, including my wife," he said.

By any name, Red delivered the last second heroics at Washington and Jefferson. It would prove to be the final basketball action he would ever see at Villanova. The changing world and changing responsibilities in Red's life would soon see to that.

Despite or perhaps enhanced by events in Europe and the Pacific, Red's and Gloria's love was now in full bloom. Upon completion of the season, there was no hesitation. The couple eloped on February 28th. They recited their wedding vows at City Hall in Gloria's current town of residence, Vineland.

"I asked her to marry me and when she agreed, we didn't waste any time. We didn't know what the future was going to hold for us. All we knew for sure was that we wanted to go into the future together."

Red's 18-year-old sweehheart Gloria Stein,
Atlantic City High School's first drum majorette.

Red suited up for the Philadelphia Sphas shortly after
signing with Philadelphia's pro basketball franchise in the
American League.

Chapter 6

Paid to Play

Gloria and Red's decision to make their union official was spontaneous, yet did not escape notice. Red's celebrity status remained in full effect. One of the local papers ran a small news story rather than the usual wedding announcements on the "society pages."

The non-bylined article, clipped from a Vineland newspaper, stated some facts about the wedding and made prophetic commentary on Red's status as a student and a future soldier: "Gloria Stein Wedded to Louis Klotz," the headline stated. "Mr. and Mrs. Herman Stein…announced the marriage of their daughter, Gloria, to Louis "Reds" Klotz, star Villanova College basketball player. Klotz, a sophomore at Villanova, was reported to be preparing to leave his studies with in (sic) a few weeks for induction into the U.S. Army. He was one of the college team's outstanding players during the past season after a sensational basketball career at South Philadelphia High School."

Red wanted to resume his studies and basketball until the call for induction came from Uncle Sam. He returned to the Villanova campus in September of 1942, but he wouldn't be staying very long. The Army wouldn't intervene just yet; it would be the administration at Villanova. One day after classes, Red was called in for a meeting with one of the residence hall supervisors, a priest Klotz recalls only as Father McQuaid. "He called me into his office and I was flabbergasted to hear him tell me about a rule they had at the time: No married men were permitted to live in the dorms. I couldn't believe it."

Vineland, where Gloria had moved recently with her parents, was a small community and word had gotten around quickly. A rabbi from the local congregation mentioned the nuptials to a priest from the area. The unidentified priest in turn contacted Villanova officials.

Father McQuaid was polite, but firm: "Reds, we have been informed you were recently married. You are welcome to stay in school, keep your scholarship, and remain on the team," he said. "Rules are rules. You can't live in the dorm."

Red was incredulous. "But Father," he protested. "The married guys are the cleanest guys on the team!"

It didn't matter. There would be no married men living in the dorms at all-male Villanova. Even if one of the men happened to be named Red Klotz, the rule would stand. The decision would spell the end of Red's collegiate career. "There was no way around it," he said. "I couldn't afford to pay for off-campus housing for myself and for Gloria, go to school full time, and play basketball. I wouldn't have been able to go to college in the first place were it not for basketball and the scholarship. It was pretty clear: I had to leave school and begin earning a living. The truth of the matter is I probably wouldn't have lasted at Villanova much beyond the basketball season anyway. I knew I was going to be going into the service."

Before Red received his "greetings" from the U.S. Army, he fielded a call from none other than Eddie Gottlieb, coach-owner of the Philadelphia Sphas. Eddie, like Robert Klotz, a Russian Jewish immigrant, had carved out a niche as one of the preeminent sports promoters of the era. Not only had the basketball team he cofounded, coached, and owned won numerous championships in the Eastern and American pro leagues, predecessors to the NBA,

Gottlieb promoted games in the Negro Leagues in baseball and owned the Philadelphia Stars of the Negro Leagues, and promoted boxing and wrestling matches and semi-pro football.

A former gym teacher at Thomas Jr. High, where Red first played the game, "Gotty" was well aware that Red had won Public League titles and a City Championship at Southern, his alma mater. He had continued to follow Red's exploits at Villanova. Klotz also had played for a time with the Sphas Reserves, an elite developmental squad under Gottlieb's control. Given Eddie Gottlieb's eye for talent, he may have noticed Red all the way back to his days with the Outlaws, the youth team that played preliminary games to the Sphas' contests at the Broadwood Hotel.

"They called him 'the Mogul' for good reason," Klotz said. "Eddie knew the game. He knew it inside and out. He knew the business side, and he knew talent. He certainly followed the local college game. It didn't take him long to reach me once the word got out that I had left school. He probably knew that I was recently married, would be starting a family, and could use some extra money."

Their first meeting was brief. "There was no negotiating with Eddie," Klotz related. "He was fair, but very tough. He told you what you were going to make and you either agreed to it or you didn't. You shook his hand. There were no contracts. He paid you after every game. He would hand you the money in a small envelope. He took the cash right out of the gate receipts. The joke was, his office was his hat. He always kept notes and scraps of paper there and in his pants pockets. Whatever notes he needed, they were right there on his person and he knew exactly where they were."

The Sphas paid their players between $1,200 and $4,000 a season at that time. Although Klotz cannot remember what the initial offer was, it is hard to imagine him earning more than the low end of the scale as a rookie. Nevertheless, it was decent money in the Depression and World War II years, especially for playing a game he would gladly play for free.

Putting on the uniform of his boyhood heroes did not seem real at first. High school and collegiate glories aside, playing pro basketball for the Philadelphia Sphas represented a new career peak for the five-foot-seven playmaker. "I was awestruck when I joined the team. Every kid in my neighborhood dreamed of playing for them, and I was living that dream."

Reds' feelings certainly were justified. He was a player who mastered the game's fundamentals, studied its nuances, and was influenced by its top players. By the time Red joined the team, it had annexed five championships of the American league and four in the old Eastern loop. At a time when the baseball Phillies and Athletics were both in down cycles (the Phillies may have been the worst team in the majors) and the football Eagles were in their infancy, with some local high school teams drawing bigger crowds, the Sphas put Philly on the sports map. Of the pro teams in Philadelphia, there was just one winner: Eddie Gottlieb's Philadelphia Sphas. Their resume also included competitive play in the World Professional Tournament in Chicago, a little get-together that included the best regional teams of the era, including the all-black New York Renaissance and the flashy group from Chicago who called themselves the Harlem Globetrotters.

In those earliest days of the marriage, Red and Gloria's life together could best be described as unsettled. They lived with Gloria's parents in Vineland, knowing Red could be called for military duty literally any day. Gloria was attending Vineland Business School, attaining skills that, coupled with keen deal-making instincts, would serve the couple well for decades to come. As they waited for the next chapter to unfold, Reds' occupation was pro basketball player. His income, small as it was at the time, was still a welcome contribution to the household.

Red soon found that playing professionally was much different than his previous experiences. For the first time, Red Klotz was not the focal point of the team. He wasn't even the only "Red." George

"Red" Wolfe, 37, had been with the team for 14 seasons and had been a part of eight championships. Wolfe was joined by Ossie Schectman, a New Yorker who would go on to record the first field goal in NBA history with the New York Knickerbockers, and Louis "Inky" Lautman, a crowd favorite with an assortment of unorthodox shots. There was also a third "Red" on the squad, Red Rosen.

Another big change was the manner in which his new teammates comported themselves. These were, for the most part, mature men with families and responsibilities. Basketball was much more serious to these guys. The money wasn't the main thing. "Being professional" was. Lateness for practice or a game or mental mistakes during a game simply were not tolerated. For the most part, the players policed themselves.

In spite of all the talent and experience surrounding him, young Red Klotz found a place on the team and in the hearts of the fans. Teammates saw his dedication, friendly nature, and work ethic, and they soon were won over. This was not your usual rookie. Fans marveled that such a small man could excel against the giants of the game. "I took a train all the way from Reading, Pennsylvania, more than 100 miles away, to see the Sphas," said Alan Kalish, a die-hard fan who in later years would found one of the East Coast's most successful advertising agencies, Kalish and Rice. "As a Jew, the Sphas interested me because of all the Jewish players competing at a high level against the greats of the game. But the main reason I got on that train was to see Red Klotz. The man was a team player. But boy, could he ever shoot."

Just as he had at 'Nova and Southern, Klotz used his speed, his ability to operate off screens, his pass-first mentality, and the old standby, his deadly two-hand set shot. On the cover of Sphas' *Sparks*, the team's program and newsletter, Klotz' photo appeared on the December 19, 1942 edition. "Perpetual motion performer," the caption read. "(Klotz is) already showing signs of stardom. He is expected to blossom into one of the best local products."

Philly sportswriter Don Basenfelder previewed the season, the Sphas' twenty-fifth anniversary campaign, in the *Philadelphia Record*. "Gottlieb attributes much of the Sphas' success to giving the fans what they want," Basenfelder wrote. "The customers demand action," the Mogul was quoted as saying. "The professional basketball follower is hard to fool. They know the game and what to expect from the players. They want to see them earn their money by moving around the floor, passing the ball and (they) desire plenty of scoring."

Thrilled as he was to be playing the game for the Sphas, controlling the game with the ball in his hands on his beloved Broadwood Hotel ballroom court, and as satisfying as it was to receive compensation for playing the game of basketball, Red knew it was all temporary. Chuck Drizen already had completed his basic training with the Marine Corps and had been shipped out to the Pacific Theatre. Red and Gloria dreamed of owning a home and building a family. The war took priority, and the young couple knew their plans would have to take a backseat. First they would move again, this time back to Atlantic City and the Inlet section on the North side of town.

"My father moved around a lot," Gloria recalled. "Times were tough. America was at war, and we were just coming out of the Depression. My father went wherever the work was."

Unsettled as things may have been at the time, Red and Gloria were happy, mainly because they had each other. "When you're young, nothing seems to bother you," Red maintained. "Looking back on it, times might have seemed a little tough, but it just didn't seem that way at the time. You did what you had to do, and nobody complained. There was always somebody who had it a lot worse than you did."

After Gloria, basketball continued to be the most constant, stable aspect of Red's life. He could hop a train from Atlantic City to Philadelphia for Sphas' home games and travel with the team via train or car to places like Wilmington, Trenton, and of course, New York City. It was an exciting basketball adventure. Gottlieb frequently drove the car along with his constant sidekick, public address announcer Dave "the Zink" Zinkoff. Zinkoff routinely stretched out across the rear floorboards of the car to accommodate additional players in the back seat. Zinkoff was Gotty's right-hand man, traveling secretary, confidant and all-around gofer. If Eddie couldn't be two places at one time, having Dave Zinkoff along was the next best thing. "Zink was a dear friend and a key member of the organization," Klotz said. "He had a very distinctive style on the microphone, and people loved him."

Zinkoff, who passed away in 1985, told a story to Simcha (Sid) Gersh, President of the Philadelphia Jewish Basketball League Alumni, which illustrated Gottlieb's toughness and fairness. "When Zink auditioned for the announcer's job, Eddie told him to read a few words. He then told him to stand in a corner and read some more in a different direction. Zink was wondering what was going on, but he gets the job for five dollars a game," said Gersh. "Dave thought he was doing a really good job, and people were responding to him, so he asked for a raise to six bucks a game. He told Eddie, 'People are coming to hear me; I deserve it.' And that extra dollar meant a lot in those days."

Gottlieb said, "We'll see how many fans you bring in," and fired Zink as announcer. He told him that his new job was to hand out programs. After a couple of weeks, Zink couldn't stand it any longer and asked for his old job back. Gottlieb scanned the sold-out throng at the Broadwood and said, "OK, OK. But it looks like firing you didn't cost us any customers." However, when Zinkoff opened his subsequent pay envelopes, they contained six dollars. Eddie had made his point, and he agreed that Zink deserved a raise.

Philly fans loved the Sphas, with most games selling out the 2,000-seat ballroom. After the game, Sphas' forward Gil Fitch hastily changed out of his playing togs into a suit and tie and led his big band with vocalist Kitty Kallen. In wartime Philadelphia, Saturday night at the Broadwood wasn't just a basketball game, it was a social event.

Jerry Decker, a former ball boy who sat on the Sphas' bench, agreed the atmosphere was special, even if he was a little young to appreciate the postgame dance. "These were the best professional players in the world. For a kid growing up in the area, they were the guys. They had that special quality that you only see in championship teams. Red was a winner, and he brought the same kind of mentality with him from Villanova to the Sphas. That's probably why he was so readily accepted by the veterans. Everybody loved Reds, and they still do."

In 1942-43, the Sphas had all they could handle from the Trenton Tigers. The New Jersey capital city's team boasted a lineup featuring two well-known Philly area stars: Mike Bloom from Temple University, who went on to play in the NBA, and Matt Goukas, a future NBA player with Gotty's Warriors. Goukas' son, Matt Jr., would star at St. Joseph's, play on the NBA champion Philadelphia 76ers in 1967, and have a long career as an NBA head coach and national broadcaster. His son, Matt III, starred at St. Joe's.

Trenton won the regular season championship of the ABL, with the Sphas finishing a close second. There was little doubt the rivals would meet in the playoff finals. Trenton had defeated Philly for the championship in the final season of the old Eastern League, and the squads split their four regular meetings with a combined scoring differential of just four field goals, according to Sphas' *Sparks*.

The teams did indeed meet up in a championship round, which proved to be just as close. The Sphas took the decisive game in the seven-game series. Red did not start, but was called off the bench to provide offensive punch, a new role he handled with aplomb. "If somebody was tired or in foul trouble, or if the team just needed a lift, Eddie called on me. The moment wasn't too big.

The bigger the moment, the better I liked it. I certainly wasn't intimidated to come into a big game at a big time. I wanted the ball in that situation," Red said.

In the end, the result was a sixth American League title for the Sphas. There was no parade, no championship ring. There was the satisfaction that Red was once again a champion. Just as he had been at previous levels of the game, Red Klotz found himself and his team at the top of the mountain. This time it was at the sport's highest level.

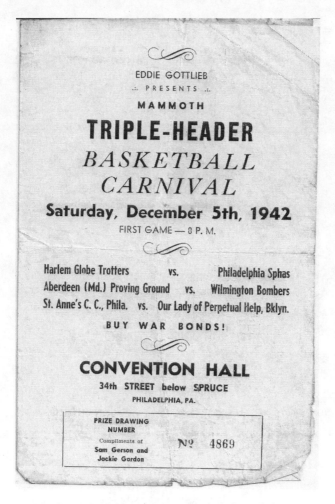

Program from Red's first game against the Globetrotters.

Red was a star on a team representing his Army base
during World War II.

Chapter 7

Sacrifice and Survival

Historians now say the tide of World War II had turned by the time Red Klotz was called into service in the U.S. Army in the spring of 1943. Germany's advance into Eastern Europe had slowed, and Allied Forces were making progress in the Pacific Theatre, albeit at a huge cost of lives. The end of the war in Europe was less than two years away, yet the end did not appear to be in sight for those who served or their loved ones. On the home front, people picked up their daily newspaper with dread and prayed that a friend, family member, or acquaintance was not among that day's list of casualties.

Like most patriotic young men, Red Klotz wanted to be on the front lines of the conflict. He attempted to join the Marine Corps with Chuck Drizen. Though both were superb athletes, the Marines accepted only Drizen, who reported to boot camp in Parris Island, South Carolina. He was shipped to Hawaii and eventually deployed to a ship at an undisclosed location in the Pacific. Red, meanwhile, was rejected summarily by the Marines due to his severe nearsightedness.

"My eyes were so bad, they would not even consider me. Half the time on the court, I couldn't see the scoreboard. I'd keep the score differential in my head, and I developed a sense of the clock. It's something I learned from playing so much." Red, who never wore glasses (except sunglasses during some outdoor games) on the court, also seemed to know where all of his teammates were and where the basket was, regardless of the state of his eyesight. The "sixth sense" that served so well on the basketball floor did not translate to the battlefield, at least in the opinion of the Marine recruiters. Instead, it was the Army, and Klotz was assigned to work in its communications combat units. Red would receive training on how to use the voice technology of the 1940s, unwieldy radios used in the trenches. He would learn how to string wires in the field to enable those on the front lines to converse with headquarters in the field.

Basic training was at Camp Crowder, Arkansas, in the Ozark Mountains. A few months prior, another major event took place in Red and Gloria's new life together: They became parents. Ronee Yon Klotz came into the world on February 13, 1943, in Atlantic City. The baby's unusual middle name was a promise kept by Gloria. "Dad wanted a boy," Ronee said, "and I was supposed to be Ronald."

The middle name came out of a friendship her mother had with a young man she had known in Atlantic City named Anton Yon. When Yon was afflicted with a terminal illness, a family member made an unusual request of Gloria: "Knowing the family surname would die with their brother, a sister asked my mother to name a child after Anton. She agreed. The middle name on my birth certificate is a tribute to a family from Atlantic City. Equally important, it illustrates my mother's integrity. She is a woman who never made a promise she did not intend to keep."

Red was quite pained to have to leave his young family. However, volunteering for service was the norm. "Nobody was happy about leaving family behind. It was what you did for your country. I wasn't alone. Plenty of people with responsibilities had to put them aside and do their part for the war effort. I was one of the lucky ones. I came back."

The luck was something that would follow Red Klotz throughout his life, and certainly for the duration of the war. Ronee believes it is more than good luck. "The term 'charmed life' may be overused. In my father's case, it really applies. I like to say he and my mom's lives have been sprinkled with some kind of magic dust."

The magic dust, or for that matter any kind of dust at all, was not immediately evident when Red arrived for basic training. Camp Crowder was a dank and miserable place. Located near Neosho, Missouri, the facility was originally designed to be an armored training center in 1941. During its construction, it was redesigned to be a training ground for the Army Signal Corps.

Cartoonist Mort Walker of "Beetle Bailey" fame had been stationed there, and it was said Camp Crowder was the inspiration for "Camp Swampy," the setting for the popular comic strip. The new soldiers were met with horrible conditions. "There were copperhead snakes all over the place, and we bunked in small tents, two men to a tent," Red recalled. "I wasn't having anything to do with that. I crawled into the back of a large truck to sleep, off the ground."

Toward the end of basic training, conditions became even worse. Torrential rains caused extensive flooding throughout the facility. "It seemed like it rained for something like eight straight days and there was nothing but mud around. Just about everywhere, it was cold, wet, and muddy. One of the officers asked for a volunteer, and when that happens, you don't normally raise your hand. You are usually going to get stuck with some terrible duty. I volunteered though, and the officer told me to report to a nearby barn. I was really happy to get out of the rain."

Red tentatively entered the barn. It was dry, filled with hay and the smell of freshly brewing coffee, and perhaps, a hint of that magic dust Ronee would speak about years later. Red cannot remember the name of the officer he reported to, except that he was a major and former professor at the University of Pennsylvania. A Philadelphian!

Red: "The major looked at me as if he knew who I was. He didn't say he knew, but I'm pretty sure he did. He said, 'Private, go over to that table and set up the communication for A company, B Company, and our headquarters.' I didn't know what he was talking about. I didn't know one piece of equipment from another. I knew nothing about any of it. I was just getting out of the rain. The major asked if I had a problem, and I told him I had never seen equipment like this set before, and he laughed at me because they were all alike."

The major instructed Red on what to do: "It's really quite simple," the former Ivy League professor said. "Plug this wire in for headquarters, and wait for the next call. Use this wire for Company A, and the other wire for Company B." Then the major sat down and asked, "Would you like a cup of coffee?"

"I couldn't believe it. Everyone else was out in the rain. I was warm and dry chatting with the major and having a fresh cup of coffee. I thought I was in heaven."

A few days before the completion of his basic training, the magic dust may have shown up again. Klotz was once again with the major, who said he had received a request for Red to be transferred to serve as a physical education instructor at Camp Luna in Las Vegas, New Mexico. The request was signed by one Captain David "Cy" Kaselman. Captain Kaselman just happened to be one of the greatest professional basketball stars of the era, and one of Red's teammates on the Philadelphia Sphas.

"Ordinarily, I would never approve something like this, but I'm going to okay it," the major said. I wouldn't mind okaying it more if I were going with you." Magic dust, indeed. Red would later learn that many of his fellow trainees had been wiped out during the Allies' initial invasion of Germany.

Las Vegas, New Mexico, was a sleepy town with a colorful past. It was a central area of dispute during the Mexican-American War of 1846 and it boomed during the heyday of the American railroad. Along with prosperity came lawlessness and such Old West legends as Jesse James, Billy the Kid, and Doc Holiday. Camp Luna, where Red was assigned, was the site of an infantry post used in Kit Carson's famous Navajo campaign of 1863.

There were no such desperados or famous military figures in sight when Private First Class Louis H. Klotz arrived in the summer of 1943. Klotz trudged down Las Vegas' main street with a heavy duffel bag slung over his shoulder, searching for the headquarters building to which he was supposed to report. He soon came upon an unbelievable sight: "There were soldiers setting up cots along the street, and they were lying down and sunning themselves!"

Among the sunbathing soldiers were none other than ex-Sphas' teammate Petey Rosenberg and Nate Comer, a fellow all-city Philadelphia high school basketball player. "I traveled all this way, and here were these Philly guys I knew, relaxing and sunning themselves on the town's main drag. I couldn't believe my eyes." It turned out that Rosenberg, who would later go on to play for the Philadelphia Warriors' 1947 NBA championship team, was instrumental in talking Cy Kaselman into requesting that Red join them in Las Vegas.

"There was a beautiful gymnasium, and Cy made me a physical education instructor and put me in charge of the gym. The camp had a heck of a basketball team and also a very good baseball team." Joe Gordon, a Hall of Famer from the New York Yankees was stationed at Camp Luna, as were several members of one of Red's hometown teams, the Philadelphia A's.

"I was on the main basketball team, and we traveled all over to places like Amarillo, Texas, Denver, all of the air bases in New Mexico, and all over the West. We played against all the military bases, the MPs (military police)…We beat everybody." Camp Luna's commanding officer, Colonel Harry S. Berry, was a highly competitive individual. "Col. Berry wanted a winning team. He hated to lose. We were a winning team, and Col. Berry appreciated it. All of the commanding officers liked to have their bragging rights, and we certainly provided them."

In spite of Red's first impression walking down the main street of Las Vegas and the abundance of pro athletes, Camp Luna wasn't a glorified sports camp. The base personnel trained for air transport support, including Red's specialty area of communications. Most of the soldiers stationed there eventually were shipped out for combat duty.

Red: "The one thing I could never figure out was why we were an air base without airplanes. Our camp and places like Roswell and a bunch of the other so-called air bases had no aircraft. We had no idea these places were set up for protection and deception for what was going on at Los Alamos."

What was going on, of course, was the development of the first nuclear weapons. Under the command of Brigadier General Leslie Groves and the Army Corps of Engineers, American Physicist J. Robert Oppenheimer led a team of scientists from all over the world for what would be known as the "Manhattan Project." High-level security measures were installed as Oppenheimer's lab designed and began the construction of atomic bombs. Though more than 100,000 people were involved in the Manhattan Project, very few really knew its ultimate purpose. What was obvious was the level of heightened security around the site. The labs were isolated and accessible by guarded dirt roads and hidden behind fencing topped with barbed wire.

Red: "We went into Los Alamos to play the MPs and we asked those guys what was going on. They told us it was the development of some weapons to combat German submarines. Little did they know what was really happening. Nobody knew except the enemy. Our outfit and the other air bases without aircraft were decoys for what was going on at Los Alamos."

Red's work as a physical education instructor, and no doubt as a slick-passing, sharpshooting guard on the base basketball team, earned him swift promotions. By 1944, PFC Klotz had advanced all the way to Staff Sergeant Klotz. As such, he earned the right to live off base. Gloria and Ronee soon joined Red at a small apartment near the camp. "We had a very modest living quarters. Living with my family, however cramped, sure beat the heck out of living in the barracks," he said.

Once again, good fortune came Red's way. He was sent to an instructional course at Washington and Lee University in Lexington, Virginia. While away from New Mexico, many of his peers were shipped into European combat zones.

Chuck Drizen did not experience the same good luck as his best friend. Commissioned as a lieutenant following his graduation from Villanova, Drizen went off for combat training at Parris Island. He took his advanced training in California, and then was sent to Hawaii for a brief stopover. From there, Chuck was dispatched to an unknown vessel in the Pacific Fleet in a secret location to prepare to lead a Marine infantry unit.

Japanese forces still held many islands in the South Pacific. Cut off from supplies, huge armies were dug into fortified bunkers and caves, prepared to die for the Empire. Allied forces launched one island invasion after another, inching closer to the main Japanese homeland, and at a staggering death toll.

Chuck and Red had exchanged letters throughout the war. Drizen, assigned to the invasion forces, wrote letters of an increasingly grim tone as the fighting continued. His correspondence drove home the realities of war. "Chuck was writing that he was smoking cigars and drinking a little bit," Red said. These were vices in which Drizen never indulged during the friends' days on the peaceful and leafy Villanova campus.

"It was as if he knew," Red said. "Chuck had a sense he wasn't coming home."

Drizen also sensed a better future for his friend. "Keep up with your basketball," Chuck wrote. "I believe you are going to be quite successful, and it will take you a long way." It was the last correspondence Red would receive from his friend.

In October, 1944, the United States planned its assaults on the islands of Okinawa and Iwo Jima. Iwo Jima is a home island of Japan and would be defended tenaciously. Securing the island was a priority for the American brain trust. Iwo Jima and Okinawa were envisioned as staging areas for an eventual invasion of the main islands. The Japanese had fortified both islands with tens of thousands of troops and installed heavy artillery in the hope of inflicting as many casualties as possible.

Only two months later back at Camp Luna, personnel was being deployed to Germany to counter the Nazis' final gamble. As American forces dwindled, every available man was needed for what would become known as the Battle of the Bulge. "Every spare man was called, and quite a few who couldn't be spared," Red remembers. "Cooks, typists, clerks, it didn't matter. Everyone was being shipped out. I was a rifle expert and fully expected to go."

Red was among a large group of soldiers ordered to assemble in a field where they stood before Col. Berry himself. "We were asked to volunteer, and I stepped forward with everyone else," Red recalled. "The colonel walked down the line. He came to me and for some reason said, 'Sergeant, step back.' I really didn't know why. The only thing I could figure out years later was that it was probably because I was a hell of a basketball player. That fact probably saved my life, because once again, many of those guys never came back." While his buddies went off to the European fronts, Red was sent to Fort Totten, New York. By this time, Gloria was pregnant with the couple's second child.

Halfway around the world, Lt. Chuck Drizen was among four U.S. divisions landing on Iwo Jima, beginning on February 19, 1945. A member of the "Fighting Fourth" Marine Division, Chuck led his outfit onto the island where one of the bloodiest and most strategically important battles of the war in the Pacific took place.

Four weeks of horrific combat resulted in heavy American losses and the loss of virtually all of the 21,000 Japanese there. Only about 200 were taken prisoner; the rest either were killed in the fighting or died in ritual suicides. For the Americans, 6,825 men were killed in action.

Chuck Drizen led his squadron of 13 men safely behind enemy lines, although they were cut off a quarter mile from their unit, according to a military press release quoted in a Philadelphia newspaper. Chuck's squadron succeeded in destroying three Japanese tanks and killing 12 enemy soldiers, the article stated. Marine Lt. Neil Deighan, was quoted as having written Chuck's parents, Mr. and Mrs. Jacob Drizen of Frankford Avenue in Northeast Philadelphia. Deighan wrote that he had met the Drizens' son on the island in the first days of March, 1945, and that Chuck was killed in action on March 6. He "died instantly by concussion from a rocket mortar," according to the article. Drizen was laid to rest in the Marine Fourth Division's cemetery on the island.

Long before Deighan shed light on the circumstances of Chuck's death, Red knew his friend had not survived the fighting. Red, devastated by the loss of his best friend, still welled up discussing it nearly 70 years later. "He was a hero and I still think about him quite a bit," he said. "It makes you think about how senseless war is. This was such a waste of a very talented human being. Chuck was a brilliant guy, a great athlete, and a fine student. He had a commerce degree and would have been a big success in any business he chose. He could have played pro basketball. But he never had the chance to grow old as I have, or to get married and have children and grandchildren."

"Even worse," Red went on, "the lessons of that war were never learned. Wars continued to be fought in Korea and Vietnam and Iraq and Afghanistan. It is as terrible a tragedy for the countries involved as for the families affected. I lost my best friend. And people are still losing family members and friends."

Approximately four months following Chuck Drizen's death on Iwo Jima, the products of the secret Manhattan Project near Camp Luna were delivered. At atomic bomb was tested in the New Mexico desert on July 16, raising a mushroom-shaped cloud estimated to be eight miles high with an explosion estimated to equal nearly 20 kilo tons of TNT.

President Harry S. Truman approved the use of the bomb on targets selected on the Japanese mainland. First, on August 6, the B-29 bomber Enola Gay dropped a bomb over the city of Hiroshima, instantly killing more than 80,000. Despite the fact that such destruction never had been seen before, Japan rejected the call for unconditional surrender. A second bomb over Nagasaki was dropped on August 9, wiping out an additional 25,000.

Six days later, the Japanese finally called it quits. The war was over, but for Red Klotz and an entire generation involved, its effects would resonate to this day.

Chuck Drizen

Red (number 20 at right) with his Air Transport Company team,
Camp Luna, Las Vegas New Mexico, 1943

Red scores a layup against the Trotters with the Sphas barnstorming
team. Klotz coached and managed the team on an interim basis for
owner Eddie Gottlieb.

Chapter 8

It's a Living

V-J Day was a big event in the lives of Red and Gloria. Not only was the war over, meaning Red soon would be returning home, but the couple would celebrate the birth of their second child.

President Harry S. Truman had ordered an end to hostilities in the Pacific on August 14, 1945, two days after Japan's unconditional surrender was received. The following day was an undeclared national holiday as millions poured into city streets across America awaiting the official word. News reports finally came in at about 7 p.m., setting off wild celebrations everywhere.

In Atlantic City, the Haddon Hall Hotel, which still stands today as Resorts Casino, had been converted into a makeshift military hospital. "Everyone was jumping up and down, screaming and cheering. The amputees were waving their crutches and going crazy along with everyone else," Red recalled. Gloria and Red's V-J Day was doubly joyous, as Gloria delivered a healthy baby boy in the Haddon Hall's nearby maternity ward. When the gender was discovered, there was no doubt as to the baby's name. Chuck Klotz was named to honor Red's Marine hero best friend, Herman "Chuck" Drizen. Though young Chuck never would have the opportunity to know his namesake, he emulated him decades later by joining the Marines.

"We named Chuck after Herm, and my Chuck always idolized him," said Red. "When it was time for Chuck to do his military service, there was no doubt which branch."

Shortly after Gloria's pregnancy had been confirmed, Red was shipped from Fort Totten, NY, to his final assignment, the air base in Newfoundland, Nova Scotia. Once again, Red's old Sphas' team-mate Captain Cy Kaselman played a role in the young staff sergeant's official military orders. Kaselman had accompanied Klotz from Camp Luna to Fort Totten.

"Cy took me aside and said it looked as though we were going to be shipped out," Red said. "Cy said he would be going to Paris, which made a lot of sense, because he was quite a ladies' man." American troops were helping to reestablish order following France's 1944 liberation and were being received warmly by the French people. "That was perfect for Cy, who asked if I wanted to go. I said, 'not particularly,' and asked him if I had a choice. If I could avoid being that far away from my family, that's what I wanted."

His friend informed Red that he did have a choice: he could opt for Newfoundland, at an American base that served as a major staging area for transatlantic flights throughout the war. There was a delay in the paperwork for Red's orders, causing him to arrive days late at his new base. He did not receive a warm reception.

"Several units knew I was coming and were bidding on my services for different basketball teams," he said. "The team that wound up with me was mad because they had lost games during my absence."

Red's stay in Canada, his only time outside the United States during the war, was a short one. Gloria's pregnancy was difficult, and sympathetic Army nurses helped him to secure several leaves, enabling him to return home for visits. His "final" excused leave came about three weeks prior to his son's birth. "I exhausted the first leave, and asked for an extension, which was approved," he recalled. "She still hadn't given birth, and somehow another leave was granted. Chuck was finally born, and it was V-J Day!"

When Red returned to the base, his superiors were not amused, until Red explained himself and presented his paperwork for the multiple leaves. In one final wartime example of Ronee's so-called "magic dust," Chuck's birth would prove to be the ticket back to civilian life for Red.

The Army used a "points" system to determine which soldiers would be discharged first. GIs received credits for things such as financial hardship, marriage, and children. When Chuck Klotz came into the world, Red suddenly had the minimum amount of points needed to apply for his release. It was granted, and Red was sent to Fort Indiantown Gap, Pennsylvania, for his final processing and honorable discharge.

As delighted as Red was to come home, he again was faced with the economic realities of having to support a young and growing family. He returned to the Sphas, for whom he had played a few games during previous wartime leaves. One such appearance against the famed New York Renaissance in December, 1944, earned notice in *Sparks*, the team's newsletter-program. "It was pleasure to see little 'Red' Klotz in action against the Renaissance last Saturday night," the item gushed. "The Red Head showed plenty of ability while he was on the court and entertained the fans by his fast and clever ball-handling."

With his discharge, Klotz was able to play for the duration of the Sphas' schedule, and he also played as a mercenary player in several semi-pro leagues. "There were games that would spring up here and there where players were needed, and they would pay you a few bucks. We were young and having a good time. We didn't know we were poor. We did know that every dime counted. Playing ball for a couple of bucks? Easy call!"

Despite playing for the Sphas and hustling as a barnstormer and 'ringer,' basketball money had to be considered a bonus. It wasn't a real job. "The Sphas may have been one of the best teams in the world. We weren't paid accordingly. Everybody on the roster did something else besides basketball. You did what you had to do to make ends meet."

Klotz knew that Atlantic City held opportunity for hardworking entrepreneurs who were willing to take risks. Postwar, pre-casino (at least pre-legal casino) Atlantic City boomed with a tourism industry centered around the beach, ocean, and boardwalk, as well as in entertainment venues, such as Skinny D'Amato's 500 Club, where Frank Sinatra and the comedy team of Dean Martin and Jerry Lewis were regulars. The Club Harlem drew a growing African American clientele from all over the East Coast. The Steel Pier attracted thousands every day and night with dozens of attractions for families and for individuals of all ages. The most famous was the high-diving horse with a lovely bathing-suit-clad rider. The horse plunged from a platform into a tank of water on an hourly basis. A large crowd had gathered for the dive almost every time.

Atlantic City, located within a short drive or train ride of the majority of the United States' population, boasted huge and stately European-style hotels along the boardwalk. In the summer months, the lodgings were occupied by the rich, famous, and beautiful, who delighted in taking in the boardwalk sights and healthful "salt air." Some were pushed along in richly-upholstered wicker "rolling chairs" pushed by hustling small-time business-men, many of them African American. The not-so-rich could find adequate lodging in hundreds of smaller inns and boarding houses around town. Even those who could not afford overnight accommodations took part in the fun. Thousands arrived daily on the train from Philadelphia and New York, carrying a change of clothing and premade lunches often carried in shoe boxes. These day-trippers came to be known as, "shoe boxers," and eventually, "shoobies," a term still used derisively by some area residents to describe the tourists. Though some locals looked on the seasonal visitors with disdain, savvy business people were getting rich off of them.

Red and Gloria had the entrepreneurial spirit and the ability to make a business work. Before the war, Red had convinced his old high school coach Doc Ker to bring his South Philadelphia High squad to the resort for a game. Red's pitch, ostensibly so that he could see his future wife, had a built-in gate appeal. The Philly Public League champs taking on one of South Jersey's best teams was a natural draw. In college, he organized a college all-star game, and sold tickets. A large crowd showed for an event that if staged today would have cost Red and all the participants their NCAA eligibility.

"He knew all about promoting a basketball game, way back when," Gloria said, not mentioning her own business expertise learned at the business school in Vineland. "Gloria had been to school, but it was much more than that. It was that she was good at (business)," Red would say. "She had a feel for it, and she still has the same feel. Gloria always seemed to know the difference between a good investment and a bad one."

Doing business in Atlantic City then as now, was not for the faint of heart. Just a few decades earlier, the resort was known as a "wide open" haven where Philadelphians and New Yorkers traveled to escape the social mores of the day, not to mention sidestep the Volstead Act. Beginning with the start of Prohibition in 1920, "rum runners" brought illegal booze into the various docks and marinas. Speakeasies, back room gambling operations, and brothels thrived under the political thumb of Republican Party boss "Nucky" Johnson.

Following Prohibition's repeal in 1933, legal bars and taverns opened or reopened and much of the illegal activity was toned down. Nevertheless, Atlantic City still boomed as a tourist destination, and during the postwar years, the reigning boss was New

Jersey State Senator Frank S. "Hap" Farley, who presided over the region's continued success as a resort town.

Red and Gloria and Ronee and Chuck were now living in the Inlet section in the north end of the barrier island city. The family lived in a few rented rooms of a small house. Red, who had been coming to Atlantic City for almost as far back as he could remember, and his wife, a longtime resident of the area, knew what they wanted to do: open a boardwalk business. That meant dealing with Hap Farley.

Red: "Hap Farley controlled everything that went in there. You didn't do business on the boardwalk without Hap's approval. Luckily for me, basketball would again become instrumental in any success I would enjoy. Basketball came before we approached him about a business. Hap owned a team (fittingly named the Atlantic City Senators). They played at Steel Pier and in Convention Hall. We had a good team and beat most of the opponents we faced."

Red's stint with the Senators was concurrent with his time with the Sphas. Red had a difficult time giving an opinion on which owner was tougher, but he said Farley was arguably as strong-willed as the Sphas' Eddie Gottlieb. One time, the Sphas were in Atlantic City to take on the Senators, with a pair of games scheduled over a weekend. "I played for the Sphas in one game and the Senators in the other. The teams split the two games, each winning on the night Red played for them. "Eddie was really mad about it, and I had to remind him that he gave me permission to play for the Senators. He made it clear that was the last time I was allowed to play for the Senators against the Sphas."

In addition to Red, one of the best young backcourt performers in the game, the Senators had a charismatic young player named Chuck Connors. Connors eventually would become a successful Hollywood actor, known to a generation of baby boomers for his 1960s' TV series, "The Rifleman." Before finding fame in Hollywood, Chuck would make it to the NBA and play briefly for the

Boston Celtics, and have a short stint in the major leagues with his hometown Brooklyn Dodgers and then with the Chicago Cubs. He also was drafted by the NFL's Chicago Bears, although he never signed with them.

"Chuck was a talented guy and a real character," Red recalled. "He was tall and handsome and he made a real impression when he walked into a room. He was one of those guys who entered a room and all eyes were on him. He was a good basketball player, not a star. By the time he was done talking to you, you thought he was a star," Red said, laughing.

Connors showed his acting ability when he was still an athlete. "Chuck would make money at banquets, where he would be hired to speak and he did a 'Casey at the Bat' routine that people loved." Connors would recite the famous Ernest Thayer poem with such dramatic flair that even though the audience knew how it would end, they would hang on every word.

Connors was also in the habit of reciting passages from Shakespeare in public, according to Charley Rosen's book, *The First Tipoff*. To say that a six-foot, five-inch man walking around quoting Shakespeare was unusual in the late 40s might be understating things a bit. "But Chuck Connors was the kind of guy who could get away with it," said Red.

Connors was a tough forward who could score and rebound and who helped the Senators win games. "I really can't remember us losing except for that one time to the Sphas. I'm sure we lost once in a while, but there was no doubt we were a very good team."

The Senators held a special place in Red's heart during that era. They weren't the Sphas, but they were a pro team based in his adopted hometown. Red didn't need to *schlep* a long distance to play professionally. He could hop a jitney from his home in the inlet area of Atlantic City and play in front of friends and customers. Red became a local hero.

Like all good politicians, Hap Farley liked to win. Though he was no Eddie Gottlieb, Hap knew that having Red on the team meant all the difference. So, when the young star of his team approached him about a store on the boardwalk, Farley knew what was in everyone's best interest. The response was affirmative.

"We got this little tiny store that was really not much more than a stall," Red said. "We were able to make it work. There was a whole list of things we were not allowed to sell because it would be in competition with other (Farley-controlled) businesses. We could only sell items that were not being sold in the established shops." That meant no "real food," such as hot dogs or hamburgers, no clothing, or anything else being sold on the boardwalk.

"We looked at the tourists in their rolling chairs, and those sunning themselves on the beach, and we tried to envision what they might want. It turned out to be a little bit of everything." The store sold fruit and nuts and small snacks, but no meals. It also offered newspapers and magazines. A shoeshine chair was installed, as were a couple of pinball machines. The couple tried to make every square inch of the place usable to generate income.

Red: "The first thing we did was go in there and clean the place up. We got some of that gray Navy paint they used to paint the decks of the battleships, and we painted the wooden floor with it. Gloria ran the place, kept the books and handled all the receipts and made the numbers work. Every morning, I would go to the farm markets and purchase the fruit, and a dealer would deliver the magazines and the newspapers from out of town. We had the Atlantic City paper, but we charged a little extra for the Philly, New York, Washington, and Baltimore papers. People wanted to read their hometown news, and that was something we could provide. We were working hard every single day. That's just what you did. You just went out and you earned a living. That was our start as businesspeople. It all began in that little stall on the boardwalk. One time (NBA referee) Riley Pitkoff came in there and asked for a shine, and I grabbed the rag and then he recognized me. He said, 'Red, what are you doing here?' and I just went to work and said, 'Well, right now, I'm shining your shoes.'"

Professional basketball still played a role in helping the Klotz family to make their way in the postwar world. Red was an established pro, contributing regularly to the Sphas and Senators. However, sometimes the stints as a "ringer" were the most exciting.

"You might get a call from somebody who needed to win a game," is the way Red put it. "They might offer you 30 bucks, and that was good money at the time. Thirty dollars bought a hell of a lot of groceries."

During the 1946-47 season, Red Klotz received such a call. The Penn State Pro League was a rough-and-tumble group of squads competing in the equally rough-and-tumble Northeast Pennsylvania towns such as Scranton, Wilkes Barre, Larksville, and Pittston. A representative of the Pittston franchise called one day, and the next night, Red was on a train to Scranton and a doubleheader featuring the hometown Scranton Miners against the Laksville Larks. Red would be suiting up for Pittston in their game against the Carbondale Pioneers.

Carbondale was favored, but if Pittston could pull off the upset, it would vault from third place in the league standings to a three-way tie for first with Carbondale and Plymouth. The twin bill attracted 1,048 paying customers to Scranton's Watres Armory, according to a faded newspaper clipping of a story by sportswriter Al Williams.

"The first thing I noticed was it was a pretty rough crowd," Red remembers. "You had a bunch of coal miners, and there was gambling going on." Most of the action seemed to be on Carbondale, and the local fans certainly were not expecting a five-foot-seven sharpshooter from South Philly to be bolstering Pittston's attack. Things went as expected in the first half when Carbondale raced to a 31-25 lead. "I wasn't there just to collect a check, I wanted to win the ball game," Red remembered. "I began to shoot more in the second half, and most of what I was throwing up there was going in."

"Little 'Red' Klotz put on a one-man show in the third and final periods to take the heart out of the game Pioneers," Williams wrote, "and turn the contest into a rout."

"A diminutive, carrot-topped veteran of the wooden way stole the show." Williams waxed. "Klotz, the smallest man on the court, went to work as the third period got under way…Two successive field goals by the fast-moving 'red head' and another by Johnny Muha deadlocked the score after three minutes had elapsed." After a Carbondale foul shot, "the little fly in Carbondale's ointment,' Klotz, broke through the Carbondale defense to lay up a two-pointer and send Pittston out front for the first time since late in the opening period."

The remainder of the article and box score are cut off from the 67-year-old clipping. However, Klotz said his hot hand never cooled in the 54-45 upset. Most of those betting on the game were not amused. "These fans knew the league and that I wasn't one of the regular players," Red said. "A lot of boos were raining down, a lot of foul language. And then some guys started coming out of the stands after me."

Luckily for Red, there was a strong police presence and the men in blue escorted Red, with three crisp $10 bills in his pocket, all the way back to the train station. "I'm pretty sure I wouldn't have gotten back to Atlantic City in one piece were it not for those policemen," he said.

Sphas Sparks

VOL. 6 — No. 9   SATURDAY, DECEMBER 25, 1943   PHILA., PA.

Break In League Schedule Brings Renaissance Team Here New Years Night To Battle Sphas

CPL. HERMAN "RED" KLOTZ
Will be seen in Sphas uniform next Saturday, while home on furlough.

Another thrilling game will be the feature of the New Year's Holiday night attraction at the Broadwood court next Saturday, January 1, when the famed Renaissance Club, perennial Negro champions, return to renew their rivalry with the Sphas.

When these two teams meet a super-sensational contest is always sure to result.

The New York Negro quintet has the best passing attack in the game, and their speed and tricky antics are something to look at!

The Rens have always been popular here, and contests between them and the locals are in demand by promoters all over the country, because these games are pleasing to the fans, featured by snappy passing, good shooting and plenty of exciting moments.

Eddie Gottlieb will have an opportunity to use this game as a means of getting his team ready for the strenuous second half schedule, which the Sphas are determined to win.

Get your ticket orders in without delay!

PRIZE DRAWING NUMBER

No. 725

Compliments of Sam Gerson and Jackie Gordon

Red featured on the cover of the Philadelphia Sphas program for a game against the New York Renaissance.

In a 1950 outdoor night game in Spain, Red guards Globetrotter Nat
"Sweetwater" Clifton, who later that year would become the first
African American to sign an NBA contract, with the New York Knicks.
Number 36 at left is the Trotters' first famous showman, Goose Tatum.

Chapter 9

Pro Basketball Grows Up

Just like a ball spinning on one of Harlem Globetrotter legend Goose Tatum's long fingers, the second half of the 1940s saw the basketball world rotating at a much faster pace.

At first, things looked just as they had before the war. Red Klotz enjoyed his status as an established pro, and the game he loved was not showing any signs of the seismic shift that was about to come. There was still no NBA. Professional basketball was a conglomeration of regional leagues and barnstorming teams. The Harlem Globetrotters did not belong to any league, but they were at the top of the food chain, drawing large crowds as they beat up on most opponents on tours through the mid and far West and the occasional East Coast swings. Besides forward Tatum, the Trotters' reigning showman and a future Hall of Famer, there was Marques Haynes, an accomplished player who gained fame as the greatest dribbler in the world, and who would join Tatum in the Hall.

Abe Saperstein's troupe enjoyed a proven, winning formula with its mix of straight basketball and comedy, not to mention exclusive pipeline to the very best black players. The NBA wouldn't get around to integrating until three years after Jackie Robinson shattered the color line in baseball. The Trotters of this era were arguably the most talented team in basketball and unquestionably the most entertaining. They could play a thrilling tight game against the highest levels of competition, or they could roll up a big lead against the local all-stars and then roll out the comedy reams. With the Depression still on everyone's mind, a ticket to a Globetrotters' game was a safe buy for a good night out for all ages and both genders.

Meanwhile, the game's first "giant" caused a sensation. There were players as tall or taller who came along before six-foot-ten George Mikan. There were none who played with such graceful ball handling or with such an ability to dominate a game. Mikan, who had a strong college career at DePaul University in Abe's hometown of Chicago, now was gaining attention for the pros with the Minneapolis Lakers of the National League.

The Sphas, with whom Red won an American League title in '43, finished second in 1946 with the redhead back in the fold. Much was different now, as soon would become evident. For starters, no longer was Eddie Gottlieb overseeing every phase of the operation. The natural-born promoter was ahead of the entertainment curve and was sensing the premium soon to come on leisure time and the acceptance of a heretofore unknown concept: disposable income. Eddie was sniffing out new and much bigger opportunities. Despite a healthy ego, Eddie knew he was just one guy spread very thin between his 10-time basketball champs, the Philadelphia Stars of the Negro National League in baseball, boxing and wrestling matches, rodeos, track meets, and anything else to which he could sell a ticket.

Oh yes, the Mogul also was heading the investors group that was attempting to buy the Philadelphia Phillies. While all this was going on, the Sphas were never more popular. There were now some gentiles on the roster, but still no blacks. They were packing them in at the Broadwood and would barnstorm against the best, from the Renaissance and Original Celtics of New York to that team from Chicago that claimed to be representing Harlem. The Sphas also competed in the World Professional Tournament in Chicago.

Despite such increases in visibility, the pro leagues were low on the consciousness radar of the American sports fan. Baseball was still king. College football, boxing, horse racing, and yes, college basketball all dwarfed the pro game in popularity. The so-called American League was really the "Northeast league," and the National League was in effect, the "Midwest league," with most games happening on weekends. They were hardly big-time.

The pro leagues at the time had no structure or unity. There was the annual World Professional Tournament in Chicago, but everything else was a crazy quilt of changing owners, new franchises, folding franchises, and players moving wherever they could make their best deal. "The buildings we played in were small and dingy and usually in a bad neighborhood," said Klotz. "You hung your clothes on a nail in the wall, might have to take a cold shower, and it was nothing to go into a locker room and see a rat running around."

The Harlem Globetrotters were the pro sport's one big exception. Their success was the residue of years of hard work by Abe Saperstein. This might explain why Abe couldn't help but notice the backcourt ace of the Philadelphia Sphas. The tiny redhead wearing number three seemed to be right in the middle of the action when the Trotters hooked up with the scrappy Sphas. On one such occasion in Philly, Red dribbled the clock out to preserve a small lead. "I pulled a Marques Haynes," he said. Tatum met Red at half-court. "That won't happen again," said the Clown Prince of Basketball, suddenly deadly serious. It did in their next meeting, though. Philly not only won its second straight over the Chicago barnstormers, Red and his crew won their opponents' respect. Around that time, Gottlieb was at the forefront of an abrupt U-turn in the vision of a group of owners.

Red: "The thing was, guys like Abe and Eddie saw something. They had the foresight and knew basketball was a great game with the potential to be much bigger. They believed in what basketball could become. They were ahead of their time, not just for basketball, but for *all* sports. They knew they had a great product, an exciting and entertaining game. They thought the public would enjoy it if basketball was packaged differently. They acted on that belief. And they were right."

Gottlieb was among a group of interested parties that gathered at a New York City hotel in 1946 to discuss the formation of a "major" pro basketball league. The time seemed right. College basketball doubleheaders were flourishing at Madison Square Garden in Manhattan and at the Arena and Convention Hall in Philly. Owners and operators of these larger buildings were filling them with customers to watch pro hockey, ice shows, rodeos, and of course, boxing. There were too many "dark" nights at these large venues, and basketball was seen as a viable way to fill the void. Little did the men know they would be acting as the "founding fathers" for today's multibillion-dollar, worldwide pro basketball empire.

The group's main proponents were Walter Brown, owner of the Boston Bruins NHL hockey team, and Al Sutphin, who owned the Cleveland Barons of the American League. Madison Square Garden impresario Ned Irish joined in, but reluctantly. The college game was a gold mine, and his plate – and building – were full. New Yorkers were eating up most of the entertainment options he was offering. Why did he need some new pro basketball league? It was said by NBA historian Leonard Koppett that Irish felt he would be competing with his own college games and that he went along with the plan solely to prevent an outsider from moving into his territory.

Eddie Gottlieb pictured the league being a go, and he already had been hired by Pete Tyrell to coach and manage the Philadelphia entry. Tyrell, who headed the corporation that owned the Philadelphia Arena, was there too. In addition to the other National Hockey League cities of Chicago, Detroit, and Toronto (French-speaking Montreal was the exception, having no interest in the American court ball game), other cities represented were Pittsburgh, home base for one of the reigning ice skating shows at the time, St. Louis, and Providence.

The basketball community, small and tightly-connected as it was, did not take long to filter word of the new enterprise down to the players. "We knew what was happening, and most of us were excited and had great hopes," said Red, who was expecting a call from Gottlieb. "I was one of the fastest, if not *the* fastest player in the game. Why wouldn't he call me?"

What Red didn't factor in was that as much as Eddie respected Red as a player, the Mogul had more admiration for his entrepreneurial streak. Gottlieb was aware of Red's boardwalk business, and his ability to suit up and travel and play well under difficult conditions. If Red Klotz said he was going to be some place on a handshake, he would find a way to get there. It was a reputation he would burnish throughout his professional career. "If you hire me, the last thing you have to worry about is whether or not I will show up. If they know you will always show up, that is something businesspeople really respect."

It turned out that Gotty had big plans for Red, but not as a player. Red Klotz was the top name on his short list of people to keep his older, more established basketball enterprise going. Gotty would offer, and Klotz would accept, the job of interim player/coach of the Philadelphia Sphas. In Red Klotz, Gotty knew both the business and basketball sides of the Sphas' operation would be in good hands. This would free Gottlieb to center the bulk of his energies on the new basketball team, which he named the Warriors, his Negro League baseball operations, and his bid to buy the Phillies.

"I was a little disappointed by (Gottlieb passing him over as a player)," Red said. "I knew I could play in that league or any league. Gotty was favoring more of the players from outside of Philly." The only local player selected from the Sphas was Red's old Army buddy Petey Rosenberg. Still, the team did have a core group of names that would play quite well in the hometown. Red's other local Army chum Cy Kaselman became Gottlieb's assistant coach. Former Philly college stars Howie Dalmar from the University of Pennsylvania, and Matt Goukas, Sr. and George Senesky both of St. Joseph's made the roster.

One of the ideas behind the new league was to move away from pro basketball's rough image and to concentrate on the clean-cut "college boys" and their fast-paced style of play that drew the big crowds. Local players on each team also were thought to be good for the turnstiles. Red seemed to fit the mold with his South Philly and Villanova ties, but at five-foot-seven, Klotz' height may have worked against him in Gottlieb's mind.

"I didn't want to use (a majority) of Sphas' players because (the Warriors) were stepping up from a representative club to major league status," Gottlieb was quoted as saying. "That required players from other geographic areas, too."

The Mogul may have had a point. However, it is likely he knew the entire venture was shaky and he wanted to keep his Sphas as intact as possible in case the new league failed. Red represented continuity and stability and name recognition for his established team. Meanwhile, he brought in for the Warriors Art Hillhouse from Long Island University, and a relatively unknown six-foot-five forward from Murray State in Kentucky named "Jumpin'" Joe Fulks. A sensational shooter off the dribble who used the newfangled one-handed shooting method with either hand, Fulks would become the league's first superstar. He poured in an average of 23 points a night, an unheard of number at the time, and his flashy style caught on quickly with the Philly fans.

When the newly-christened Basketball Association of America began play in the 1946-47 season, the very first recorded field goal was scored for the New York Knickerbockers by a former member of the Sphas, Ossie Schectman. The goal accounted for two of his 11 points as the New York team defeated the Toronto Huskies 68-67 at Maple Leaf Gardens. Although Gotty's Warriors had only the fourth-best overall record in the league's regular season, they peaked at the right time. The Warriors defeated St. Louis and New York respectively in best-of-three quarterfinal and semifinal playoff series. The Chicago Stags knocked off the regular season's best team, the Red Auerbach-coached Washington Capitols, in the other semifinal. The Stags didn't seem to have much left for the finals, and the Warriors wrapped up the BAA's first title in just five games of a best-of-seven. A one-point loss in Chicago averted the sweep.

For Red, it didn't hurt too badly to see his hometown's first "big league" team celebrate the first "world championship." He was just too busy earning a living, feeding his growing family and leading the still-popular "minor league" Sphas.

"I had too much going on to worry about it," Red said. "Remember, I was still playing and coaching the Sphas, putting in stints with the Senators, and getting more calls for single games as a ringer. I was a working player, and in that respect just as good as anybody playing in the BAA. None of those guys were doing it full time. I was a professional player, and I also had a real job. Just like they did."

It wasn't that way for long. The new league still was finding its way and trying to identify and sign the best available talent. The Boston Celtics, destined to become one of the marquee franchises of what soon would be known as the National Basketball Association, were coming off a sad first year. Walter Brown had done a great job of getting the fledgling league off the ground, but not so well at establishing his Boston franchise.

Things got off to a dubious start before the very first game at the old Boston Arena. The Celtics and Chicago Stags had just completed their pregame warm-ups when Red's old Atlantic City Senators teammate Chuck Connors heaved a 40-foot shot that tipped the front iron of the hoop and shattered the backboard. By the time a replacement goal had been fetched from Boston Garden across town, the game had been delayed two hours and much of the crowd had gone home.

The Celtics limped to a 22-38 record that first year, tying for last in the Eastern Division with Toronto. For all the owners' talk of "going big league," the Celtics' average paid attendance was 1,682, and its total gate receipts probably amounted to what present-day NBA franchises spend on meal money. For the Celtics second season, Coach John "Honey" Russell was searching for new blood. An old-school coach who favored the slower and more physical pace of the regional leagues, Russell had coached the Cleveland Rosenblums of the ABL and had coached against Red with the ABL's Wilmington entry. Honey knew of Red's reputation and that he might be available.

"He invited me and wanted me to be part of the club," Red said. Russell's training camp was rigorous, and Red delivered his typical solid effort. In fact, he might have been the best guard in camp. "I shot well and made plays and fit into the team concept they were trying to build. I felt that I had made the team."

Ed Sadowski, the Celts' starting center, agreed. A six-foot-five, 240-pound bruiser, Sadowski had played college ball at Seton Hall, one of Honey Russell's previous coaching stops. "Ed came up to me at the end of camp and said he was looking forward to the coming season with me on the roster."

Unfortunately for Red, talent didn't seem to be the only consideration. Even at that time, marketing played a role, and there was a general feeling that teams would be better off at the box office if they employed well-known former college players from the area. Honey Russell's roster did not have the local flavor of say,

Eddie Gottlieb's champion Philadelphia Warriors. In addition to Sadowski and Connors, who also played collegiately at Seton Hall, Russell had his own stable of Philadelphia players, including Mike Bloom and Jack Hewson from Temple, and Art Spector from Villanova. The majority of the remaining spots were sewn up by players from New York and the Midwest. Among the guards, Russell was left with a choice between the Philly-bred Red and Saul Mariaschin, a five-foot-nine guard from Harvard. Philly fans and insiders looking for a ringer knew the name Red Klotz. When it came to box office, Mariaschin's name played better in Beantown.

"Honey asked to meet with me at the end of camp and told me the situation. They had a guy from Harvard who they felt would help them sell tickets. They weren't drawing, and I wonder if Honey really knew the way to sell tickets: to put the best possible team on the floor and win games. Honey didn't see it that way and wanted the local kid."

Russell left the door open a crack. "You could help us, but we have to see how (Mariaschin) works out," the coach told Red. "We'd like you to stick around for a while, and you could still wind up on the team."

"I told him, 'That's no good, I can't do that.' I couldn't afford to wait around on a promise. I had a family, and Gloria was stuck in Atlantic City keeping things going and caring for the kids. I had to go home."

Red's assessment of Honey's decision turned out to be prophetic. The Celtics went 20-28 in the regular season, good for third place in their division, and then were bounced unceremoniously from the playoffs by the Chicago Stags. Mariaschin barely played. The Celtics still couldn't draw many fans. Honey Russell would be fired and eventually replaced by the former coach of the BAA's talented Washington Capitols, that other "Red," Auerbach. As it would turn out, Red Klotz' exclusion from the new league wouldn't last for long.

A CHAMPIONS   BALTIMORE BULLETS—1947-1948

Red, second from right, with the 1948 champion Baltimore Bullets.

Chapter 10

Number One...With a New Bullet

The *Baltimore Sun* article was foreshadowing exciting things to come for that city's vagabond pro basketball franchise. "BULLETS GET SPHA PLAYER," the headline's print boldly stated.

At the time this seemingly innocuous item appeared, February 11, 1948, Baltimore's entry in the Basketball Association of America was mired in last (fourth) place of the Western Division behind the front-running Washington Capitols, second-place Chicago Stags, and St. Louis Bombers occupying third. The Bullets' 10-15 record would have placed them second in the East, just 41 percentage points behind the New York Knickerbockers. With 14 regular season games remaining, Baltimore was looking up at the rest of the conference and was fighting for its playoff life. Changes were needed if the Bullets were to reach the postseason.

"Balked in their efforts to purchase Fred Lewis from the Sheboygan (Wis.) Redskins of the National Basketball League, the Bullets got busy yesterday and made a deal with the Philadelphia Sphas for the purchase of Red Klotz," the article stated.

The piece did not carry a byline but was in all likelihood penned by the *Sun's* Seymour S. Smith, a beat reporter covering the Bullets. "Klotz, who has played with the Sphas for four seasons since coming out of Villanova College, is no giant by current tall-boy standards," the story continued. The Bullets believe his lack of height will be offset by his shooting and floor work."

At the time, Red definitely wanted to prove he belonged in the BAA, yet was not sitting around and waiting for his phone to ring. His hands were full with a wife, growing family responsibilities, and the boardwalk store. At age 28, he still had plenty of opportunities to augment his income, basketball-wise, and was embracing his role as Sphas' player-coach and road manager. "Look, I knew I belonged and wasn't sweating it," he said. "I saw some of the names of guys in the league and knew I was better than many of them. But I was doing okay. We were getting along financially, and I was still playing lots and lots of basketball."

With all that in mind, it was still an easy choice. When the Bullets finally did come calling, Red and Gloria said, "Why not?" without hesitation. If anything came up in the family, Baltimore was only a couple of hours away by train or car. Gloria told her man not to worry about the family business and sent him packing.

While Red's acquisition may have seemed underwhelming to the *Sun* sportswriter, he got the part right about Red's ability to command the floor. The move would coincide with a turning point in fortunes for the moribund Bullets. Ticketed by player-coach Buddy Jeannette as a backup ball-handling guard, Red immediately was welcomed by his new teammates. They either knew about him as an opponent or realized right away at practice that the fast, slick-passing redhead could distribute the basketball and was not intimidated by playing in the top pro league. Red did not have a problem facing off against much taller athletes, either.

"I fit in with the rest of the team because I always had the ability to pick up on a guy's tendencies," Red said. "I could figure out pretty quickly how to get the ball in a guy's hands when he was in position to do something with it. That's what a coach wants in a backcourt guy."

For his part, Harry Edward "Buddy" Jeannette certainly knew what he was getting in Klotz. Regarded as one of the best guards in the game, Jeannette's playing career was in decline by 1948. ,

He could still score, however, and he knew talent. In addition to playing and directing the squad as coach, Buddy essentially served as GM as well. He played against Red in the ABL and understood he would get a return on management's investment when he offered to plunk down $100 a game for the five-foot-seven ball handler and shooter from South Philly. Jake Embry and co-owner Tom Tinsley (who also owned local radio station WITH) probably made whatever deal on the side they needed to with Eddie Gottlieb to take Red off the Sphas. Sportswriting of the day did not focus on details of such a move. However, Klotz' price turned out to be feasible for the Bullets to handle, while Lewis' was unworkable. The *Sun* article vaguely alluded that the Bullets, "moved to get Klotz... as soon as they learned they were unsuccessful in their move to land Lewis."

Fred Lewis had built his reputation and won a championship in the NBL with Sheboygan, one of Jeannette's old teams. A rival league franchise, the Indianapolis Kautskys, blocked the Bullets' bid for Lewis when the Indy club, "arranged for his purchase." A versatile six-foot-two player from Long Island University, Lewis could man the backcourt or play the small forward position. He would go on to become better known as the head coach at Syracuse University. A great offensive mind, one of his Orangemen teams flirted with becoming the first college team to average 100 points a game. While at Syracuse, Lewis also would mentor future NBA superstar Dave Bing.

When Baltimore's plans to obtain Lewis fell through, only a few hours remained before the BAA deadline for trading or adding players. Buddy needed to move quickly to secure Red's rights and Gottlieb had Jeannette over a barrel. Not only was Gotty the owner/coach of a league rival that was defending the championship, he still owned the Sphas, for whom Red was doing an excellent job playing and managing. It is highly doubtful the Mogul, who was known to drive a hard bargain, would have let Red go without compensation or future considerations of some kind. Still, Gottlieb was a deal-maker. He knew Klotz wanted to play in the BAA, and he may even have experienced a guilt pang or two for never giving his loyal employee a chance to play for the Warriors. If he blocked the move, Red always could quit the Sphas and work his own deal. At least this way, he would get something in return.

For his part, Jeannette wanted to shore up his roster and make a run at the postseason. Although best known for his exploits in the NBL, Jeannette had been through the pro basketball circuit. In 1941, he was MVP of the World Professional Tournament for the champion Detroit Eagles and played in the ABL for a time. The two main pro loops frequently staged non-league games, and Buddy had evaluated Red's skill set thoroughly.

Ball security was huge in the postseason, and Red had a reputation for milking the clock off the dribble. Though not known for his defense, Red's was above average, especially given his size. And the word turnover was not in his vocabulary. Jeannette knew that he wouldn't hurt his team by inserting Klotz into a game's late stages. Buddy wasn't getting any younger, and Klotz would provide speed that had to be defended, and a sound basketball mind to go with the fresh legs. It really didn't matter that he was the shortest guy in the league. "Red was just a complete guard in a compact package," said future teammate Sam Sawyer. "The Bullets made a smart play in picking him up when they did."

The transaction was completed. "If (a side deal with Eddie Gottlieb) happened, I wasn't aware of it," Klotz said. "Eddie picked me to run the Sphas because he knew how good I was. The guy never had to worry about the team arriving on time for a road booking. And he never had to worry about how the Sphas would play. The problem was I never made any money doing it, and like most players I wanted a shot at the BAA. Gotty was a really tough negotiator. But when I had the chance to play in the new league, Eddie did not stand in my way."

Whatever the scenario for his departure from the Sphas, Red was now a Baltimore Bullet and full-fledged member of pro basketball's "big leagues." The prospect of earning $1,400 extra for 14 basketball games in little more than a month, a significant amount of money in postwar America, was not lost on the hardworking Red and Gloria. "It didn't matter if it was basketball or picking up newspapers and fruit, you did what you could to earn anything you could and keep the show going," Gloria said. "Besides, I couldn't say no. Basketball was what he loved to do."

Klotz' addition to the roster was the final piece, dwarfed by a shocking trade made days earlier. The move shipped fan favorite Meyer "Mike" Bloom, a six-foot-six center from Temple, to the Boston Celtics in exchange for six-foot-eight Connie Simmons. Though probably the major impetus for Baltimore's turnaround, the move, "almost sparked another Civil War," Jeannette said. Bloom, along with his player-coach, were the lone holdovers on the Bullet squad from the franchise's days in the ABL, and Mike was beloved for his ferocious defensive play.

Red boarded a train south from Philadelphia's 30th St. Station and took up residence at team expense at the Baltimore YMCA. He arrived in time to join practice before the February 12 home game against the first-place Knicks. Not only were the New Yorkers atop the Eastern Division standings, they had a 10-game winning streak going, and it had been more than a month since their last loss. The Knickerbockers also had the league's top rookie in Carl Braun, a six-foot-five forward from Colgate who came into the contest averaging 15 points per game.

None of that seemed to matter to the new-look Bullets. They appeared to be instantly transformed in a shocking 96-86 upset of the Knickerbockers, and Red made an impact right away. The Bullets took a 27-23 lead in the first quarter and then scored five straight points in the second to take control. In the pre-shot clock era, teams with the lead legally could freeze the ball. Red was brought into the game to do just that and performed admirably. "After holding the ball so as to retain possession when fourth period hostilities resumed, the Bullets dumped in three quick baskets," Smith documented in the *Sun*. The scoring burst made it 81-70, the night's largest lead, and Baltimore cruised the rest of the way.

"Newcomer Connie Simmons got six points," Smith wrote of Bloom's replacement, "while little Red Klotz, the other new Bullet member, turned in some fine ball handling along with a lone point – the ninety-sixth." The scoring total was just four points shy of the all-time franchise record at the time. Fans were questioning which was more surprising: the win itself, or the ease with which the Bullets dispatched the front-running Knickerbockers.

Still, there were problems to overcome for the team. "We played in the worst arena in the league, which was located in a tough neighborhood, and the accommodations for the players were terrible," Red remembers. "The thing was, it just didn't matter. I was happy to be playing at that level."

The Bullets were the original stepchild franchise of the Basketball Association of America. Initially denied entry in the league because of the size, condition, and location of their home arena, the Baltimore Coliseum, the Bullets were admitted into the league only because the Toronto, Pittsburgh, Detroit, and Cleveland franchises all had folded. In that first year, the owners of the BAA teams were aligned with hockey arenas of the National and American Hockey Leagues generally three times the size of Baltimore's home base.

The new "major" basketball league had survived its initial season, but just barely. Only the champion Warriors and the Knickerbockers, from the nation's largest population center, drew more than 100,000 fans for the season. That's five games' worth of fans for a successful NBA team today. With only seven surviving teams, nobody would have been surprised if the entire league decided to shut down.

While Gotty's Warriors were winning the first championship, the Bullets (named after the Bata Bullets canvas basketball footwear) had advanced to the ABL's championship round. When an invitation came to play in the Chicago World Professional Championship tourney, the Baltimore team pulled out of the ABL finals to do so. The ABL brass was not happy with Baltimore, yet still acknowledged them as the winners of the disputed series, which they led at the time of their pull-out.

The following year, BAA Commissioner Maurice Podoloff needed an eighth team if the league was to make another go of it. Podoloff looked directly across the bridge Embry had burned with the ABL to find his fourth squad for the Western Division. The Bullets allowed the league to soldier on despite an awkward geographic alignment in the "West" featuring natural rival Washington in the same division with St. Louis and Chicago. With the BAA's very survival on the line, the filthy and small Coliseum and its basketball tenants no longer seemed toxic.

Jeannette had absolute control of the team from a basketball standpoint. "Buddy was in charge, and he had one of the biggest names in pro basketball at the time, and the owners loved him," Red recalled. It didn't hurt that as player, coach, and de facto GM, Jeannette saved Embry and Tinsley two salaries. "Buddy was a tough guy, and he ruled with an iron fist. His word was the final word. I thought that I deserved more playing time, but I took the minutes I received and used them the best I could to help the team win."

Lest anyone think Baltimore's new-found chemistry had kicked in on a permanent basis, an ugly 69-63 loss to the Bombers in the league's westernmost outpost of St. Louis would dispel the notion, as would back-to-back road losses at Washington and Philly following a hard-fought 79-76 overtime win against lowly Boston at the Coliseum. For Baltimore fans, this stretch of games was highlighted by Bloom's return to town with the Celtics. "Main attention

will be paid to how Bloom fares against his former teammates,"
opined a *Sun* article. "The one-time Temple All-American has
scored 24 points in a trio of contests while performing for Honey
Russell's Eastern Division Club."

Bloom would prove to be just a footnote, as Baltimore held
Mike to just three field goals in a game with 23 lead changes and
21 ties. Klotz was scoreless, but again was called on to spell Jeannette and distribute the basketball. Steals, assists, and minutes
played are statistics that were not yet kept. However, Red remembers being brought into pressure situations and knowing what to
do.

"They didn't use the term point guard in those days, but that's
what I was. I understood there were some big, talented guys out
there. I had a lot of confidence in my shot. That really didn't matter if I could get the ball to a guy who was close to the basket."

The 1947-48 Baltimore Bullets were a collection of old pros
and hungry young bucks. Red was a hybrid, a pro veteran still in
his mid-twenties. Jeannette was 31, with a well-nurtured rep as
the best all-around scoring guard of the era, and for good reason.
The native of New Kensington, Pennsylvania was on three NBL
championship teams and was a four-time first-team All-NBL performer. His performance in the World Professional Tournament
in Chicago may have had an influence on Baltimore's decision to
bolt the ABL playoffs with the Bullets in 1947 to compete in the
tournament one last time.

Simmons, the "beanpole center," according to Smith, had zero
college experience. However, when teamed with another six-foot-
eight presence, the burly Clarence "Kleggie" Hermsen, the six-
foot-seven, 215-pound Oklahoman Grady Lewis, and Purdue
rookie Paul "Bear" Hoffman, the Bullets had a front line rotation
as formidable as there was in the league. Guard was set with Jeannette and his old Ft. Wayne Zollner Pistons teammate Joseph
"Chick" Reiser. A great set shooter, Reiser was not as accurate as

Red's two-hander, nor was he Klotz' equal in speed or creativity off the dribble. Reiser's 11.5 average in the American League in 1946-47 was his career high. Years later, while touring with the Globetrotters and facing admittedly loose defenses, Red would consider anything less than 20 points to be an off night, and 30-point games were not unusual. "I couldn't score from the bench, though," he would say. Reiser had a championship resume in the NBL, and at five-foot-eleven, four inches on the speedy newcomer. He also was thought to be Jeannette's closest off-the-court basketball advisor. Thus, Reiser was the second guard and Red had to be content with his role as a key reserve.

Red: "You have to understand, Reiser was three years older than Buddy, and I knew they were going to need a blow during the game. I was going to get my time. Each time I was out there, I had to prove myself. At this stage of the season, almost every possession and stop on defense was big. I really didn't mind. I was on the team and making a contribution. It was a lot of fun once we started winning."

The squad also included six-foot-two swingman Carl Meinhold, the rugged Dick Schultz, and Herman "Dutch" Fuetsch. Though they were big and physical, the Bullets had the ability to play finesse basketball. Ball movement and the classic "give and go" were offensive staples. "We were a team in every sense of the word," Klotz recalled. "I don't know what it was like before I got there, but during my time there, it was about sharing the ball, team defense, and watching each other's back."

Things were darkest before the dawn. At this point, the Bullets were 2-3 since Klotz joined them, and 1-3 in their last four. They were 21-18 overall and were mired in the West basement, three full games behind Washington in the loss column. However, something odd happened in the Warriors 83-71 thrashing of Baltimore at the Arena in West Philly. Red Klotz started the game, and it completely unnerved Coach Eddie Gottlieb.

"Red Klotz, hustling newcomer, started the Philadelphia clash. Tossing in a pair of baskets while holding the dangerous Angie Musi to a like number," the *Sun* reported.

"I could hear Eddie telling his guys to watch me, and he switched things up." Eddie ordered Musi, a five-foot-nine sharp-shooter out of Temple, to abandon his perimeter game and take Klotz underneath the basket. "He made Musi take me in the hole, and it took their offense out of what it did best, which was to give Joe Fulks room to create."

As a result, Baltimore played the favored defending champs evenly for most of the first half. It was tied after one, and Philly held a three-point edge at halftime. Even though the Warriors pulled away in the second half, Fulks, the league's leading scorer, was held to eight points, 14 below his average. Baltimore, "got into Eddie's head, and we knew that we could play with them on their home court," Red said. "In fact, we knew we could beat them."

The newfound confidence translated in the eight remaining regular season games and the playoffs. Eight of Baltimore's nine remaining games were at the Coliseum, of which they would win seven. Among them was a thrilling 64-62 triumph over the Warriors on March 13. The Bullets could have locked up a playoff berth by beating Washington on March 18, but Auerbach's Caps prevailed, 71-64. Then, in a must-win finale, they steamrolled Providence, 75-58.

The win left Baltimore in a tie with Washington and St. Louis for second place in the division with identical 28-20 regular season records, forcing a complicated series of elimination games to determine the postseason matchups. In its tie-breaker game, Baltimore slipped past Washington, 75-72, to secure a spot in the postseason. The Bullets then topped the Knicks, 2-1 in the best-of-three quarterfinals, and swept the Chicago Stags 2-0 in the semis. This set up a Baltimore-Philly final, as the Warriors defeated

St. Louis in their semifinal series. There was one more piece of drama before the finals were to begin.

The rookie Hoffman was averaging 10 points a game and was a key to the Bullets' hopes. That didn't stop him from jumping the team to be with his wife, Mitzi, who reportedly had the chicken pox. "Mitzi never liked the idea of her husband running around in short pants," Embry told *Sun* sportswriter Alan Goldstein 40 years later. "I went to his house and pleaded with both of them, but they were adamant. Paul's season was over, playoffs or no playoffs. I had (Commissioner Maurice) Podoloff call him from New York and warn him he would be blackballed from basketball if he didn't play in Chicago. Even that didn't help."

The rest of the team left on a 6 p.m. flight to Chicago, and the Bullets' owner took one last crack at the Bear. "There's a train at 11 o'clock," Embry told Hoffman. "If you're not on it, your career is over." Hoffman showed up in the Windy City just before the opening tip, scored 16 points, and the Bullets advanced. "I don't think Mitzi ever forgave him!"

The final series was a classic matchup. Although they barely had squeaked into the postseason, the Bullets were 7-2 in their last nine regular season games, 5-1 in the postseason, and 14-6 overall since acquiring Connie Simmons and Red.

The Warriors were defending champs and had the league's leading scorer. "When you have (Joe) Fulks and (center Chuck) Halbert and (Howie) Dallmar under the basket and (George) Senesky outside, you've got a pretty good ballclub," Hoffman told NBA.com decades later.

A crowd of 7,201 turned out at the Philly Arena to watch Gotty's champs coast to an 11-point victory in Game 1. It looked like it wouldn't be a series at all when Philly jetted to a 41-20 halftime lead in the next game. "In those days, if you got behind that far, the game was over," Jeannette said. "There was no 24-second clock to help you come back. But somehow, we did."

Fulks went into a rare cold streak and the Bullets cut the lead to 48-40 in the third quarter and Baltimore dominated the final session. "We were up by one with four seconds to go and I tapped in a missed free throw," said Hoffman.

The remarkable comeback resulted in a 66-63 win and the split in Philly. It was a huge psychological lift for the Bullets, who knew they had to win a game on the road, and a crusher for the Warriors, who still hadn't recovered physically from their semifinal series. In the bizarre playoff format of the day, the first-place teams in each division were matched up in a seven game series, while the Bullets were in a best-of-three, which they swept. As if that weren't enough, Gottlieb opted to have his team travel by train, a 24-hour trip each time, instead of flying. Sensesky told NBA.com the decision was due to the weather, but given Eddie's frugal reputation as a businessman, one must wonder.

Regardless, the momentum was with Baltimore, who took a commanding series lead with home wins of 72-70 and 78-75. Back in Philly, the champs staved off elimination, but it was just a brief reprieve. On April 21, the Bullets took the city's first major sports championship with an 88-72 blowout.

For Red, it was another triumphant career milestone. "I won in high school, college, and with the Sphas in the ABL," he said. "Finally, I was a champion in (what is now) the NBA."

Basketball signed by the 1947-48 champion Baltimore Bullets
(Red signature toward bottom right)

Red instructs his Cumberland Dukes of the All American Professional
League in his first official stint as a pro coach.

Chapter 11

The Duke of Cumberland

As the clock wound down on the Baltimore Bullets' shocking BAA championship series win over Eddie Gottlieb's Philly Warriors, the Bullets' loyal fans began an early celebration. "We had some of the loudest and most boisterous fans in the league," Red remembers. "Our building was small and cramped compared to arenas in the rest of the league. That made things loud. Sometimes you couldn't hear a thing other than the crowd noise. It gave us a big advantage and made (the Baltimore Coliseum) a very difficult place for opponents to play."

The title-clinching game gave the Bullets 12 wins in their last 13 home games. They did not lose a game in the playoffs on the Coliseum floor. All of the home playoff games had been sold out, and according to the story by the *Sun's* Jesse Linthicum, scalpers were getting double the face value for tickets out on the seedy streets surrounding the building.

Klotz, who is credited in the box score of the final game as a non-scoring participant, remembers dribbling around to deafening cheers, passing off for an assist and the crowd noise volume going up even more. "I did not think it could get any louder, but it seemed to every time we scored."

The Warriors got to within 67-60 early in the final stanza, but it was all Bullets after that. The home team went on a 21-13 advantage the rest of the way. "FANS NOISY AS GAME ENDS," the

Sun's headline proclaimed. "Fans slapped each other on the backs when the buzzer signaled the end of the game and the basketball season. Few conceded (the Bullets) a chance to win the rugged series," Linthicum wrote. "I'm glad it's over, because I couldn't stand much more of this torrid action," he quoted one fan as saying. The story also documented that a large contingent of Warriors fans in attendance not only left disappointed, but lighter in their wallets. Bettors among the Philly crowd reluctantly spotted two points to the Bullets in the belief their defending champs would win on the enemy hardwood to force a game seven.

Members of the Baltimore team celebrated in a restrained manner. After whooping it up in the locker room, the squad gathered for a late night meal at a neighborhood deli. "There wasn't much celebration," Jeannette said. "None of that crap of shooting champagne over everybody. It was just another game to us."

The trappings of the win also were modest. The players received a pen and pencil set and a tie clasp, and their wives were given a cloth coat...no diamond-encrusted championship rings. "That's okay, we knew that we won, and that was what mattered," Red said. "That and the playoff shares."

According to the *Sun*, the league gave out a total of $50,000 in playoff money, of which the Bullets received $9,385. They also received approximately $6,000 for winning the semifinal series. Although he was with the team for only 14 regular season games plus the postseason, Red was voted a full share of playoff winnings, reported variously to be from $1,800 to $2,000 per man. Even at the low end, the money more than doubled what Red had made throughout his Bullets tenure to that point.

"That was pretty serious money at the time," Klotz said. "It sure was to me, anyway. That extra cash came in handy."

Shortly after the season, some of the players came to management seeking a raise, and most of the roster summarily was fired. "It was reasonable to want more money after winning the championship. Nobody was really making anything to speak of, and we weren't asking for much more. But they canned us," Red said.

Only Jeannette, Reiser, and Simmons came back to the Baltimore roster the following season. The Bullets were moved into the Eastern Division, and went 29-31 in the regular season to finish third behind Washington and New York. The Knickerbockers bounced them out of their three-game playoff series, 2-1. So much for a repeat championship in Baltimore.

Red's final BAA stat line read 17 games (11 regular season, six in the playoffs), nine field goals made, three free throws converted, eight assists, and six personal fouls. He averaged 1.4 points per game in the regular season, and 1 point per game in the playoffs. As had been the case throughout his career, the numbers really didn't tell the whole story.

"I was on the bench most of the time, but I was still a contributor to a championship team. I knew what my role was, and I gave them exactly what they were looking for. I'm proud of my contribution. More importantly, my teammates were happy with me. That's really what mattered. If they weren't thinking that I had helped them, would they have voted me a full share?"

With his season over and being among those cut in the Bullets' roster purge, Red nevertheless returned to Atlantic City with a champion's swagger. He didn't know exactly where he would end up in the next season. There could be no doubt, though, that the game he loved would find a place for him.

"I wasn't worried about it," he said. "I was just happy to be back with my family. I knew I would be playing ball some place."

"Some place" wound up being Cumberland, Maryland, where Red signed a one-year contract as player-coach of the Cumberland Dukes of the All American League. "I could have tried out for any number of the NBA teams (the newly-named league absorbed the Minneapolis Lakers, Ft. Wayne Pistons, Indianapolis Olympians, and Rochester Royals) and don't have any doubt I would have caught on someplace. But I was approaching 30 years old and was beginning to think that my future in the game would be as a coach and not a player. Besides, I really didn't like coming off the bench, and that is how most of the teams would have wanted to use me."

As a result, when Cumberland Dukes' President David Kauffman came calling, the opportunity appealed to Red on several different levels. He had helped Eddie Gottlieb by pinch-hitting as the Sphas' coach and he had been the de facto coach of his high school team. The Cumberland Dukes represented the first "official" coaching job of his career.

Unlike playing for the Sphas or even the Bullets, there was no direct train service from Atlantic City to the western part of Maryland. Red would have to bid his family adieu for most of the 1948-49 basketball season. He wasn't happy to leave, especially knowing that Gloria was expecting the couple's third child. One again, Gloria insisted that he pursue his basketball dreams.

The All American "Pro" League was technically semi-pro. Red said that each team was limited to two "outsiders" of the league territory. The rest of the talent came from the ranks of former local high school stars and blue-collar workers. In addition to the Cumberland team, franchises represented Washington, Altoona, Butler, and Pittsburgh in Pennsylvania, and Wheeling West Virginia. "It was a very tough, competitive league and well-respected among basketball people," Red said. "It could only enhance my career if I went out there and did well."

Klotz was by far the biggest name on the Cumberland squad. "The Dukes are indeed fortunate this year in securing the services of Louis H. 'Red' Klotz as playing coach," stated an item in a Dukes' game program. The story touted his career at Villanova, "a hitch in Uncle Sam's Army," and his championships with the Sphas and the Bullets. The team played its home games on the court of Saints Peter and Paul High School, and most of the contests were sold out. The local residents loved their Dukes.

The *Cumberland Evening Times* cartoonist, identified only as Marvin, described Red Klotz as the clever player-coach of the Cumberland Dukes. "Making up in speed, cleverness, and accuracy in shooting for what he lacks in height...Klotz is a real inspiration to his basketball team. A playmaker deluxe and a great favorite of local fans, the 'little redhead' is a big reason for the Dukes' strong bid for the All American Basketball League crown."

As for Red's living arrangements, Kauffman found his new coach a room upstairs at Keegan's Café, a local saloon that dated back to Civil War days. The café's owners were also advertisers in the team's program, and its customers were rabid supporters of the squad. Some of the regulars at the bar were old enough to be from the Civil War era themselves, Red joked, and they were as rough as the terrain surrounding the nearby hillsides. Still, the personable coach somehow fit in and enjoyed the company of the bar patrons.

Cumberland was a source of coal, iron ore, and timber during the industrial revolution, and was at one time the second largest city in the state. By the time Red joined the Dukes, the population was already in decline from its 1940 census peak of nearly 40,000 residents.

"It was a little rough around the edges, but the people were hardworking and very nice to me," Red recalled. "They worked in mines and in factories. Just good, honest, hardworking people." When the team wasn't playing, Red would sit with the group at the bar, where he would have his dinner. Usually it would be a steak or a fine home-style meal.

Red: "They would ask me what I wanted to drink. They would feed me a great meal. Then they would ask me again what I wanted to drink. I told them the same thing: I wanted a glass of milk. They laughed at me. They said I was the first person to ask for milk in there, and the only person to drink milk there. They thought I was kidding. But I held my ground, and they went out and got it for me. Eventually I didn't have to ask any more, and they just brought out a tall cold glass of milk with my meal. I'm sure it helped that we were a winning team."

Cumberland's other legit pro was Ken Haggerty, who was best known as captain of the 1947 Holy Cross College NCAA championship team. One of Haggerty's Crusader teammates was a flashy guard named Bob Cousy, who went on to become one of the all-time greatest players in NBA history. Their best "local" and most popular player was Bob Pence, a star forward best known as football coach of the local high school, Allegheny High. Pence had been named Maryland Coach of the Year for guiding Allegheny to an undefeated season. On the basketball court, he was a dependable scorer and a rugged rebounder.

The Dukes quickly adapted to Red's coaching philosophy of working to get open shots and sharing the basketball. They battled the Butler club for the top spot in the league standings for most of the season, and eventually finished second.

In addition to putting together their regular league schedule, General Manager H. R. Whip arranged for two exhibition games to round out the Dukes' slate. The first was against the NFL champion Philadelphia Eagles basketball team, which featured future Hall of Famer Pete Pihos, and his teammates George Savitsky, Bosh Prichard, and Alex Wojciechowicz among others.

Whip was able to score a real coup when he booked the Harlem Globetrotters for the other practice game. The highly-anticipated game might not have counted in any standings, but it was important to Red and the Dukes. The Trotters were fresh off their second straight win over the Minneapolis Lakers and had such stars as Goose Tatum, Ermer Robinson, and Nat "Sweetwater" Clifton on their roster that season.

"The Trotters expected to come in there and walk all over us. I told our guys to, 'make them respect you,' and they responded.

They took what I said to heart. And they played with a lot of pride."

Cumberland came out shooting well and playing hard-nosed defense, forcing the Trotters to abandon their reams and concentrate on playing. No account of the game can be found, and Red's memory fails as to which unit of the Trotters showed up that night or what individual players. However, Klotz vividly remembers his role in the game: "I had a nasty infection on my neck, a 'carbuncle,'" Red said. "I didn't think I was going to be able to play. But once the game began, my guys were playing so well I felt I had to get out there. We had a chance to win."

Red remembers feeling weakened by the infection, but it did not affect his ability to shoot the ball. Pence, Haggerty, and company fed the hot hand, and Red scorched the nets for much of the game. There were very few reams going on due to the closeness of the score. The Dukes and Trotters slugged it out on mostly even terms for the entire game, and when the buzzer sounded to end regulation play the score was knotted.

"The Trotters had left the court, believing they had won," Red remembers. "They couldn't believe they had not beaten a minor league team playing on a high school court. But they hadn't. They didn't want to look at the scorebook. All they wanted to do was get dressed and head out of town and make it to their next game."

General Manager H.L Whip had other ideas. "He went into their dressing room and told them if they wanted to be paid for the game, they would return to the court."

The Trotters did indeed return, and proceeded to run the Dukes into the ground during the extra period. "They finally did to us what they should have done in the regulation time. We gave them a tough way to go."

Afterward, Trotters' owner Abe Saperstein was informed of his team's narrow escape. He was none too pleased about it, Red said. He also was not surprised to learn that Red Klotz had given his team all that it could handle.

Even though the Dukes had lost, Red felt confident about their chances in the upcoming playoffs. "We were the hottest team in the league at that point, and playing with a great deal of confidence. After nearly beating the Trotters, we felt like we could pretty much beat anybody. We were entering the playoffs fully expecting to win the championship."

Unfortunately for Red and the Dukes, it was not to be. Gloria went into labor as Cumberland embarked on its championship series. "I don't have any doubt we would have won that title if I had been in a position to stick around and play," Red maintained.

Instead, Klotz hustled back to Atlantic City just in time to greet the arrival of his third child and second son, Glenn, born on March 6. There would be no return to Cumberland, either. The league folded during the 1949-1950 season, according to the American Professional Basketball Research website.

Even though there was no championship to celebrate this time, Red looks back fondly on his season in Western Maryland. "It was a unique experience. I learned about coaching and relating to players. We did well in a very competitive league. I always knew that I could play. But now, for the first time, I knew for sure that I knew how to coach."

Once again, Red was a man without a team and no immediate prospects for one. Little did he know that his basketball life was about to take on an entirely new direction, one that would define his career.

Cumberland Dukes program.

Abe Saperstein and Red in West Berlin during the 1952 European tour.

Chapter 12

Abe Saperstein Calling

The Cumberland Dukes' near miss in the All American League playoffs did not dampen Red's desire to stay in the pro game. Life circumstances and a sense of family responsibility seemed to be pulling him away from the game and back home to the Inlet to tend to the growing brood.

The birth of his son Glenn not only interrupted Red's participation in the Dukes' postseason, "and my absence probably cost us the championship," he said, but Glenn's arrival also meant more resources were needed. The small apartment was now too small, and the food bill was getting larger. However, a funny thing happened on the way to his full-time career as a fruit, nut, and newspaper salesman on the AC boardwalk. The basketball world reached out and grabbed at Klotz once again. This time, that world would include parts of two continents he never had seen before.

Abe Saperstein reportedly heard about his team's near-upset in Cumberland and Red's role in the game. Once again, Klotz had been the central figure. But unlike his dribbling prowess, which closed out a Sphas win over the Trotters in 1942, it had been Red's shooting that could not be stopped this time.

Red: "After I got to know Abe, I could imagine how he reacted to that game. He wouldn't have reacted well. I was red hot and doing the bulk of the scoring. We took away their show plays and forced them to play it straight. He was probably thinking to himself, 'There's that Klotz guy again. Who is this guy?'"

"If they were going to leave me open, I was going to shoot it all night long. If they double-teamed me, that just meant somebody else was open," Red said. "We were a good team, and we were on our home court. They knew they were fortunate to get out of there with a win."

To put the performance in context, one must recognize that the Trotters were at this period in history not just the most popular and entertaining basketball team in the world, they were also unquestionably the best. They had beaten George Mikan and the mighty Minneapolis Lakers the previous February, 61-59 on a 30-foot bomb at the buzzer by Ermer Robinson, and they were less than a month away from repeating that feat with a 49-45 win.

The Trotters also had begun to expand their geographic horizons. The regional white pro leagues were still around and the top loops boasted very good teams and players. The Trotters dispatched most without breaking much of a sweat, and local patrons howled with delight watching the various reams and show plays despite the fact they came at the expense of their local heroes. The Lakers were something altogether different. They were the only current squad with a plausible claim as the best team.

Both Laker games were played before large, racially mixed and charged crowds at Chicago Stadium. The all-white Lakers were NBL champs in 1948, and joined the BAA the following year, a season before the league would merge with several other NBL franchises and change its name to the National Basketball Association. The Lakers were favored heavily each time, but the Trotters put their bag of court reams on the shelf (save the fading moments of the 1949 game) and won the tense, closely-contested battles. The 1948 game, played before more than 17,000 fans, was thought by some to be a fluke, which generated even more interest for the rematch the following year. This time, more than 20,000 showed up, a new Chicago Stadium record.

In 1949, Abe had his most talented team ever with Pressley, Marques Haynes directing the offense, and Goose Tatum throwing in his deadly hook. All three were veterans of the first Laker win, as was Robinson. Fans who normally saw the "Golden Goose" star in the "baseball" skit and other antics were even more amazed to see him in straight basketball action against the Lakers. Tatum used his long arms to grab rebounds or keep plays alive off the glass. "He had the longest arms I ever saw," Red marveled. "It made it funny as hell when he rolled a ball across his back and down his arm. But those arms also made him an outstanding player. His hook shot was deadly and almost impossible to block."

Goose was somewhat of a defensive liability though, and putting him on the six-foot-ten Mikan proved to be a mismatch. George was the first big man to play with the athleticism of a small forward. He took his game right at Tatum early and scored a pair of easy baskets as the Lakers jumped out to an 8-1 lead. However, Abe wasn't merely a promoter. He knew the game and switched the defensive assignment over to Nat "Sweetwater" Clifton, a six-foot-seven Chicago product who effectively shut down big George, holding him to just two field goals for the rest of the game. Clifton displayed the skills that would land him with the New York Knicks in 1950-51 as one of the NBA's first African American players.

The Trotters, who couldn't buy a basket early, seemed to be energized by the defensive switch and began to hit their shots at the other end. Ultimately, they ran up a 12-point lead late enough to roll out a few show plays at the end, as they would have if the opposition had been a bunch of local stiffs. However, these were the mighty Lakers, not some team of coal miners or loggers with a ringer or two in the game. The show plays, which developed as a means to not humiliate local opposition, was now the signal the game was over. It was a huge embarrassment to Mikan (the BAA's leading scorer at 28-plus points per game) and his teammates, none of whom scored more than six points against the brash barn-stormers.

Not far removed from Jackie Robinson's historic breaking of the color line in baseball, the Trotters' made their own statement for equal sports opportunity that was quite bold. Unlike Robinson, a single player on an otherwise white squad, the Trotters were all black, taking on a team of whites. Also, basketball was a faster game with more physical contact. Both teams wanted the victory badly, and play was intense. Sometimes during scrambles for a loose ball or positioning for rebounds, it looked like a fight might break out. Instead, the players held their emotions in check. It proved ironic that the Trotters' show plays, designed not to humiliate, did just that against the mighty Lakers.

That the reams came at the expense of the team widely regarded as the game's best was heightened by the presence of newsreel cameras and national press. Millions of fans would witness the Trotters' superiority themselves the next week in theatres across the land. The 49-45 final score was not as close as the numbers would lead one to believe. Mikan scored eight of his game-high 19 points from the field. The Trotters had balanced scoring, with Tatum getting 14 points, followed by 11 each from Haynes and Clifton, seven from Babe Pressley, and Robinson, the previous year's hero, getting six. The Trotters clearly outplayed the white champions.

Red: "The newsreels showing them beating the Lakers was a huge step in building the Globetrotters' name and legend. Remember, most people still didn't have television at the time. Moving pictures were the next best thing to seeing live action. Everyone could see for themselves how good the Trotters were. It wasn't a matter of black team against white team at this point. The Trotters were just the better team, period. They beat the Lakers not once, but twice. Just (the newsreels) being on there legitimized them in the eyes of many white people who weren't familiar with them or the pro game. All the big-time writers were there. The Trotters were national at this point. They weren't just those black guys on a tour coming through town once a year. They were in the big buildings and their best players were becoming household names."

Newfound celebrity notwithstanding, the Trotters' stock-in-trade continued to be their viability as a traveling road show at outposts around the country. By this time, Abe was touring two separate units for the U.S. tour, and the East unit expected no major resistance when it rolled into Cumberland. When it didn't work out that way, Abe began to think about a different approach. Rather than taking on whatever competition was available, he considered bringing regular competition along on the tour. This would give him more control over the tour and logistics, and it would eliminate the need to deal with local contacts to raise a team to face the Trotters.

Red: "Sometimes it worked out well with local competition. We certainly proved in Cumberland that a less talented team could give them a run. More often though, local teams were proving to be an embarrassment. Even with the reams, which people were coming to see, they wanted some basketball action, too. The Trotters had simply become so good they couldn't bank on a good game. Fans were becoming more sophisticated too. Nobody wanted to pay good money and watch a bunch of guys out there who looked like they didn't belong on the same court."

The following year, the nationwide tours still would go on, but in addition, there would be an 18-game "World Series of Basketball" against some of the nation's best former collegians, and the final triumph: a jaunt to the British Isles and the main European continent, as well as parts of North Africa. The famous Harlem Globetrotters now truly were living up to their name.

As they planned to go into areas where basketball virtually was unknown, Abe was going to need opposition, and there was little doubt Klotz would be asked along to be part of the ambitious plan. Wasn't this guy a protégé of Abe's close friend Eddie Gottlieb? Hadn't he won a BAA title already? Hadn't he coached a pro team in the All-American League and managed the Sphas' touring unit? Didn't he always seem to turn up when the Trotters found themselves in a tough contest?

Saperstein knew Red off the court as well, having bumped into him many times in the course of doing business. Gottlieb was busy managing and coaching the Philly Warriors and helping to keep the NBA afloat. The Warriors had won the first BAA championship and lost to Red's Bullets in the finals the following year. The consummate booking agent, Gottlieb, along with the other BAA owners, knew putting the Trotters on doubleheader bills would help draw customers.

The Sphas remained a known entity in their own right and could play on par with most other barnstorming and league teams. They still had a strong base among Jewish fans, and in recent years had become more diverse ethnically (though still all-white) and were popular opening game attractions for BAA teams, for the Trotters, or in the nightcap against the Trotters. The Mogul needed someone to keep the team together on and off the court, not to mention book the hotels, distribute meal money, and drive the car and players to the next date.

Saperstein kept running into the little redhead from Philly, be it with the Sphas, managing them, or the Dukes or Atlantic City Senators. "Wherever he ran into me, he seemed to be impressed. I was either doing a good job on the floor or I was doing a good job running the team, whatever team I was representing. He knew I was a professional." Later in the season, Saperstein would show just how much he respected and valued Red's approach to the game as a player and a manager.

First, there would come an entirely new concept, the "World Series" of Basketball, pitting the Harlem Globetrotters against some of the greatest graduating seniors in college basketball. The college game had caught on faster than the pro version, and games were selling out places like Madison Square Garden in New York and Convention Hall in Philly. With their credibility of beating the Lakers, fans were excited to see how they would do against a squad of collegiate all-stars.

The College All Americans' tour of 1950 featured future Boston Celtics' great Bob Cousy of Holy Cross, the tour's leading scorer, six-foot-seven power forward Don Rehfeldt of Wisconsin, three-time Notre Dame All-American guard Kevin O'Shea, and the MVP of the tour, Villanova's Paul Arizin.

The World Series was an instant smash hit. The All-Americans, coached by Hall of Famers Ray Meyer of DePaul and Clair Bee of Long Island University, gave the Trotters good competition and the matchup drew capacity crowds. Thirteen of the 18 games were sellouts. The buzz of Trotter wins over the Lakers was fresh, and large audiences were willing to come out and see some great basketball, and reams if the score allowed. The Trotters won 10 of the first 15, and their losing margins were no greater than eight points during that span.

Perhaps looking ahead to the European tour, the Globetrotters dropped two of the final games in Buffalo and Philly, before closing out the series with a convincing 77-64 decision in Washington D.C. The 18 games in 17 cities tour (Los Angeles hosted two games) proved to be the latest sports triumph for the Trotters' owner-coach-promoter. It wasn't so much that the Globetrotters again had proven their superiority on the basketball court, but that huge, predominantly white audiences were clamoring to see them. Postwar America was in the middle of a great industrial and overall economic boom, and workers had disposable income for entertainment.

Abe and his squad reaped the rewards in accolades, if not dollars. He made it a point to give the ticket-buyer added value with a floor show featuring some of the great musicians, comedians, and vaudeville-style acts. Big-name athletes and movie stars also found their way to Globetrotter games. Abe would provide courtside seats in exchange for a few bows to the crowd. Boxing great Sugar Ray Robinson went so far as to dress with the team and join the "magic circle" warm-up routine.

"People always thought Abe was getting rich, but he kept putting all the profits back into the business and building the name," Red asserted. "He did great advance work. He'd go out and buy extra newspapers and send the accounts of the previous night's game to the papers, radio, and TV stations in the next city. He also wined and dined the top sportswriters and held a big party for them every year. The publicity began to feed off itself and the Trotters were becoming more famous at each and every stop."

The Sphas, meanwhile, had become one of the Trotters' regular tour opponents at stops in larger cities or where there was no local opposition available. Red seemed to have a knack for keeping his team in the game but not upstaging the Trotters, for whom the paying customers had come to see. "I wasn't afraid to play along with the reams, which some of the other players just didn't have a feel for," Klotz said. "I became adept at chasing the dribbler, usually Marques, and anticipating his moves. It got to be like a ballet out there with the two of us."

The acclaim Abe's team would enjoy on its North American tour, its triumphs over the Lakers, its three wins in Cuba, and the series against the All-Americans was about to pale. The Trotters soon would become true world travelers and true United States diplomats. First, they had to come up with a new team to provide the opposition. The Sphas had their own scheduling commitments and would not be available for the trans-Atlantic tour. Thus, Abe needed to put a squad together.

There was no doubt that Red would be invited, along with the likes of Yale University All-American Tony Lavelli, who since had broken into the NBA with the Boston Celtics; Bob Karstens of the New York Celtics, an independent team, who later would become the first white man to play for the Globetrotters; Leo Barnhost of Notre Dame; Ange Acuna, who had played for his native Mexico in the 1948 Olympics; and Leo Mogus of the Warriors. They formed the core of the squad. The team was coached by George Mikan's brother Ed, a fine player and technical basketball man in his own right.

Abe's invitation to tour with the Trotters would mean another extended separation from Gloria and his family. Klotz can't remember the exact circumstances of the invitation, only that it came directly from Abe himself. "That's the way he did things. He wouldn't hand that down to an underling. Besides, he ran most of the operation himself, anyway."

"He probably took me aside and mentioned it to me one night after a game against the Sphas," Red went on. "Or he may have called me at home. We would have so many more conversations over the rest of Abe's life, I just can't remember. But I can tell you one thing: I was thrilled he asked and had a feeling we were in for some special times."

Still, it was a tough call for Red to confirm his participation. "I wasn't going to get rich off this tour. It represented an opportunity to do something I always had dreamed of, to see the world. And to do it with the best team in the world. That's a hard thing to turn down when you love the game as much as I do."

It was a much simpler decision for Gloria, and one that could be considered unusual for a woman tending to a large family and a business. "This was something he wanted. He had the ability to play at the highest level and here was an opportunity to pursue his passion," she said. "Basketball was his first love. I wasn't about to stand in his way or try to hold him back. Besides…we were young and we didn't know any better," she said with a laugh.

With Gloria's full blessing, Red boarded the TWA flight out of New York's Idlewild International Airport and joined Abe's traveling party for the first time. The Trotters brought Marques Haynes, Goose Tatum, Ermer Robinson, and Babe Pressley, as well as Red's Philly homeboy "Rookie" Brown, a graduate of Ben Franklin High School.

"This was undoubtedly the best team in professional basketball at the time," Red said. "They proved it night after night, and the audiences in those countries were anxious to see them in person." He had no idea just how anxious, but was about to find out.

Even though basketball was a little known sport in Great Britain, crowds flocked to the games at London's Wembly Pool Arena and throughout the English countryside. The announcers frequently mispronounced names and misstated basketball terminology. None of that seemed to matter. The Trotters let their skills and their comedy acts speak for themselves. The formula translated just as well when the tour hit the main European continent and the Americans had to overcome a language barrier. Audiences loved the Trotters. They also appreciated the efforts of their hardworking opponents.

"I was always up for adventures," he said. "Basketball was about to give me more adventures than any human being has a right to expect in their lifetime."

Abe Saperstien meets Soviet Premier Nikita Khruschev in 1959. At left is Trotters publicist Walter Kennedy, who would go on to become NBA Commissioner. Eddie Gottlieb is between Abe and Khruschev.

Argentina's first couple Juan and Evita Perone (front and center) pose with the Harlem Globetrotters and U.S. All Stars. Red is second from left, at bottom.

Chapter 13

Evita and the Ambassadors

The Trotters' European triumphs were just the beginning of a long series of "firsts" for Abe Seperstein's team. The 1950-51 season would see the first ever tour to Central and South America, an ambitious nine-country foray in the spring and early summer. Red could have signed on for a second tour of Europe and North Africa, in which the Trotters were opposed by longtime barnstormers the Boston Whirlwinds. Instead, he opted to accompany the delegation headed for the Southern Hemisphere and opposed by a group known as the U.S. All Stars, comprised of recent college grads and established pro stars.

Red's thinking was that South America would present new and more varied thrills, as the tour would mark the first time the American pro game had visited Argentina, Brazil, Chile, Colombia, Panama, Ecuador, Peru, Uruguay, and Venezuela. He had returned from his first European tour as a different basketball player and a different man. The lure of the exotic locales he only had heard of proved irresistible.

"It felt very satisfying to have helped introduce the game in Europe, and quite educational to see firsthand many of the countries that had been devastated in World War II," he said. "It felt better to finally come home to my family and Atlantic City, and made me better appreciate living in the United States. But when

Abe told us about plans for his newest tour, I was probably one of the first guys to sign up for the South American schedule."

Already a champion at every level of the sport, nobody would have blamed Klotz for feeling as if he had seen and done it all. Given the evolution of the game at the time, Klotz had amassed a resume unmatched by all but a select few. However, Red exhibited some different attitudes than most athletes. For one thing, he felt he just was getting started as a pro, despite his veteran stature and the fact he was advancing on the age of 30. At a stage of his career that signaled the start of the downside for many elite players, Red was in the best shape of his life and injury-free. He was still one of the fastest players with a basketball in his hands and still a clever playmaker. If anything, his years as a pro only had sharpened his keen basketball acumen.

More importantly, Red Klotz shared Abe Saperstein's sense of pioneer spirit. "Traveling to new and different places broadens you as a person and sharpens your appreciation for life," he said. "It also gives you a perspective on humanity. People around the world may be different than we are in many ways. But they are more similar than different. Fans want to escape the real word for a couple of hours, see a good game, and be entertained. News of the tour to Europe the year before had reached these people (in South America), and we thought they were ready to embrace the game."

Those feelings would be reinforced when Red, his coaches, and his teammates boarded a plane with the Trotters that left from Miami's International Airport on April 26. The group was off on the first leg of a 46-game, 59-day whirlwind covering 18,000 miles. It mattered little the Trotters won all 46 games. What mattered was the game was played for the first time in outdoor bull rings, on soccer fields, and before Argentine President Juan Peron and his glamorous wife Evita. On one magical night in Brazil, it would be played in front of the largest crowd in the history of basketball.

"One similarity between this tour and Europe was that soccer had been the dominant team sport," Red recalled. "Also, people were ready for something new in sports, and basketball certainly provided that. The major difference was the people of South America were louder and less reserved. In England, the audience appreciated the game just as much, but they'd sometimes sit on their hands. In these countries, the people made it clear. They weren't shy about letting you know when they were having a good time. They'd let you know if they felt the opposite way, too."

Klotz was having a pretty good time himself. In Argentina, the basketballs provided were unlike anything he had seen before: essentially soccer balls built to a basketball's circumference and weight. Klotz practiced with the new ball and found the unusual seams allowed his deadly set shot to be more accurate than ever. "The balls were easier to dribble and shoot," he said. "I practiced with them a bit, and I became pretty good with them. They looked almost exactly like a soccer ball, except larger."

As a result of his familiarity and comfort level with the new ball, Klotz shot more often and more successfully against the Trotters, further building his reputation, keeping the scores close, and proving his squad of all-stars to be worthy opponents. On some nights, the U.S. Stars played in a split-squad format with an opening game against a local or national team. The games were more fun for the Americans than their hosts.

"We gave them a lesson in basketball," Red recalled. "These were countries that enjoyed the game and were getting to know it. Their development was behind ours, and in the backcourt especially, the South American players didn't have the skills we did, or know our tricks of the trade." Consequently, Red's defensive abilities, probably the least-heralded part of his game, were clearly on display. "I knew where their guards were going to be in certain situations, which allowed me to get there first, or at least be in the neighborhood. Then I would use my speed and quick hands and knock the ball away to one of my teammates, or steal it myself. I also had the luxury of being on a pretty good team. I could take more chances on defense because of the other guys we had out there. If I overran the play going for the steal, I knew there was someone backing me up. We came at them in waves. The Trotters were our only competition. We beat the hell out of many local teams and national teams on that tour."

An action photo from the tour captures Red in the process of sneaking behind an Argentine guard and stripping the soccer-style basketball while Lavelli looks on with a bemused expression. The Argentine wears a look of outright horror.

If the enlarged soccer ball proved easier to handle for Red, imagine its effect when held and shot by the likes of Goose Tatum, who possessed long arms and huge hands. "A regular ball looked small in his hands, and his long wingspan (84 inches, reportedly the longest of any player in the game at that time) allowed him to accentuate all his tricks and to make his hook shot more accurate," Red recalled. "The fans loved him. He was a very good player and a great showman, probably the greatest of all time. Goose's hook was deadly to begin with. We knew Goose was the greatest showman in basketball. Now the world was seeing it, along with his many skills as a player."

Any doubts that Red had chosen the correct tour in 1951 were dispelled when they arrived in Rio De Janiero, Brazil, and the traveling party checked into a hotel just steps from the famed Copacabana Beach. "It was first class, and we were treated like royalty," said Red. "Many of the guys lounged by the pool or went to the beach or just relaxed in their rooms. I could never do that. I had to find a tour of the city and look at something educational. It was always important to me to get something out of the trip besides basketball and partying."

The reason for star treatment soon was verified. The Stars and Trotters had been booked to play 10 dates in the massive soccer stadium known as Estadio Maracana, which accommodated over 200,000 fans at the time. None of his previous basketball experiences prepared Red and the Trotters and Stars for what they would see on May 5 when they entered the massive structure, opened the year before to host the 1950 World Cup.

"We walked through the tunnel and saw the court had been set up down at one end of the soccer field, and we couldn't believe how many people were there," he said. "A moat filled with water had been set up to separate the players from the fans." Red said the dressing rooms were equipped with oxygen for the players, something unheard of in 1951. "That place was well ahead of any stadium or facility in America at that time," Klotz said.

The announced attendance of 50,041 was the largest throng ever to witness a basketball game. The previous record was set earlier the same year at the Rose Bowl near Los Angeles, where more than 36,000 saw the Trotters win. The crowd in Rio also exceeded the combined attendance figures of the six American baseball stadium tour dates that year, by more than 3,000. In all, more than 217,000 watched the Trotters and U.S. Stars in Rio over the 10 dates, according to Red Smith's report in the *New York Herald Tribune*.

From Rio, the tour stopped at four other Brazilian cities, with games staged in smaller venues but filled to capacity each time. Red was having a hard time wrapping his head around the phenomenon. "For a kid from South Philly who came up on the playgrounds, it was hard to imagine. And it wasn't imagination. It was happening right in front of us."

Things were pretty impressive off the court as well. "The players were the toast of the town," said Bob Finnegan, a Chicago radio broadcaster who served as a referee during the tour. "They willingly signed autographs and displayed their famous basketball tricks, sometimes using the hotel lobby as a court."

While in Sao Paulo, the party received an invitation from President Getulio Vargas to return to Rio for a command performance, to which they agreed. Vargas was the longtime dictator of the nation until his first democratically-elected term as president the year of the Trotters' visit.

The shaky political situation in Brazil was downright stable compared to what the Trotters and Stars would encounter when they arrived in Argentina. Along with wildly enthusiastic capacity crowds, the traveling party encountered a nation that was just five years removed from a military government imposed with the help of strong-arm tactics by the current president, Peron.

Peron was in the first of his three stints as president, none of which would amount to a fully completed term. Many of his countrymen considered Peron to be a bully and a dictator. Fully aware of this, Red and the rest of the Trotters arrived in Bueno Aires with more than a little bit of trepidation. What they received were flowers and gifts, including letter openers in the shape of a sword bearing Peron's signature. They were received officially at a state luncheon, and then would go out and play before capacity crowds each night. "That was the thing with going into some of those countries," Red said. "It could have been dangerous, and looking back on it all, it *was* much more dangerous than we realized."

The meal with the Argentine president and his wife came at a time when Peron was promoting Evita as his vice president, despite opposition from rivaling factions in politics and the military. "They gave us tons of political literature and propaganda speeches," Red recalled. "His wife was a beautiful woman and seemed to like basketball. The luncheon they gave us was wonderful, but I think most of the guys weren't so interested in the politics and just wanted to get out there and play ball."

Grainy home movies of the luncheon show the smiling Juan and Evita, who was still looking vibrant despite being in the last months of her life, due to a battle with cancer. Members of the Trotters and U.S. Stars appeared to be reserved yet relaxed in the film as they are honored by the Perons.

"Abe always told his players and management of the opposition that he expected everyone to represent the United States, not simply your team," Red said. "Most of the guys took it to heart, and those who did not were sent home." This was a credo Red adopted when running his own operation in future years. "There is enough other stuff to worry about without worrying about the character of your players," he said.

There were no such issues on the first trip to South America. Although Argentina had never seen the likes of the Trotters, the country had a strong basketball history. The nation hosted and won the first Federation of International Basketball Association (FIBA) title in 1950, the year before the Trotters arrived. The country's love of the game endured and decades later, the Argentines would beat the United States en route to the 2004 Olympic gold medal. Argentina also has contributed outstanding players to the NBA. Even during that first visit by the Globetrotters, the Argentine fans held high expectations for the Harlem team and for the national team's appearances with the U.S. pros.

The American basketball ambassadors did not disappoint Peron and Evita. "We went over exceptionally well there," Red recalled. "They loved the Trotters and the show. They just embraced the game, and they knew it was American. We represented something to them they had never seen before." Evita was so taken by the Trotters' "Sweet Georgia Brown" theme song, she ordered it to be played before all national games in Argentina.

The playing conditions in Central and South America were unlike any others the Trotters or Red ever had encountered. Local officials may have received the traveling party like royals, but there was nothing that could be done about the weather or the relatively primitive facilities that existed outside of the major cities. Most games were played in stifling heat and humidity, and in dingy, overcrowded arenas. In Guayaquil, Ecuador, the teams overcame the trials of playing in the thin air of a city situated at an altitude in excess of 3,000 feet. This was in stark contrast to what they had seen in Rio.

On the next-to-last date of the trip in Caracas, Venezuela, the game was rained out at an outdoor bull ring. Taking their ambassador's orders seriously, the following day, the Trotters and Stars played though a drizzle to accommodate the fans. They then boarded a flight and flew all day to make it in time for their final tour date in Panama City.

The Trotters now had played in 27 nations and the U.S. Territories of Alaska, Hawaii, and Puerto Rico. They had been blessed by the Pope. A movie, "The Harlem Globetrotters," starring "Rookie" Brown and the beautiful Dorothy Dandridge as his love interest, featured Thomas Gomez as Saperstein. The film opened to good reviews and box office success. The World Series of Basketball recently had wrapped up, and had proven to be quite popular.

At home, the tour had not gone unnoticed. Nor did the American press miss its impact on race relations and foreign diplomacy. It was being written how the "all negro team" was proving that democracy and equality existed in the U.S. They received an official government welcome home at the airport in New York. The general population was beginning to see and appreciate what the Trotters were doing beyhond the game itself.

Although not yet welcome in every state, the Trotters were officially an international sensation and an asset to the United States Department of State. During a Cold War era in which Communist nations were quick to characterize blacks as second-class U.S. citizens, the Globetrotters' tours indicated something quite different. Here were young, athletic men staying in the same hotels as the well-heeled and well-educated, and given extensive plaudits for doing so.

"In our own way, we were helping to state a very strong case against segregation," Red said. "Nobody was accusing any of us of being the 'Ugly American.' We were embracing the culture of each and every place we visited. People can tell when somebody is a phony. And it didn't matter about the language barrier, they could sense we were genuine."

Saperstein quoted an official state department communication as reported in the military newspaper *Stars and Stripes*. "The Globetrotters have proven themselves ambassadors of extraordinary goodwill wherever they have gone," the letter stated. "On any future tours, please call on the State Department of the United States for any help we can give."

Red may have been on the opposition's side for the first European and South American tours, but he was an integral part of them both. "There are 10 men on a basketball court, not five," he stressed. "As well as the Trotters played, they had to be pushed. That's what we did, and a big part of why the Trotters played so well. At the same time, we received our fair share of compliments. We made consistently good plays, many great plays, and we heard about it. Our guys were All-Americans and successful pros in their own right. They had a ton of pride. They played smart and they played hard all the time. The fans knew, and the Trotters certainly found out on the court, that we were a very good team."

The concept of pushing the Trotters with an all-star team was not lost on Abe Saperstein, nor on Red. It was a concept that would serve them both well for what was about to come next.

At Idlewild International Airport in New York before taking off for a European tour. Red is third from the right at bottom. Just to the left of Red is Goose Tatum.

Chapter 14

Berlin, Ballparks...and a Proposition

Red's right to brag for having played in the best-attended basketball game of all time lasted much less than all time; it lasted exactly 107 days. While the U.S. Stars and Trotters' western unit were blazing new trails throughout Central and South America, the eastern squad was staging a triumphant return across Europe. They did so with a veteran opposition squad of barnstormers known as the Boston Whirlwinds.

In a contest that would prove to be a milestone not only for the international acceptance of the sport, but also a major victory for U.S. diplomacy, the Trotters would play before an amazing throng of 75,000-plus at Berlin's Olympic Stadium. The game, played on August 22, 1951, catapulted the Globetrotters to new heights both in popularity and as goodwill ambassadors for the United States.

Although Red wasn't there, one of the few key moments in the last 60 years of Trotters' history he was not a witness to, word immediately got back from Abe and the players who were there. "If you could imagine a crowd of that size watching basketball on one of the Trotters' portable courts with portable goals, equipment Abe basically invented, in a place where we had been at war...Well, you probably *couldn't* imagine it," Klotz said.

Abe, who hopscotched the hemispheres to observe parts of both tours, now realized the Trotters were the preeminent draw in the sport and among its top teams. Having beaten the Lakers a second time in 1949, their court credentials were impeccable, and their comedy element set them apart. You really didn't need to be a basketball purist to enjoy a Trotters' game. Male fans brought their wives or their dates, and parents brought their kids. It seemed as though everyone wanted to watch and be entertained, even if they "didn't know a dribble from a Dodge," to borrow a phrase from tour secretary Dave Zinkoff.

Abe fully understood the days of playing against local challengers were nearly over. There were exceptions, usually in the form of the national team representing the nation the Trotters were passing through. Sometimes those teams weren't an embarrassment going up against the likes of Sweetwater Clifton, Goose Tatum and Marques Haynes. More frequently, the Trotters would roll up a big lead and put on the show to avoid outright humiliation.

In some places, the show could carry them. Basketball was so new to the audience that they ate it all up. Sometimes it was simply the fact they were watching the world-famous Harlem Globetrotters. Other venues were more sophisticated about the sport. The laughs were great, but they also wanted to see shooting, dribbling, and passing. This was true of the opposition as well. In order for the game not to be an insult to these crowds, the Trotters' opposition had to do a credible job. "Very few teams were out there that could stay with the Globetrotters, and fewer who didn't get in the way of the show," said Red. "It was up to the Trotters to build up a lead, and then they were free to put on the show."

With the Globetrotters' success, basketball was catching on as a major sport. Stateside, the BAA had absorbed several of the NBL franchises, including the Lakers, and renamed the circuit the National Basketball Association. Crowds still mostly were sparse compared to the college game. The one exception seemed to be when there was a basketball doubleheader scheduled: the NBA game, followed by the Trotters against *anybody*.

"The NBA owes us a debt of gratitude," longtime Trotter Tex Harrison said. "We kept them afloat. People came to see us, not some new pro league."

Regional pro leagues such as the ABL still managed to carry on by playing preliminary to the NBA contest or in small venues; however, their days were numbered, and they would not survive much longer. The Philadelphia Sphas, still owned by Eddie Gottlieb and now managed by Red, were the exception. They'd play regular league games as well as "exhibitions," which were real games against top non-league opponents, such as the New York Renasannce and of course, the Harlem Globetrotters. A great action photo of this era shows Red in a Sphas' uniform, beating a Globetrotter down court for an easy layup, as a packed house in Los Angeles watches.

"Opposed to the Trotters will be the ever-alert-up-and-at-'em Philadelphia Sphas," Cleveland News sportswriter Ed Bang wrote. "(they) have enough oomph when it comes to playing basketball to make the best of them hustle to the limit and that goes for the Harlem brigade."

There were a few other "usual suspects" teams that could give the Trotters a run. Besides the Sphas and Whirlwinds, there were the New York Celtics (not to be confused with the "original" Celtics of New York, or Boston's NBA franchise, which made Red Klotz its last cut of the 1947-48 season). There were also all-star professional teams, such as Red's squad that was traveling through South America, and the College All-Stars could make a credible contest of it.

Abe began to think about soliciting other teams to accompany his squad, although the consideration was not at the top of his mind. During the summer of 1951, he still was trying to complete arguably his greatest season ever. All eyes in the basketball community were on Europe, Saperstein's biggest hit yet. A series of games at London's Wembly Pool Arena were sellouts to kick things off before the party embarked for the main continent.

Among those watching closely were high-ranking officials of the U.S. Department of State. They had noticed the acclaim foreign countries afforded a team of black players and were well aware of the positive public relations aspects. The Trotters breezed through Holland, Italy, Portugal, Spain, Switzerland, and Belgium prior to their foray into Germany. In Rotterdam, their portable court was laid atop the soccer pitch, where Abe assumed a perch on the grass.

In Rome, the Trotters were received by Pope Pius XII. The Pontiff proved to be somewhat of a basketball fan. "He was seen tapping his feet along to Sweet Georgia Brown," longtime Philadelphia sports broadcaster Bill Campbell said.

Always ahead of his time, Abe turned the games into entertainment events for the fans who shelled out their hard-earned cash to buy a ticket. Tony Lavelli jumped from his spot on the U.S. All-Stars to join the Whirlwinds and also to play his accordion in the halftime floor show, which featured, "baton twirling lovely, Dotty Grover," a singing and dancing trio, and "table tennis" experts Doug Cartland and Marty Reisman.

The Whirlwinds also featured the famous Clark twins of Andrews, Indiana. The Clarks were not precursors to Tom and Dick Van Arsdale, the NBA's most famous set of twin brothers. They were their own *team* of six twin brothers. Of Harvey and Gertrude Aker Clark's 11 children, eight were four sets of twins, and the only non-basketball players among them were the youngest, girls Mildred and Margaret. The boys' basketball team won two National Family League championships in the late 40s before joining the Whirlwinds. Bob and Ross were the oldest, followed by Dale and Don, and finally, Jim and Joe. *Life* magazine wrote them up, which caught Abe's attention, and the young men soon were trading shots and elbows with the most famous team in the sport. "Those guys were a novelty, but they could also play," said Red.

As if that weren't enough value added for the ticket-buying

public, track star Jesse Owens, who had won four gold medals for the U.S. in the 1936 Olympics in Berlin, was on hand. Owens set up and conducted track clinics for local youngsters at each tour stop. Middleweight boxing champ Sugar Ray Robinson was another key component of the tour.

The German itinerary called for stops in Munich, Stuttgart, Mannheim, Hamburg, Dusseldorf, Hanover, Breman, and Frankfurt, where U.S. High Commissioner to Germany, John J. McCloy, tossed the ball up for the ceremonial opening tap. Unbeknownst to Abe, McCloy previously had received a wire from Secretary of State Dean Acheson, asking him to secure the Trotters for a game in Berlin.

Abe was not keen on the idea. Berlin had been the scene of riots following a championship fight between Robinson and local challenger Gerhard Hecht. Judges ruled that Sugar Ray had landed an illegal kidney punch and disqualified the champ, spurring the crowd to shower the ring with bottles and other debris. The next day, the local boxing commission overruled and declared the fight a no-decision. Abe justifiably was concerned with how the residents of Berlin would react to Robinson and to Jesse Owens, who famously was snubbed by Adolf Hitler at the 1936 Olympics in the same stadium where the Trotters would perform.

Postwar Berlin was a city divided, with the Western portion belonging to the host country and the Eastern section designated a tiny island controlled by the Communists. A concrete wall guarded by machine-gun-carrying elite troops was the line of demarcation. Adding to the tension were two youth rallies going on simultaneously in the eastern and western sectors. The East Berlin event featured concerts, art exhibits, and sports demonstrations, along with anti-West propaganda.

Despite his misgivings, the patriotic Abe granted McCloy's request and agreed to the game. All parties concerned agreed it would be a great message to show Communists and free Euro-

peans alike that African Americans could be accepted and celebrated. Syndicated columnist Earl Wilson wrote: "all we Americans felt very nationalistic about the team." Wilson singled out a
number of American journalists covering the tour, and a private
individual by the name of Walt Disney.

Honoring McCloy's request was not only a gutsy move, it was
difficult from a logistical standpoint. August 22 was the only open
date left in Germany and the teams needed to travel 175 miles
from Hamburg to get there. After Berlin, they were required to arrive in Paris on the 23rd in order to wrap up the tour.

McCloy, grateful for Abe's agreement to play, promised to handle the transportation, and arranged for three C-119 aircraft to deliver the teams and their court and equipment in time for the 2
p.m. game. With only two days to promote the Trotters' appearance, nobody was expecting a large crowd. McCloy issued a press
release announcing the game and the appearance of Jesse Owens.

Abe, the Trotters and Whirlwinds, head referee Elliott Hasson,
and the traveling party that included Gottlieb, Dave Zinkoff, and
promoter Harry Hannon experienced a collective nervousness as
they made their way from the airport in a bus and car caravan to
the stadium. They noticed the streets lined with people pressing
forward. "They didn't know if this was a friendly or hostile environment," said Red.

It soon became apparent the throngs were smiling, laughing,
and singing. They were intent on gaining the best position within
the crowd to try to catch a glimpse of the American players. When
the players' bus finally arrived at the stadium, the stands nearly
were filled.

"(McCloy) had offered free admission to the game, and those
kids showed up," Klotz said. "Many of them were from East Berlin,
and they found a way to get past the wall. The 75,000 Germans
were all there to watch American basketball. A crowd of that magnitude had never happened anywhere before."

At halftime, the sky began to buzz, and a U.S. Army helicopter appeared over the stadium. The craft landed on the field next to the court, and out stepped Jesse Owens, dressed in an elegant, light-colored suit. As a thunderous ovation continued, the Trotters, including Goose Tatum and Marques Haynes, formed a circle around Owens to shield him from view, and he emerged wearing his U.S. Olympic track uniform. The ovation grew even louder and longer. "I have not seen anything like that before or since," Haynes said in an interview decades later.

Owens took a lap around the track and pointed to the box where Hitler had stood 15 years before. He made a gracious speech to the German fans, and paid tribute to Lutz Long, who had lost the broad jump competition to Owens and openly embraced him, further embarrassing Hitler. Long had been killed in battle during the war.

Walter Schreiber, the mayor of West Berlin, took the microphone and stated: "Hitler did not offer you his hand. I offer you both of mine." The wild cheers grew louder still, and finally the Trotters and Whirlwinds settled down to the business of finishing out the game, and another Trotter win. The U.S. Air Force picked up both teams and all the equipment and transported everyone to Paris for the final contest of the frenetic 14-country, 92-game tour, with the Trotters winning them all.

The State Department was thrilled with the results of the Berlin game and the tour in general. "The Trotters were doing a great job of selling the American Dream and the idea that people could make something of themselves in the greatest country in the world. America was the land of opportunity, and regardless of color, everyone had that opportunity," Red said. "At least that was the message being communicated."

When the teams returned to the U.S. they were greeted at Idlewild Airport like conquering heroes. Wendel Smith wrote in the *Chicago Herald American*: "They were given a tumultuous re-

ception and welcomed by New York civic officials and other dignitaries of prominence. It was truly a great homecoming for this
band of fabulous basketeers...they spread goodwill for America
every place they went."

Amazingly, Abe's triumphant 1951 season wasn't finished.
After two U.S. tours with separate units, after a 14-4 domination
of the College All-Stars series, and after the tours of South and
Central America, Europe, and North Africa, Abe had yet another
outside-the-box idea: He would play a series of outdoor games at
major league baseball stadiums.

Red was invited to play on the all-star opposition coached by
George Mikan. He jumped at the chance. "We had already proven
we could play under all kinds of conditions," he said. "It was
pretty easy to adapt our style and to playing at night in ballparks."

 Klotz was joined on the opposition team, which kept the
"United States Stars" moniker, by Lavelli, Mikan's brother Ed, Ray
Ragelis, Bob Karstens, and a few other pro veterans.

The six-game tour included several big-league parks and a
one-point All-Stars win September 1 at the minor league Park-
way Field in Louisville, Kentucky. "Abe hated to lose, and it
was rare for the Trotters to lose. You didn't see that side to him
that often," Red recalled. "He would get steamed on those rare
occasions."

Whatever anger Saperstein felt was short-lived, as Harlem finally wrapped up their triumphant season with wins in Indianapolis and Fort Wayne, Indiana. Almost every one of the ballpark
series of games were contested closely, and Red Klotz seemed to
be in the middle of the action once again.

The series represented one more subtle but important triumph
for the founder and owner of the Harlem team. "Up until then, basketball was considered by most people to be a minor sport," Klotz
said. "Baseball was by far the biggest, and boxing was big. Horse
racing was still big at that time. College football was big. Basketball

was pretty much an afterthought. But times were changing. You could see people liked the teamwork, skill, and fast pace of basketball. And here we were, going into major league baseball stadiums, and thousands of people were coming out and paying to watch."

The next year was Klotz' third straight touring with the Trotters as they headed back to Great Britain, Europe, and for the first time, to the Far East. In Osaka, Japan, a gigantic, four-story poster greeted them featuring Goose Tatum's image. While in Luxembourg, Red was with the Trotters when they visited the grave of General George S. Patton in the U.S. cemetery there. It's still hard for Red to look at the picture of the basketball players solemnly placing a wreath on the final resting place of one of the country's most revered military figures.

More than 27,000 showed up in Tokyo to watch Harlem stomp all over a local college alumni squad. Upon their arrival, as they departed the plane, they were greeted by a line of Kimono-wearing young women. In Cairo, Egypt, the players were photographed between games riding on camelback.

Red's and the nation's thoughts never were far from the war. Virtually everyone had suffered loss and incredible sacrifice in the name of freedom. He would think of his lost childhood pal Chuck Drizen as he looked at the still-fresh bullet holes on buildings across Europe and city blocks that had been leveled by bombs and not yet rebuilt.

Through it all, Klotz comported himself as the consummate professional. Abe and Red had hit it off as friends from the beginning, and the Trotters' owner might have seen something of himself in the industrious point guard and family man. Red managed the Sphas with businesslike precision in a manner that endeared him to Gottlieb, but he still was hired help. Abe viewed Red quite differently. Here was an experienced pro coach with the Sphas and Cumberland Dukes, who also happened to be a savvy point guard with the ball in his hands when the buzzer went off at the end of several rare Globetrotter losses. At the conclusion of the 1952-53 season, Saperstein knew the time was right to make his pitch. He wanted Red as a partner, not an employee.

"Abe called me up," Red remembers. "He asked if I wanted to form my own organization and to go out on the road with him. Part of me couldn't believe it was happening. A break of a lifetime. I had always felt bad about leaving my family and now we were talking about more time away than ever before. Abe's offer also had the potential to mean better money and more things we could offer the kids.

Gloria was always supportive and this time it was no different.

In addition to leaving my family, I now would have more responsibilities than ever. I would have to select the players and handle a thousand details. My head was swimming."

Red was never one to back away from a challenge and with Gloria backing him up, he never hesitated.

"How could I possibly pass up the chance of a lifetime? I couldn't."

London, the birthplace of Abe Saperstein, was the traditional first stop on the Trotters' and Generals' overseas tours. Red (third from left) is standing next to Eddie Gottlieb. At the far left is publicity director Walter Kennedy, who would later serve as Commissioner of the NBA.

Red Klotz in publicity photo from the early 1950s.

Chapter 15

The Generals are Born

Before Red could begin his new direction as a basketball player and a businessman, he needed to settle up some loose ends with Sphas' owner Eddie Gottlieb.

It was the end of the 1951-52 season when Klotz brought Gloria along for the hour's drive from Atlantic City to Philly and a meeting at the Mogul's offices on Chestnut Street. Most of Gottlieb's time now was devoted to his NBA franchise, the Philadelphia Warriors. He also was promoting boxing and wrestling matches and his next big thing: exploring the possibility of putting an ownership group together for a bid to buy the Philadelphia Phillies. Gottlieb was involved in the ownership and promotion of the all-black Philadelphia Stars, and no one better understood what Jackie Robinson's signing meant for the long-term prospects of the Negro Leagues.

The Sphas, he knew, were probably on their last legs as well. The days of regional weekend pro basketball leagues were just about over. Still, the Sphas' name meant a great deal in basketball circles, and with Klotz managing things expertly on and off the court, Gotty was getting a five-man management crew for the discounted price of one. The Sphas were instant credibility for the opening game of a doubleheader with the Warriors in Philly or the Knickerbockers in New York.

171

"Eddie didn't have to worry about me, or the Sphas," Red said. "I was doing everything: coaching, playing, managing, booking the hotels, driving the players to the next date in Eddie's green DeSoto, which could fit eight men inside. I ran that team as if it were my own. Maybe that's what Abe noticed before he decided to give me the biggest break of my life. I was doing all that, and I was always a hard guy for him to beat in the game."

As excited as he was for his new project, Red approached Gottlieb with some mixed feelings. Klotz idolized the Sphas as a child, played in preliminary games with his boyhood team, the Outlaws, and then with the Sphas' reserves. Eventually he would make the varsity and star as a homegrown fan favorite. When he took over management of the franchise, Red considered himself to be caretaker for a Philly basketball institution. The Sphas had evolved from Gotty's vision to a dominating force in the pro leagues of its day. With hoops taking on more national presence since the Globetrotters-Lakers game, that meant one more re-invention of the franchise: opposition on the Trotters' U.S. tours.

Red was a loyal guy, and adding to his angst were the facts that Eddie Gottlieb was a fellow South Philadelphia High grad, and had signed Red to his first pro contract. The Mogul also had helped open the doors resulting in Klotz' selection to the U.S. All Star teams for the Globetrotter tours. At the same time, Klotz was being paid, "very poorly for all that I was doing," Red said in 2013. "It was embarrassing. I wasn't being paid much more than a top player. Eddie had a reputation as being tough but fair, but he was also very tight and a hard negotiator. Every negotiation was a battle."

When Red informed Gottlieb of his plans to form his own team and oppose the Trotters, the Mogul was incredulous. "He smirked and said, 'What are you talking about?' He told me not to believe Abe. 'That will never happen; Abe likes to say he's going to do something and then not do it. You can't believe any of this.'"

Red bristled. "I looked at Eddie and said, 'This is too important for me not to believe him.'" It was the end of Red Klotz' long association with the Sphas. There was no gold watch, no thanks for a great job, and not even a single word of encouragement from Eddie Gottlieb.

Klotz said Abe's offer represented a big step forward in his pro basketball career. "Opportunity doesn't come along all that often," he said. "You never know how long it can be between opportunities. I don't think I knew at the time this was going to be the biggest chance of my career."

Knowing where he stood with Eddie left him needing just one more thing from the Mogul, a rather large thing in the scheme of making his opportunity move forward, quite literally. "I asked him about the DeSoto. We used to call it the Green Hornet," Red said. "I asked him if he could throw it in as part of my compensation. I was going to need it to transport my team to games. Eddie just said, 'We'll have to see about that after we get this whole situation straightened out.' At that point, I knew he wasn't going to let the car go without money. Money that I did not have."

Gloria, who was a witness to it all, could not believe what she was hearing. "It was all about money to (Gottlieb)," she said. "These two had been through so much together, and to (Gottlieb) all that mattered was the bottom line. We're talking about people here, and the most important thing was a number."

Red wasn't into burning bridges. If there was any lingering bitterness or resentment, it soon would fade after a conversation with Abe, recounting what had occurred at the meeting. "Abe said not to worry about it, that he would take care of it," Red said. Saperstein would provide a no-interest loan to pave the way for Red's acquisition of the Green Hornet.

With the deal done on a handshake, Red's mind was racing. Now he knew that he had to build a team, and one that could compete with the world-famous Harlem Globetrotters. Before he was too far along in the process, Klotz received a call from Hall of Fame Coach Clair Bee. Bee, who had won three national championships at Long Island University, including a pair of undefeated squads, had coached the College All-Americans in their tour with the Trotters and was presently in charge of the NBA's Baltimore Bullets.

Bee had left LIU after his team was mentioned in connection with the infamous point-shaving scandal centered on the City College of New York. "Clair Bee told me about a player he thought would be good for my team, but who was 'too short' for the NBA," Red laughed. "Well, I'm the wrong guy to be telling that anybody is too short to play."

The player was Bennie Purcell, an All American at Murray State in Kentucky, who, at five-foot-eight, was an inch taller than Red. Purcell was a two-time Ohio Valley Conference All-Star, and had led the Racers to the OVC title. However, what put Bennie Purcell on the national radar was his performance in the postseason National Association of Intercollegiate Athletics (NAIA) Tournament.

"There were scouts at the tournament, and Mike Bloom was there for the Bullets and recommended me to Bee," Purcell said. "What really set my game apart was my quickness. My first step with the basketball was as fast as anybody's. Still, I wound up being the last man cut by Baltimore."

Clair Bee, who also was known to a generation of young readers as the author of the Chip Hilton book series, had coached Purcell with Ray Meyer on the 1952 College All-Americans squad that opposed Harlem in the 1952 World Series of Basketball. Bee may have been one of the greatest college coaches of all-time, winning at a .950 clip between 1931 and 1951, including 45 in a row during one stretch, but his talent assessment of Purcell was more indicative of his 34-115 career record in the pros.

Purcell still wanted to play. He had a chance to do so in the Eastern League, which was attracting top pros at the time, or to go the AAU route and take a job with an oil company to play for the Phillips 66 squad. When Purcell heard about this chance to play for a new team that would tour with the Globetrotters, he was intrigued. "I knew some of the Trotters from the World Series of Basketball and I knew what their tour was about," Purcell said. "The prospect of joining up with a new team to play against them appealed to me."

Purcell did have one reservation, and it was major in his mind. "Bennie told me he would be interested in joining with me, but only if he played a lot. I laughed and told him he would be playing more basketball than he ever had in his life," Red said. "I'm not sure he fully understood what the schedule was going to be like."

Klotz wasted little time securing Purcell's talents. With Bennie and player-coach Red Klotz, the team started out with a superior backcourt. Klotz used his extensive contacts to land the rest of his first-year roster. Former Bullets' teammate Carl Meinhold from the 1948 champs, and Jim Coyle, a Brooklyn native considered to be one of the best prep standouts in the country were signed as forwards. Red's friendship with DePaul coach Ray Meyer gave him inroads to pick up six-foot-five Bill Schyman, a Bullets draftee, and Bill Carroll was a young forward from Atlantic City. Red knew him well, having seen Carroll in action with the Atlantic City High School Vikings. "It wasn't that unusual for guys to sign with the Globetrotters or their opponents right out of high school," Purcell recalled. Even though the money was not great, the lure of playing basketball for a living at an elite level appealed to players who felt they could make the grade.

"We didn't have a budget to speak of, but we were able to sign guys on the strength of the Globetrotters' reputation, the success of their tours, and the lure of adventure," Red said. "I would tell guys they would have more experiences and excitement in one season of touring with the Trotters than in all of their college careers and probably more than they would have in the rest of their life."

The team would be based out of Red's Atlantic City home in the hardscrabble Inlet section of the city. Gloria would handle the books. He decided to call the squad the Washington Generals. The name was a nod to General Dwight D. Eisenhower, who was elected as the nation's thirty-fourth president the previous November. Eisenhower was Supreme Allied Commander in Europe during the war. Red designated "Washington" as the Generals' fictional home base, because that city recently had lost its NBA team, the Capitols.

"It was just good timing, and the name had a good sound to it," Red said. "Washington Generals! It just sounded like a team, and we were going to be a team." He selected green and gold as the team colors. "I always gravitated to the Boston Celtics and loved the green. I had bright red hair, and a lot of people who met me for the first time assumed I was Irish; that is, until they learned my last name was Klotz."

Upon securing the Green Hornet from Gottlieb, Red installed a wooden luggage rack on the roof where the players placed their bags. He covered that with a canvas tarp to protect the luggage and other belongings from the elements. In the back of his mind was the disturbing thought that the items on the roof were vulnerable to theft or becoming dislodged in an accident. "The baggage went up on the rack, but uniforms had to stay in a smaller bag with each player inside the car. They can play without their street clothes. They cannot play without sneakers and uniforms."

Klotz did most of the driving himself. One night on an icy North Dakota road, it all nearly ended before it really had a chance to begin. "For all the grief Eddie gave me about buying that car, it wasn't exactly a creampuff," Red would chuckle. "It always was a challenge to keep it going, mechanically."

The Trotters and Generals were battling icy roads as they pressed forward toward a date on the regular schedule. Red was at the wheel, attempting to get traction to climb a hilly stretch of two-lane highway when the car stalled. "The guys got out and tried to push while I stayed in the car to steer. We weren't making much progress. There must have been three inches of solid ice covering the entire surface of the road. I heard an engine's roar and saw lights beyond the horizon of the hill. When the vehicle crested the hill, I saw it was a gigantic tractor trailer hugging the center line of the lanes. The truck was bearing down on me, and I was pretty much a dead duck."

The Generals bailed from pushing the car and jumped in snowbanks along the road as the truck driver hit the brakes. The incident, which probably took less than five seconds, was playing out in slow motion in Red's mind. "The driver hitting the brakes probably saved me. Instead of going over me, the truck jackknifed and the trailer was swinging around toward me like a baseball bat."

Meanwhile, the Generals reunited with the Trotters "under the snow," Red said. "Their bus had broken down too, and they were all right there in the same snow bank." The Trotters and Generals held their breath as the trailer swung past the Green Hornet, missing it by inches, and coming to rest diagonally, blocking both lanes. The state troopers who eventually arrived on scene could not believe that no one was seriously hurt in the accident.

"Calling it a close call really doesn't do it justice," Red said. "But that's what we went through on the road. I never ever missed a game because I didn't show up. Missed a few because the Trotters didn't show up. But I always managed to get where we were supposed to be with my team."

The Generals' very first game in 1952 could not have been on a bigger stage, Madison Square Garden, considered the national mecca for the sport. They were scheduled to play the Trotters in the opening game of the 1952-53 schedule. Tatum and Haynes had left the organization by then, but Abe still had a very good squad, including deadeye set shot ace Clarence Wilson, six-foot-eight pivot man J.C. Gipson, who was the high school player of the year in Los Angeles a few years prior, and "Showboat" Bob Hall, a six-foot-two forward and center who loved to mix it up with much taller players.

"I had my guys meet at a restaurant across the street from the Garden, which was then located on Eighth Avenue between Forty-Ninth and Fiftieth streets in midtown Manhattan," Red said. "We didn't have a training camp or even a practice. We needed to eat, but the real purpose of that dinner was to introduce the guys to each other and to give them an idea that their job wasn't just about playing."

Red told his new team not to get in the way of the Globetrotters' show. "This is not always an easy thing for players to understand, but it's very important. The people who are coming to this game are coming to see the Harlem Globetrotters, not us. I told them to look to me if they had any doubts. By cooperating with the show, you become part of the show yourself."

Bennie Purcell confirmed this. "As an athlete, it goes against your instincts," Purcell said. "You're taught to compete and you do compete. "It goes against everything you know and have been told, to let the other team score."

Red used this feeling the rest of the Generals no doubt shared, to deliver his longtime mantra about playing hard-nosed, tough basketball and never holding back. "The people who think we throw games couldn't be more wrong," he says. "The Trotters have never asked me to lose, and I have never asked my players to lose. I tell them: You play to win. I tell them to go out there and make people see how good you are! I tell them to make the Trotters respect you as a player. When you walk off that court after a game, you should walk off respecting yourself, and with the Globetrotters' respect and the fans' respect. That is how you build a name for yourself, and how we will build a name for our team. And that's the way we have done it all these years."

The pep talk must have worked. The Trotters won, the first in a long string of wins over the Generals that would take on epic proportions. The game was close, and the Generals comported themselves as the professional players they were. The game was credible. Red made sure the basketball part was airtight; the Trotters took care of the show. "We had good players and good people. They respected themselves and they respected the game."

Saperstein was pleased that his decision to put his trust in Klotz had paid off and his instincts about the five-foot-seven, 32-year-old dynamo were correct. This Red Klotz guy was a pro's pro, and it would be the start of a long and successful partnership.

When it was over, Abe and many of the Trotters came over to the Generals' locker room and showed their appreciation. "I think Abe liked the fact we gave them a tough game," Red said. "Abe also knew we 'got it' concerning the reams. He couldn't have been happier. He was smiling broadly and clapping me on the back. 'Losing' had never felt this good to me before. I didn't have the heart to tell him we had just met up right before the game and we had not even practiced together yet."

Bill Spivey, MVP of the University of Kentucky's national championship team, played for Red and the Washington Generals after he was banned from the NBA for alleged associations with gamblers.

Red with Clarence Wilson (left) and Bobby Milton.

Chapter 16

Generals and a President

The Washington Generals were not overnight sensations. They had plenty of competition before they became the Globetrotters' primary opponents. When Abe Saperstein mapped out the schedule for the 1952-53 regular U.S. tour season, it featured Red's new squad, and also the Toledo Mercurys, Boston Whirlwinds, and sometimes the Sphas. Gottlieb hired Pete Monska, a former Spha player from Northeast Philly, to take over Red's duties of running and coaching the team.

"For all the lip Eddie gave me when I told him I wouldn't be back, he was actually quite happy the way things worked out for all concerned, including himself," Red said. "Pete was an excellent player, a good friend, and he did a good job of running the Sphas."

The Sphas were in good hands, and the Trotters' world tours (where Gottlieb still worked as a tour manager and coach) would prove to go much smoother with Red running some things. "There were plenty of times it was tough to get to the game, and we'd always get wherever it was ahead of the Trotters, who of course had deeper pockets than we did. It might not have seemed clear to Eddie at the time. But as the season went on and things went smoothly, I became accepted." Before Red could prove himself overseas, he had to do so on the court with the regular season U.S. Trotter tour.

"Since (Harlem) beat the Lakers, and they had been received so well overseas, and the NBA was still hanging in there, the idea was the Trotters would be going into the large buildings most of the time," Red said. "Sometimes the Trotters would appear on the bill in support of scheduled NBA games, and just as frequently if not more so, sometimes as the sole attraction." What the Generals (and Mercurys, Whirlwinds, and Sphas) did was take the whole matter of the opposition off the table. "It was a huge part of planning Abe was able to address by having his opponent travel with him."

The Whirlwinds no longer had the Clark twins. They were led by Bob Karstens, and former college legend Bevo Francis, who once scored 113 points in a game for obscure Rio Grande College in Ohio. Francis also would see action for the Generals. Toledo's best player was six-foot-five Frank Evengello, who played at the University of San Francisco with future NBA greats Bill Russell and K.C. Jones.

The Generals, newcomers to the circuit, were bedecked in flashy green uniforms with "Washington" emblazoned across the front. Their warm-up silks were equally loud. Red might not have had much of a budget, but he spared no expense when it came to playing togs. The Generals were part of a show and would look the part. No doubt Gloria's influence was felt here.

"It was all about looking like we belonged out there with the famous Harlem Globetrotters," Red explained, using his favorite adjective to describe the club Abe was now calling, "The magicians of basketball." "We had to play like we belonged with them on the court, and we had to *look* like we belonged. Having nice uniforms was always an important part of us fitting in with the show. Players appreciate nice uniforms, too." To this day, Red recounts the tale of making a deal with his old high school coach: a championship in exchange for new uniforms. "Nobody likes to go out there wearing bush-league uniforms. The flip side is guys are going to play better if they think they look good."

The Globetrotters' also had (and still do have) distinctive, instantly recognizable threads: their red, white, and blue jerseys paired with red and white striped trunks, designed to emulate the U.S. flag. Their blue satin warm-ups shone under the arena lights while they trick-passed, dribbled, and spun the ball through their "magic circle" routine to start the game.

Today, sports marketing types would credit Abe for his "branding" efforts, which paid dividends as he promoted future contests. Fans attending a Trotters' game for the first time, or as repeat customers, wanted to see the recognizable outfits as Harlem took the floor, accompanied by Brother Bones' rendition of "Sweet Georgia Brown" echoing through the public address system.

The Trotters would run onto the court to deafening cheers, gather in a circle at midcourt, and pass the ball to one another after each team member exhibited a trick move or dribble. It was a dramatic and fun way to start the game and get the crowd into it. The "magic circle" appears in some of the earliest newsreels and endures to this day as a signature part of the Trotters' game-day experience for fans. It was just one of many such marketing innovations Abe would come to earn credit for inventing. Fans at a Trotters' game would have their senses inundated from the time the house lights went up until the game's final buzzer. Red knew he needed to "brand" the Generals, too, in order to help the game and show go over. The uniforms were a small but important aspect of that.

"We weren't the main attraction," said Red, "we were supporting characters. I looked at it that the supporting characters were just that, support for the main thing the fans came to see. That's always how I have looked at it. The interesting thing was, as a supporting part of the show, we built up our own name, too."

When the Washington Generals took the court, fans felt they were going to see two teams in action: the most famous team in the world (and still one of the best), and a team that looked like a professional basketball squad and could keep up with the Trotters, if not beat them. Fans would come to recognize Klotz as the face of the team: the five-foot-seven scrapper who used the old two-hander shot to score, and his quickness to steal the ball and shadow the Trotters' dribbling specialist. At age 32, some were already calling Red Klotz "old."

Uniforms were one of the rare areas for which Red could afford to splurge. He always made separate travel arrangements and always was looking for deals on hotel rooms, fares, and the many other aspects of playing the game and getting his squad to the next one. "I was paid $100 per game on the College All-Stars tour," Bennie Purcell recalls. "Red couldn't pay that much. I think I got $35 a game and was happy to get that much for playing basketball."

The Generals and other opponent teams comprised what the players called the "Grapefruit League." Three of the teams traveled with the Trotters at any given time, and Abe would promote and stage doubleheaders. If the Whirlwinds opposed the Trotters, the Mercuries and Generals would square off in the opening contest.

"The opening games were hard-fought," Purcell remembers. "The teams were pretty evenly matched. It was kind of like a night off when you played the Trotters, because you got to rest during their show plays."

Red remembers it similarly, but with a twist: "They were some good teams," he said of the other opponents. "There was no question that we were the best of the lot. We were a smart, tough club. And we understood our roles in playing the Trotters and not interfering with the show. We beat everybody else that we played. These were good teams, and we were beating them regularly and giving the Trotters their best games, too."

Abe eventually would see it that way as well and eliminate the other Grapefruit Leaguers from the U.S. tours, but in 1952-53, the

Trotters crisscrossed the United States and parts of Canada and the Alaska territory with a troupe of singers, jugglers, acrobats, musicians, and a mini pro league of their own.

"We had assembled a tough club, good enough to play in the NBA at that time," Red says, an assertion backed up by exhibition games set up against NBA teams the following year, some of which the Generals won. "There were only 10 teams in the NBA and our circuit, if you wanted to play professionally," Bennie Purcell said. "You are talking about less than 200 jobs, total. We were losing to the Globetrotters, but we still had one of the best teams in the world."

The overall landscape of pro basketball was changing along with the Trotters' new approach. The league had finally integrated in 1950-51, and was the last major pro circuit to do so. It came at a high cost to Abe, who previously had a virtual monopoly on the best black players. Chuck Cooper of Duquesne became the first African American player drafted, by the Boston Celtics. Sweetwater Clifton, a key member of the Trotter teams that defeated the Lakers, became the first to sign an NBA contract. The way the schedule unfolded that year, Earl Lloyd of the Washington Capitols became the first black man to actually appear in an NBA game.

Cooper and Lloyd briefly had been Globetrotters. Cooper played all of the games in the College All-Star series, and Lloyd a few games, before they were both drafted. Clifton had been coveted by the New York Knicks after Sweetwater did a defensive number on George Mikan in the second win over the Lakers in 1949.

Less than two weeks after the draft, Abe struck a deal with the Knicks to release Clifton from his Trotters' contract, which still had a year to run. Sweetwater reportedly had jumped previous contracts, and Abe, seeing the shifts in the basketball world, may have decided to get as much for Clifton as he could before losing him for nothing.

Sweetwater and Haynes' departures were certainly blows to the Trotters, who, after winning their first two games against the mighty Lakers, would have six more tries and never beat them again. However, Abe still had the best scouting network for black players in the game, according to the leading sportswriter of the black media, Wendell Smith, and there was a consensus at the time that no single player was bigger than the Globetrotters as a team. There was merit to the theory, as Abe had dealt with a changing cast of players since beginning the enterprise a quarter century earlier. Haynes would go on to form his own touring team, the Harlem Magicians.

The Trotters' lineup remained potent, as they still had plenty of star players. Goose Tatum was still the marquee star, while Josh Grider, Babe Pressley, Pop Gates, Robinson, and a then-19-year-old J.C. Gipson provided plenty of basketball and comedy talent. The Trotters still could play it straight when needed, and of course the show still was intact. A young Leon Hillard tried to fill the void in dribbling left by Haynes' departure, and the crowds continued to flock to watch the Trotters play.

"This was still the era of regular basketball being dominant and the show came second," Red said. "The Trotters wanted a good game, but they also wanted audiences to leave laughing, having seen the baseball skit, ball on a string, confetti bucket, and the rest."

The basketball part still came naturally for both the Trotters and their Grapefruit League opposition. These were professional players doing what they did best. The show part took some getting used to for some, including Bennie Purcell. "I was a competitor and it was hard for me," he admitted. "The main thing was, I was getting paid to play. It helped that we faced regular opposition on the nights we weren't playing the Globetrotters."

For Red Klotz, what mattered most was living up to his part of the bargain with Abe. "Sometimes," Red said, "I had to tell my players to defer to me during the show. Sometimes I had to show them the way when the reams were going on."

The Trotters had a natural foil in Klotz with his small physical stature. "They had fun with me because of my size, and I would get them back when I could with a steal when they got careless. Other times, I would catch them napping on defense and I would beat them downcourt for a layup."

Fans began to respond to Red, and not just the Trotters. "By supporting the show, I became part of the show." The Trotters would stuff a ball under Red's jersey, make fun of his height, and dribble around him in circles while he chased.

The first year flew by, with the Trotters going 168-0 during the regular U.S. tour season, and the western unit, organized a few years earlier, going to Austrailia for the first time and also to Hawaii, Malaya, the Phillippines (where they would famously play to an audience at a leper colony), Guam, Japan, Indionesia, China, Formosa, and wrapping up in Western Canada. That year's series against the College All-Americans ended with the Trotters winning 15 of 22 contests. Although the Generals did not win a game against the Trotters, they were winners in other ways: helping the Harlem team entertain hundreds of thousands of fans, to build the Globetrotters' and their own names, and spread goodwill for the sport.

Red was named to the United States All Stars squad for the 1953 summer tour of Europe. The team was handpicked and coached by Eddie Gottlieb. "One of the smallest professional players is Louis 'Red' Klotz…an average height for an average person but rated midget-like in the realm of the Trotters," stated the official program for the series of games at Wembley Empire Pool and Sports Arena. "Last season, in addition to being outstanding on the court, he also coached the Washington (D.C.) Generals. They call him 'General No. 1' because of his tactical abilities," the program write-up continued. "Klotz enjoys the reputation of being among the most scientific players in basketball."

The U.S. Stars were joined by Red's Generals' teammate Carl Meinhold, who was also sometimes called "Red," the Sphas' Pete Monska, Karstens, and Mark Workman, a six-foot-nine-and-a-half-inch former All-American at West Virginia. Workman recently had completed a rookie season in the NBA starting with the Milwaukee Hawks and ending with the Warriors following his trade.

Once again, Abe split his Globetrotters squads and sent a unit back to South America, a two-month, 10-country, 32-game jaunt that included a return to Argentina, where fans lined up outside Luna Park.

The European and North African tour highlights were quite numerous: Abe greeted General William Hoge, commander in chief of the Army's European Forces while in Frankfurt, Germany; Red was among the Trotter and opposition players photographed riding camels in front of the pyramids in Egypt; and the teams showed their willingness to battle the elements to get through a rainy tour date in Liege, Belgium.

During the foray into Egypt, Abe, the team, and the U.S. All-Stars met with President Mohammed Naguib. It no longer was unusual for the Trotters to meet with heads of state. The triumph in Berlin and resulting publicity was noticed all over the globe. Countries playing host to the Trotters responded in a way that suggested the "ambassadors in short pants" moniker mentioned in a Trotters' program of the era was not hyperbole.

The meeting with Naguib, thought by some to be a quick official hello, morphed into a two-hour conference that took place at the presidential palace. The previous year, Naguib had served as prime minister, appointed by the king, and before that, he was major general of the Armed Forces. He met with the Trotters and U.S. All-Stars during both visits.

Just months prior to the 1953 visit, the Egyptian Revolution was playing out, with Naguib leading the coup to depose King

Karouk. In a few short months, Nabuib ascended from com-
mander-in-chief of the army, to prime minister, and finally to president, Egypt's first.

"We were getting all kinds of rhetoric from him," Red said.
"He was going on about the evil forces inside and outside of Egypt,
and how he represented the forces of good." At one point in the
proceedings, Naguib opened the floor up to questions. Red decided to take advantage of the opportunity.

"I reminded him that fighting has been going on for thousands
of years in the Middle East, and I asked him if he could do his part
to actually make peace. He looked at me and said, 'Be patient.' He
lasted only a short time (actually to November of 1954 when he
lost a power struggle with Gamal Abdel Nasser) as president, and
he's telling me to be patient! Sixty years later, we still aren't close
to (Middle East) peace. Be patient, my eye."

In France, Trotter Josh Grider made a length of the court toss
for a field goal, and the French audience politely applauded, thinking it was a regular occurrence, while the players on the court celebrated wildly.

In Heidelberg, West Germany, Abe laid his plywood court atop
a stone amphitheater built by Hitler to deliver some of his most
notorious speeches during the rise of the Third Reich. The irony
of the situation was not lost on Red: "We were truly the ambassadors of basketball and American culture," he remembers. "Here
was a team of very talented black ballplayers, coached by a Jewish
guy, playing against a bunch of white guys of every nationality. It
was the idea of the American melting pot on display in postwar
Germany, on a stage previously commanded by Hitler. We were
showing the world that the American ideal of working and playing
together can actually succeed. We weren't just talking about it, we
were doing it, right in front of everybody."

Tour Secretary Dave Zinkoff described a Heidelberg moment
thusly: "The entire Trotter entourage enjoyed a breakfast (hosted

by a local organization) and a half-ton of bagel and lox disap-
peared before you could shout 'Jackie Robinson.'"

Red's patriotism was touched when the party visited the Memorial de Mardasson in Liege, Belgium, near where 76,890 Americans were killed or wounded in the battle of the Ardennes. The
memorial contained stones symbolic of the then 48 states.

When they finally returned, another baseball and football stadium tour, which Abe now touted as the "Welcome Home Tour,"
was on the agenda. Red was one player short for one of the dates,
which happened to be Yankee Stadium. He grabbed his Atlantic
City neighbor, Alan "Boo" Pergament, and asked if he wanted to
don a Generals' uniform and sit on the bench.

"Did I want to?" Pergament asked with a roll of his eyes, 60
years later. "The Yankees were my favorite baseball team."

Pergament had become friendly with Red playing games of 2-
on-2 if they had another pair of players, or "Around the World"
or "21" if they were by themselves. "He would spot us a lead, or
if I was too proud to play at a handicap, he would just miss inten-
tionally until I built up a big lead. Then he would shoot the way
he could shoot and simply would not miss in that situation."

Pergament said that despite his status as a successful pro athlete, Red never "big-timed" anyone. "He is just a nice, down-to-
earth guy who loves his family and the game of basketball. It was
always a dream of mine to see Yankee Stadium. Red gave me the
chance to see it from field level and to warm up on the same court
with the Harlem Globetrotters. I remember sitting on the bench,
watching the game from that vantage point, and looking around
Yankee Stadium and just saying to myself, 'Wow.' It was hard to
believe I was on the same field where Babe Ruth, Lou Gehrig and
Joe DiMaggio had played. I will always remember that day and be
thankful to Red for helping me achieve that dream."

Red (kneeling), accompanied by members of the Generals and Trotters, lays a wreath at the grave of General George Patton. Behind Red is longtime friend and tour secretary Dave Zinkoff.

Red's favorite publicity photo, from the late 1950s.

Chapter 17

Buzzing in the Hornet

Red was an experienced basketball road warrior, yet nothing would prepare him for the adventures of running a team, taking care of the myriad details involved, and driving all over the East Coast with eight large men shoehorned into one car.

Abe's loan to Red, the amount of which Klotz cannot remember exactly but is reported to be $1,500, had secured the services of a late 40s' model De Soto. Nobody knows who nicknamed the vehicle the Green Hornet, but the moniker stuck. "It was pretty tight in there," Benny Purcell understatedly remembered. "We all dealt with it because we loved to play basketball."

Gloria, who would tour extensively with Red in the future, was thrilled to be home in Atlantic City at this time. She tended to the still-growing brood while administering to important team business interests, such as the team payroll and expenses. Meanwhile, Red took care of business on the road and on the court. None of this bothered Gloria. "I was happy for him. Basketball was his first love before I came along. I think it was important for him to have that. It was an opportunity and something that made him so very happy. I felt it was my job to help in any way I could. We made a few dollars as we went along…very few."

Gloria cringed at the thought of the Generals on the road in the Green Hornet. "It was a big car, but these were some big guys," she said. "There was a bench seat between the regular front and back seats, and I'm thinking that mouthwash and deodorant were pretty important."

The "GPS system" at the time was a paper map from the gas station, and when the road wasn't on the map, which frequently was the case, it was stop and ask a stranger. Flat tires, an overheated radiator, dead batteries, and other mechanical issues were aggravations, not problems.

Traversing the Deep South in a traveling party that included an all-black basketball team was a different matter, regardless of the fact that said basketball team happened to be the Harlem Globetrotters. The irony is documented widely that the Trotters, who displayed the American ideals of equality and civil rights in places like Prague and Berlin, and before long, in Moscow, would return home to face the insults of segregation and discrimination. In the 1950s, the Globetrotters were treated better in Europe, Asia, Africa, and South America than in their own homeland.

"The Communist argument is that the American Negro is exploited and held in bondage," Abe Saperstein told the *San Francisco Chronicle* in 1952. "I do say we chipped at the edges and broke down a lot of opposition. Without saying a word, we refuted much of that by living at the best hotels, eating at the best restaurants, and behaving in the manner of educated men."

Despite such lofty pronouncements, the Trotters and Generals would see firsthand some of the inconvenient truths on which the Communists based their arguments. "We would go into places where the audiences would cheer enthusiastically for the Trotters, and boo us," said Klotz. "Then we'd go out for dinner, and the restaurants refused to serve (the Globetrotters)."

Red particularly was appalled by an incident that occurred just outside of Washington, D.C. After a restaurant refused service to the Trotters, the party took off with empty stomachs. "We are basically in the nation's capital, 90 years after the Civil War, and black men can't eat in a public restaurant? Come on! There were times when we would bring the food out to the car for the black guys, but this time we couldn't bring ourselves to give them our business. Better to be hungry for a while."

Out of necessity, the Generals were a mostly white team in the early years. More than a few cities and towns in the South would not allow games between racially-mixed teams. "Sometimes, they made us play two games," recalled Bennie Purcell. "We'd play for a white audience and then for a black audience. In some towns, the only whites in the building for the 'black game' were the guys on our team and the police."

The situation held true for hotel accommodations, as well. The Generals were welcomed at more expensive white hotels (which Red couldn't afford anyway) while the Trotters were sometimes relegated to "colored" rooming houses and shabby segregated hotels.

Red: "Things were bad in some towns. The Trotters were among the greatest athletes of their day, and they were forced to stay in some real fleabags. They had enjoyed the very best accommodations while in Europe. They were asked by the State Department to serve as ambassadors, and were doing a great job of it. Their reward? They were forced to hang their hats in roach-infested hotels and were denied service in restaurants, movie theatres, and stores. "

Following a few small civil rights gains later in the 50s, the separate games for black and white audiences no longer had to be staged. Atlantic City's Gene Hudgins, a longtime friend of Red's, would become one of the first black Generals in 1957. Purcell remembers "a light-skinned black guy before Gene," although he could not remember his teammate's name. Red's recall button, clear on so many details of his career, fails him on specific names of some of his first African American players. "I can't remember us ever having an all-white team," he says. "In those days, I almost always had a few local guys (most of whom were black and came off the always strong Atlantic City High School program)," he recalled.

Generals' rosters and box scores of the era largely did not survive. However, while specifics of the General' rosters of those earliest days may not be documented fully; it was known that jobs for blacks in pro basketball of the era were exceedingly scarce. "There weren't many opportunities for black ballplayers at the time," Hudgins said. "Red gave me the chance and became almost like a second father to me." Hudgins went on from the Generals to a contract and career with the Trotters.

Sporadic yet persistent indignities of the road in 1950s America would not stop Abe and the Trotters, nor Red and the Generals. They provided constant incentive and served as reminders why they were sometimes fighting for causes larger than sports. Certainly performing at a level beyond that of a basketball comedy and variety shows, they were frequently referred to as "United States ambassadors in short pants" abroad and racial barrier-breakers at home.

Red: Walk a mile in somebody's shoes, and you understand better. Traveling with these players all the time, you began to get it. You could see what was happening in this country at the time. I was being treated better than them because my skin was white. In our own way, we were helping to change things. We were making people see black and white can not only co-exist, they can do it on an equal playing field. We challenged segregation. Sometimes we didn't win, but anybody with any sense of what's fair could see that segregation was wrong. I'm proud we were a part of that."

The challenges of the road weren't always racial or philosophical. Sometimes, they simply were logistical. Red, who did not learn how to drive until he was in his twenties, soon became a savvy driver and navigator, and even learned how to make simple repairs. "It could be tough to keep that (car) on the road," he said. "We had no other choice. That car was our transportation. Somehow, we always figured out a way to get to the next date, usually ahead of the Trotters."

Sometimes, when the car was running well, the weather would not cooperate. "I remember driving in rain that had so much wind behind it that it was going sideways. Or it would be boiling hot outside, and we had eight big guys inside. That could be uncomfortable."

He recalled another near-miss with a tractor trailer. "This time, it was because the driver had a girl with him and they were doing things you shouldn't do when you're driving. And it almost killed us. Somehow, we managed to avoid the crash. This was not unusual. The roads in many parts of the country still weren't very good, and the drivers weren't very good. The cars weren't very good. We had so many accidents and near-accidents that we were all living on borrowed time. There were probably about a dozen times we all could have been gone." Meanwhile, the Green Hornet pressed on. "I don't know how many miles were on that thing when we got it, but I think it's a conservative estimate we added at least 150,000 of our own," Red surmised.

After a few years, he upgraded to a newer vehicle, but the Green Hornet remained in service on a more limited basis. "You think we junked, it? Heck no!" Gloria said. "We used that car for at least a couple more years to haul the kids around in."

In the days before the Generals split into separate eastern and western units, the entire roster, equipment, and books all would be contained within that car. Between us and the Sphas, there was a lot of basketball history in that old DeSoto," Red frequently would say.

Whatever travails faced the Generals as they went from games in remote outposts to the biggest cities, Red Klotz always could find peace on the basketball court. "It didn't matter if he was at the outdoor court down the street or at a game 2,000 miles from Atlantic City," his daughter Ronee said. "As long as Dad had a ball in his hands and a game to play, he was in his element. He may not have been actually home. He was at his second home."

Homesickness, missing his family, and missing out on his children's' school activities, birthdays and other events would be a career-long regret for Red. The feelings would be summed up in a 1952 postcard sent from Nice, France. "Sweethearts: Less than a week to go before leaving this city for the most beautiful sea resort of all, including Rio or Miami. I'll take Atlantic City right now or any time. I can hardly wait." He signed the card, "Your Red," and added the postscript, as he would do many more times over the next four decades, "kiss kids."

The kids now numbered four with the addition of Kiki. The Boardwalk newsstand/fruit and snack shop had yielded about as much as it could for the small space. Gloria began looking for a new investment and found it in a black-owned liquor store and bar in a tough part of "Uptown" Atlantic City. As Red now had a name in basketball and proudly was claimed as a longtime AC transplant, the Top Hat Lounge and packaged goods store was renamed Red Klotz' Bar and Liquors. Gloria would manage the place for years, infuse the family into the community, and deal with the situations that seemed to crop up all the time. If a paying customer wanted to run a tab or even borrow money to get to the next paycheck, Gloria made it happen. Soon, the establishment had a loyal following.

"Gloria was amazing," Red said of that time. "She was the brains and the heart and soul of that place. I still wasn't making any real money in basketball. She was the one holding the family together."

The mid-50s were a transitional time for the Generals' more famous opponents as well. Goose Tatum finally had left the team for good in 1955 after several stints spanning 14 years as the most recognizable face of the organization. The reason was a salary dispute, and Tatum would play two full seasons with Marques' team, the Harlem Magicians, who attracted some other big-name former Trotters, including Josh Grider and the NBA's first black draftee, Chuck Cooper.

Once again, Abe was not rattled by the departure of a star player, even though this time it happened to be the most famous and recognizable of all the great Trotter showmen. Many of the great reams that would endure for decades to come and are still used today, originated with Goose.

The transition was made easier by the fact that Meadow Lemon, who would gain fame as Meadowlark Lemon, was waiting in the wings. Lemon, of Wilmington, North Carolina, joined the Trotters a year before Tatum left and learned all his reams and mannerisms. Eventually, he would become better-known than the Trotters' original "Clown Prince" because of the national yearly TV exposure the Trotters would receive in the 1960s. However, in 1955, Lemon sometimes was seen as an imitation Goose Tatum. Lemon also could play, but generally was regarded as less talented than Tatum. Straight basketball was still a major part of the Trotters' games of this time period. The reams came in only when there was a comfortable lead, and when the Trotters needed to play it straight, Meadowlark needed to be on target with his famous hook shot.

"Goose was a player," Benny Purcell said. "Ermer Robinson was a player. Marques Haynes was a player. Meadowlark was a great showman. However, he improved as a player and he had a great hook shot that he had developed through years of practice."

Audiences continued to flock to see the Globetrotters, even without Goose Tatum. The NBA still hadn't caught on fully, and the college game was tainted by point-shaving scandals. Fans may have known Globetrotter games were not likely to be contested tightly, and they also knew the games still would be entertaining. Meadowlark added new reams of his own to compliment those he adopted from Goose.

The Generals' star power was heightened in the 1954-55 season when they acquired a new center, one Bill Spivey, a seven-foot, 200-pounder from Lakeland, Florida. With Spivey in the middle, and Purcell and Klotz in the backcourt, the Washington Generals had talent on par with many NBA teams, and proved it by winning several exhibitions.

Spivey was a national figure for his dominating play at the University of Kentucky in the 1949-50 and 1950-51 seasons, which earned him All-American status both years. Kentucky, coached by the legendary Adolf Rupp, won the NCAA tournament that year, and Spivey was named its most outstanding player. He was regarded as the best big man of his time, and was considered to be the heir to George Mikan. Spivey likely would have been the first player drafted in the NBA following his Kentucky career had he not become embroiled in a controversy that was not of his doing.

During the height of the point-shaving scandals that would rock college basketball in the 1950s, Spivey refused to testify against three of his teammates who admitted to missing shots that "shaved" points off games to aid gamblers. He then was indicted on perjury charges, and though never convicted of any crime, was suspended from Kentucky and banned from the NBA for life.

"All the guy did was try to protect his teammates," Red remembers. "Spivey received a terribly raw deal. He was just a kid and did not want to be the one who put his buddies (Alex Groza, Dale Barnstable, and Ralph Beard) away. He could have been one of the best NBA players of all time. We'll never know."

The NBA's loss was Abe Saperstein's gain. Spivey was signed for the "Grapefruit League" and ballpark tours played at various times for the Whirlwinds, Mercuries, and House of David squads. Then he went with the Generals full time. It was quite an upgrade at the center position from Bob Chubb.

"He was one heck of a player, as talented as they come at the center position at that time," said Benny Purcell, who roomed with

Spivey. "The problem was, he was very bitter about what happened to him, and carried that with him his whole career, and some have said, for the rest of his life. Spivey was a nice guy, but he played with a chip on his shoulder and had no problem throwing an elbow once in a while."

During Spivey's first year on tour with the Trotters, he was involved in a fistfight with Bob "Showboat" Hall during a hotly-contested game in Brisbane, Australia. According to the Association of Professional Basketball Research, Claude Overton hit a buzzer-beater to "defeat" the Trotters, until the scorekeeper "found an error" and the Trotters won in overtime.

"I liked Bill, and people were coming out to see him. It was money in our pockets," Red said. "But sometimes you are playing three games in three days, or a doubleheader on the same day, and tempers might flare once in a while."

Purcell remembered another time when Spivey got into it with the Trotters' J.C. Gipson and Walter Dukes (a future NBA star), and chased Gipson literally out of the arena. After all three players were kicked out of the game, Spivey tried to resume the hostilities in the Trotter dressing room afterwards.

Despite the rough play and sometimes sullen moods, Bill Spivey helped provide the Generals with a credibility they had not experienced before. With the newfound respect came more financial success and better travel accommodations. The Trotters also were doing better financially. Abe continued his formula of investing his profits back into the business. He always was searching for new entertainment acts, making additional bookings, and developing players. Further expansion of the foreign tours was part of the formula, with new cities and countries and more games added. Abe's lavish annual dinner in Chicago for the sporting press continued, resulting in great media relations and even bigger gates.

The coattail effect helped the Generals. They were years away from their future portrayal as hapless losers. The Generals' name appeared prominently in many advertisements hyping Globetrotter games. Said Purcell: "We were flying more with the Trotters, and Red had by then acquired a second car. We didn't all have to squeeze into one."

Red has an old color home movie that shows Spivey smiling and waving as the Generals are about to board a plane for destinations unknown as the Generals prepared to take on the Grapefruit League, any local opponents brave enough to take them on in a preliminary game, and of course, the Trotters. "We didn't get in the way of the show plays, but we also played some really tough basketball. Whoever we played knew they were in a game," Klotz said.

Side projects continued, as well. In the second Globetrotter movie in as many years, "Go, Man, Go," which starred Dana Clark as Abe, the Generals appear in action footage with Klotz among the featured players. They are mentioned in the film's script as the Trotters prepare for a fictitious championship tournament as the film's storyline moves towards its climax. In a line that would invoke laughter in future years, one of the actors states: "The Washington Generals are a really tough team." As odd as that seems today, the truth of the line resonated in the mid-50s

In 1955, Bill Spivey returned to Kentucky to complete his degree and toured the next year with Marques Haynes, Goose Tatum, and the Harlem Magicians, who named their opposition team the Kentucky Colonels (not to be confused with the American Basketball Association team of the same name that played in the 60s and 70s to honor Spivey. He would continue to kick around pro basketball's minor circuit, winning three championships in 10 seasons in the Eastern League, and spending the 1961-62 season with Abe's ill-fated NBA rival, the American Basketball League.

There, Spivey was the star attraction of the Los Angeles Jets, and later in the year, the Long Beach Chiefs, in the league's only full season. He could still score, racking up a 38-point performance for the Chiefs' 124-111 win over Oakland late in the season.

Following basketball, Spivey parlayed his name and college degree to a successful career in sales, but Purcell said he never lost the resentment for what happened to him as a young man. "He just always had a sense that he had been cheated out of the professional career he should have had, and he probably had a point," said Purcell. Though Bill Spivey's name largely would become forgotten outside Kentucky Wildcat fans of a certain age, a new force was looming that would shake up the game. Once again, Red Klotz would find himself at Ground Zero for a seismic change in basketball.

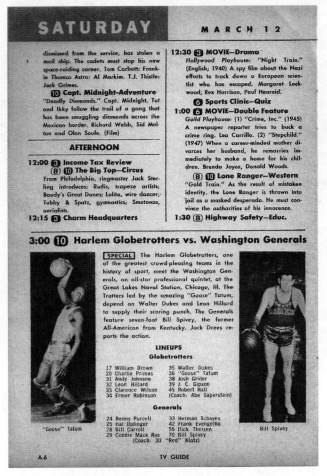

The Trotters and Generals became a television staple in the 1950s.

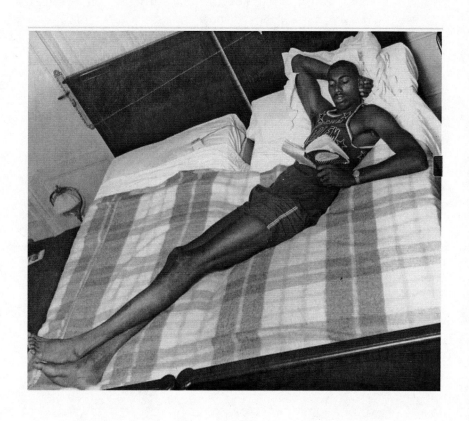

Relaxing before a Globetrotters-Generals game, Wilt Chamberlain
improvised to create a king-sized bed.

Chapter 18

Along Comes Wilt

As the Washington Generals continued to grow, basketball's next big thing was exploding onto the scene. Once again, a pivotal moment in the game's evolution was taking place in Philly. This time it was happening in the very neighborhood where the Klotz family had moved at the start of Red's senior year in high school. Had Red Klotz not jumped on two different trolley cars to return to South Philly High as a senior - a very smart decision, based on the Rams winning the city title - he would have graduated from Overbrook High in West Philadelphia, 16 years ahead of one Wilton Norman Chamberlain.

Chamberlain, dubbed "Wilt the Stilt" by a sportswriter, brought new possibilities to the game. It could be argued that no other player influenced the game more. Wilt, who stood six-feet,11 inches during his sophomore season of 1952-53 (he eventually reached seven feet, one and one-sixteenth inch) was a track and field star who used his speed in the 440 to run the floor like a guard and his high jumping ability to play above the rim. His hands were so large, he could palm two balls at the same time using just two fingers on each hand. He had a wide variety of shots and deft moves around the basket. Defensively, he was a shot-blocking machine who seldom got into foul trouble. He also had a dynamic personality and a smile that could light up a room.

Film of one of his high school playoff games shows a young Chamberlain grabbing an opponent's shot out of midair with one hand and then dribbling the ball to midcourt before executing a perfect give-and-go. The ball comes back to Wilt and he finishes the play not with a dunk, but a delicate lay-in. Then he hustles back down to the defensive end of the court. Chamberlain's basketball IQ had been developed by Sam Cozen, the same guru who had taught the fundamentals and finer points to Red when Cozen was a junior high gym teacher and coach.

Wilt, like Red, had taken Cozen's lessons seriously, and had a keen sense of the game at a very tender age. People took notice, and Wilt Chamberlain was a national celebrity by the time he turned 16.

"Young Giant is Basketball Sensation," read the headline in a newsreel showing Wilt's astonishing skills to coaches and fans across the nation. It was one of the first references to his abilities that hinted at Chamberlain's image as being almost larger than life. "I think they had no way to compare what I was doing," Wilt said years later. "It was so far out of the realm of believability, they had no way to compare."

Red had heard about Wilt since the prodigy was in junior high school, and had followed his progress. Abe Saperstein and Eddie Gottlieb knew about him too, and both wanted him under contract. Both men would get him, at different times. Gottlieb cooked up a scheme and persuaded the new pro league to institute a "territorial" draft, theoretically to allow clubs to help boost gate receipts by having the first crack at local players. At least that was the premise Gotty sold to his fellow basketball barons. In accepting it on its face, the owners were more akin to basketball bumpkins. The territorial draft was just the first of the game's rules re-written with Wilt Chamberlain in mind. It was a rule changed by Eddie Gottlieb to benefit Eddie Gottlieb's Philadelphia Warriors.

"Eddie devised a plan to get Wilt, and it wound up in his favor. But Abe wanted him, too," Klotz said. "Everybody knew this guy was fantastic. He was still a kid, and it seemed obvious he was going to be the greatest attraction the professional game had ever seen." There was good reason for the extremes Gottlieb was willing to go to obtain Wilt's services. Chamberlain showed promise far beyond that of George Mikan or Bill Spivey.

Shrewd as Gotty's new rule ultimately would prove to be, the territorial draft concept merely paved the way to pursue his ultimate prize. It provided an inside track for Wilt's services, but did not deliver the financially-savvy Wilt's signature on the dotted line. In fact, the move nearly backfired when Chamberlain worked during two summers as a bellhop at Kutsher's resort in the Catskills, a mecca for pro and college summer leagues in the 50s and early 60s. Boston Coach Red Auerbach tried to persuade Wilt, a good student at Overbrook, to attend Harvard University, where the Celtics could lay claim to the territorial pick.

In a 1956 *Sport* magazine article, former New York Knick and longtime broadcaster Bud Palmer quoted an unnamed NBA official: "I hate to admit it, but right now (prior to playing his first college game) Chamberlain is better than any player in the NBA." Palmer worked out with Wilt personally and was amazed by the kid's talent. "Chamberlain has just about every shot in the books, and is deadly with each of them," Palmer wrote. "His coordination and speed are unusual for a boy his size, and he moved around the court with the shrewdness of a veteran pro."

While Red and the Generals were helping the Trotters take the game truly global, the kid from Overbrook was looking like the best player on the planet. He was averaging 30 points a game in his freshman year at "the 'Brook." His team would win the Public League crown, defeating Northeast High and Wilt's future Warriors teammate, Guy Rodgers, who first would go on to star for the hometown Temple Owls. In his high school career, Wilt would win two more Public League championships and two City titles, his teams would go a combined 56-3, and he would average 37 points per game, breaking the record of another future NBA team-mate, and Philly homeboy, Tom Gola. As a senior, Wilt *averaged* an astounding 45 points per game, including a 71-point outburst against Public League rival Roxborough.

West Catholic prepared for one of the City championship contests by arming defenders with brooms in practice to try to swat the ball away. Although he virtually was unstoppable at the offensive end of the floor, "most teams were more intimidated by my defense," Chamberlain claimed.

"Wilt was in a whole different place," Red recalled. "Nobody had seen anything like this guy. When George Mikan came along, they said, 'Here is the first big man who can do everything,' and they were right – as far as the center position is concerned. Wilt was the first big man who could do almost everything at every position. He already looked like a guy who could become the best who ever played, and he would go on to become that guy."

Chamberlain became the first high school athlete in any sport to become the focus of intense recruiting efforts, some of which were quite dubious. News media speculated (and Wilt never denied) there was an outright bidding war for his services. In the end, he chose Kansas University, not so much for the alleged perks he would receive, but to play for legendary Coach "Phog" Allen, who was a disciple of the game's inventor, Dr. James Naismith. Also, there were no NBA teams with territorial draft rights to KU players. A rumor (never substantiated) persisted that Gottlieb worked out a secret deal with Wilt to attend a school out of the territorial draft reach of the other NBA clubs.

At first, Chamberlain seemed to enjoy his college experience. During his freshman year, the Fieldhouse later named in Allen's honor was packed with fans wanting to see him, many of whom then passed on watching the varsity and left the building. Chamberlain hosted his own jazz music show on the university's radio station, and learned about the nightlife in nearby Kansas City, Missouri, with none other than Goose Tatum. Wilt also was credited with breaking down segregation practices at restaurants and theatres in Lawrence, the town where the KU campus is located.

Wilt's dream to play for Allen never worked out. Phog was forced to adhere to the university's rule of mandatory retirement age when he turned 70, prior to Wilt's first varsity season. Chamberlain did not have the same level of respect for Allen's replacement, former Jayhawk assistant Dick Harp. Nevertheless, sophomore Wilt proved to be a sensation in his first year of varsity competition. Arenas were packed both home and away as fans flocked to see Chamberlain. He did not disappoint, leading Kansas to the NCAA championship game, as Eddie Gottlieb and Abe Saperstein looked on, imagining more packed arenas and Wilt wearing a Globetrotter or Warrior jersey.

In the national final, Kansas lost to the University of North Carolina in triple overtime. Wilt had 23 points and 14 rebounds and was named Most Outstanding Player of the tournament despite being triple-teamed most of the game. Given wide-open shots as a result, the rest of the Jayhawks shot a collective 27 percent. The final play of the game, an attempted inbound pass to Wilt, was intercepted to preserve the 54-53 Tar Heels win. For the rest of his life, Wilt would say that the NCAA title game loss was his most bitter defeat.

The next season, Chamberlain grew tired and bored with the college game. Each night he faced double and triple teams and was fouled repeatedly, and hard. In the pre-shot clock era, teams routinely held the ball against Kansas for minutes at a time to limit Wilt's offense. It was one of the only ways teams could stop Chamberlain, and it also took much of the joy out of the game for him. The physical pounding, coupled with the boring nature of the slowdown game employed by many opponents, frustrated Wilt to the point of exasperation. There also were financial considerations for his large, working-class family. Wilt felt he had played enough college ball, and wanted to make some real money. Although Gotty and the Warriors would hold his rights, NBA rules at the time did not permit a player to join the league before his class graduated. To Wilt's way of thinking, a final year at KU would be a wasted one from an earning perspective.

Wilt's mind was made up. Earlier in the season, his Kansas track and field teammate, four-time Olympic discus champion Al Oerter, had overheard a conversation between Wilt and Abe Saperstein. According to Gary Pomerantz' book, *Wilt, 1962*, Oerter heard Saperstein offer Wilt one-third ownership of the Trotters if he signed immediately. Oerter said he heard Wilt tell Abe he was not interested enough yet to sign. The key word Oerter heard was "yet."

Wilt would pack up his car soon after the Jayhawks' completion of the 1957-58 season, during which Kansas went 18-5. Three of the losses came with Wilt out of the lineup nursing a urinary tract infection. Because Kansas finished second in the Big Eight conference that year, the Jayhawks did not receive a bid to the NCAA tournament or the then-prestigious National Invitational Tournament. Wilt drove over to see Harp and deliver the news in person: He was finished at Kansas. His story, "Why I am Leaving College," was sold to *Look* magazine for $10,000, more than many NBA players made for an entire season in 1958.

Meanwhile, Red hardly was making Chamberlain-type headlines or money during this period, although his reputation as a player, coach, and team manager continued to grow. By the 1955-56 season, the Trotters and Generals were crossing the Atlantic on a chartered flight, and Abe told Leonard Lewin of the New York *Daily Mirror* that gross earnings of $6,000 after one of his early tours was, "about half of my present telephone bills." The year's transportation tab alone would be $370,000, Lewin reported. Part of his costs involved a contract for Red Klotz' organization to provide strong opposition, but the majority focused on improving the show, signing new or retaining veteran players, and increasing his marketing efforts.

"Every year, Abe started the season in the red, and he didn't start turning a profit until late. He was always planning to expand the foreign tours and to go to a few places we hadn't been to before." For a guy with such an unwieldy overhead, Saperstein saw in Wilt Chamberlain a guy who could raise the ceiling.

When he finally signed with the Globetrotters, the contract amount was variously reported from $50,000 up to $65,000, by far the most ever paid to a professional basketball player. Wilt posed for publicity pictures in his new Trotters' uniform, was touted in advertisements as Wilt the Stilt, a nickname he never liked, and he tried to fit in as just one of the guys, a difficult task given his paycheck. To put it in perspective, baseball was by far the most popular American sport in 1958, and National League MVP Hank Aaron was making a reported $35,000. Mickey Mantle, coming off back-to-back American League MVP awards in 1957, was pulling down $7,000 less than the high end of Wilt's reported salary.

"Abe pulled off quite a feat in getting Wilt under contract," Klotz said. "The Trotters were starting to become more oriented to the show and the reams, and people were excited to see Wilt. They were going to have a much better opportunity to see him with the Globetrotters than with Kansas University."

Gene Hudgins, who became the first Washington Generals' player to jump from Red's team to the Trotters, was a rookie in 1958-59 with Wilt and future baseball Hall of Fame pitcher Bob Gibson. In yet another stroke of genius, Chamberlain was tapped by Abe to play guard for the Trotters. On the face of it, the very notion of a seven-foot-one-inch backcourt man added value to the Globies' comedy routines. The fans howled with delight as Wilt dribbled the ball up the court, and dished passes with pinpoint accuracy as the Trotters ran their famous figure-eight play on offense. He would boost a shorter forward or center onto his shoulders, who would then dunk the ball, and Wilt would pick the player up to do it, showcasing his brute strength.

By playing in the backcourt, Wilt also was practicing to improve his ball handling skills, already among the best ever for a big man. Wilt often spoke of his year with the Trotters as an excellent training ground for his NBA career, especially his ability to pass the ball and move without it.

Bob Gibson, meanwhile, played with the same attitude and intensity that would help define his baseball career. It was a fine attribute for the straight-up basketball part of the Trotters' games, but a more difficult fit for the comedy side. "Wilt was a natural entertainer and showman and a great guy to hang around with," Hudgins said. "Bob Gibson, I think, was more interested in playing regular basketball."

A native of Omaha, Nebraska, Gibson signed with both the Trotters and the St. Louis Cardinals upon his graduation from Creighton University. Known for his "chin music" brushback pitches on the mound, he played just as hard on the basketball court. Sometimes he played a bit too hard for the Trotters' and Generals' need to survive a lengthy schedule. Red remembers that Gibson was playing particularly rough during several games on the European tour that year. He spoke to Gibson about it. "I told him we have many more games to play and we all need to stay healthy. I appreciated how competitive he was, but it wasn't doing anybody any good to have guys get hurt. Apparently he wasn't hearing what I was saying."

The very next night, Gibson threw an elbow that landed and felled one of Red's players. During the next stoppage of play, Red huddled his team and put the order out: The next time the ball went to "Bullet" Bob, as the Trotters called him, allow Gibson a clear lane to the basket. At that point, the entire Generals team would collapse around him and get in a few payback licks. That is exactly what happened, Red says. "He took a few punches and finally got the message and fell more in line with the show after that."

Things sometimes got a little bit rough for Klotz as well, as he was almost always the smallest man on the court; however, the comedy value made it worthwhile. One time, running the Trotter's famed "figure eight" dribbling ream, Wilt wound up at the top of the key, where Red reached in and stole the ball. "You're in my country now, Wilt," Red said, before dribbling the length of the court and flipping in a layup. Later in the game, they ran the play again, but this time Red got his legs tangled up underneath the basket and took a spill to the floor.

As he scrambled to regain his feet, a size 17 sneaker pressed him back down to the hardwood. "You're in my country now, Red!" Wilt bellowed, and both men laughed heartily. "I really got a chance to get to know him, and he was just the friendliest, most delightful guy," said Red. "He was popular with his teammates, with us, and of course with the fans. He really helped the gate."

It was another historic year on the travel front. The Trotters' ninth overseas tour took them into the Soviet Union, the first time an American basketball team had played there. During one of the Trotters' tours of Moscow, Soviet Premier Nikita Khrushchev posed with the team, and he showed up for the opening game of a series that would draw a total of more than 135,000 fans.

"This was the height of the Cold War, deep within the Iron Curtain, and here we were again, making people laugh and think better of Americans. We did a lot to tell the other side about what the people were being told in all the propaganda," said Klotz. According to one high-ranking Soviet official, "(the Trotters have) done more to help Russian-American relations than any other sports organization."

According to a basketball research website, Wilt's first game with the Trotters took place in Cortuna Da Ampezzo, Italy, on July 22 against a U.S. All-Stars team that included Red Klotz. Wilt liked playing for the Globetrotters so much that he would return, sometimes without notice, in the summers after the NBA season had ended. "He would check our schedule and catch up with us," said Red. "The Trotters never knew for sure when he would show up, but they knew he would eventually. They always packed his uniform and had it ready, because Wilt was going to make a dramatic appearance at some point."

Wilt made his United States pro debut in Chicago on October 17, 1958, scoring 25 points against the Sphas. The next night he was at Madison Square Garden for the first time as a pro, scoring 16, once again at the expense of his hometown Sphas.

According to an Internet posting, the Kansas City *Star* reported that Wilt averaged 30 points per game for the Trotters for the summer tour through the first 12 games of the 1958-59 season, Wilt's only full season with the Trotters. He reportedly scored 21 points in a Chicago all-star game won by the Trotters in his final game of the regular season. That would be the end of Wilt's full-time Trotters' career.

Eddie Gottlieb's manipulation of the league's draft rules and his patience finally paid off in May of 1959 when he announced Wilt signed with the Warriors for a reported $35,000. It was the league's highest salary, but a significant pay cut from his deal with the Trotters. Although Chamberlain wanted to prove himself against the top pros in the NBA, he continued on the Trotters' European tour of 1959. After his rookie year in Philly, he threatened to quit (citing hard fouls and unfair officiating), and mulled another lucrative offer to rejoin the Globies full time. That leverage undoubtedly helped his negotiations with the notoriously tight Eddie Gottlieb.

Eventually he would return to the NBA and rewrite most of its record book. By the middle 60s, Chamberlain was the most dominant offensive and defensive force in the game. Some of the memorable stats include a 55-rebound game against Bill Russell and the Celtics, averaging 50 points per game over the 1961-62 season, never fouling out of a game, averaging more than 48 minutes over the course of a season, and becoming the first center to lead the league in assists. Of course, his most famous feat was the 100-point game against the New York Knicks in Hershey, PA, in 1962. He would win two NBA titles during his career.

Despite his fantastic success, Wilt always seemed to come home to his pro roots with the Globetrotters. Red would face Wilt again during the ballpark series in 1963 at New York's Polo Grounds. Chamberlain appeared on the summer tours until 1968, when he was traded from the 76ers to the Los Angeles Lakers.

"I think he liked it so much because the pressure was off him," Red said. "He was able to enjoy playing basketball. He didn't have to carry a team around on his back or feel the expectations for winning every night. He was very popular in Europe, and nobody was saying things about his height, at least in a language he could understand. It was a way for him to escape. "

When the 76ers held their preseason training camps in Margate, a small beach resort city near Atlantic City, where Red and his family had moved, Wilt sometimes joined Klotz, Gloria, and the family for dinner. "He loved coming to the house and just being a nice young man, not Wilt Chamberlain, superstar," said Red. He was able to let down his guard and just be himself. He was great with my kids."

"He was so nice to us," Red's daughter Kiki would say. "I remember him playing with us and laughing with us. What I remember most was standing up next to him and staring straight into his kneecap."

On the court, Red and Wilt had a friendly rivalry. The five-foot-seven Klotz was Chamberlain's physical antithesis, and that somehow drew them even closer. "I took the ball away from him a few times and he ran over me a few times," is the way Red summed up their on-court encounters. "We respected the heck out of each other. He left us too soon, and I still miss him."

Wilt, who passed away in 1991, put it this way in a *Wall Street Journal* article: "With Red, you lose on all counts. You're supposed to pick on somebody your own size, you must always respect your elders, and you can never hit a man with glasses."

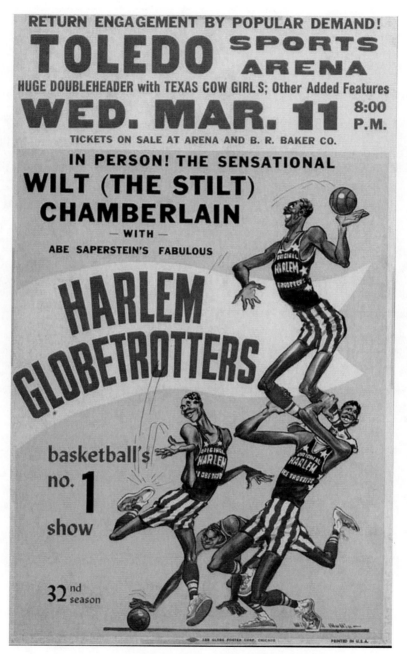

A poster advertising Wilt Chamberlain's appearance
with the Globetrotters.

Red gets a steal from an Argentine player as U.S. All-Stars teammate Tony Lavelli looks on at left. Note the soccer-style basketball used in the game.

Chapter 19

Shrinking the Globe

By now, Red was a seasoned world traveler, and an established professional basketball entrepreneur. However, the road is full of surprises, some of them not so good. The Trotters hadn't survived since 1926 by walking away from scheduled games. That meant finding another way when travel plans went awry. Red's method of operation was stricter still: He always tried to arrive at a site before the Trotters.

During a tropical storm at a venue in Brazil, the Generals found impassable roads and made their way to the arena via canoe. When they got off the boats and put the paddles away, they found a packed house, oppressive humidity, and enough leaks in the roof to flood the court. A few of the players balked at the conditions and suggested a cancellation of the date.

"The promoter said cancellation was not an option. That would risk a full scale riot," Red recalls. "The guy says, 'If this game is called off, we might not get out of here alive,' and he wasn't kidding. We needed an answer."

They found one. Crews mopped the court, and buckets were placed beneath the holes in the roof, and the game went on as scheduled.

Red: "We had to dribble around the buckets, but we got the game in. Some guys were slipping and sliding, and we just made it part of the show. It never slowed me down. I guess all those years of dribbling around the trash cans on Darien Street paid off. We played the game, and as a bonus: no riot! Sometimes you just have to find a way to deal with the situation and move on. There is always another game to get to tomorrow…or sometimes there is one later that same day. You have to deal with whatever is thrown at you and try to give the people what they want. This is how the Trotters became so beloved and why (the Generals) were able to catch on. Whatever it took to get the game in, we did it."

There were more to the trips than business. The cultural side was a big part of what kept Abe and Red on the world tours and why Abe kept looking to expand them into areas the teams had yet to visit.

In 1961, Abe sent Red a cryptic post card from Bologna, Italy: "To those who boast," he began in English, *"Come si dice in Italiano, lo avete o non lo avete. Come voi vedete bene."* The computerized translation: "As they say in Italian, did you or did you not. You see how well." More than 50 years later, Red can't recall what the reference was. Probably some inside joke. The point was that Saperstein took the time and trouble to write in the language of the country he was visiting and knew that Red, a fellow travel lover, would figure it out. It was all about embracing the culture and adapting to it, and not expecting the culture to change for a bunch of athletes, no matter how famous they happened to be.

"Abe was adventurous and loved to learn things about all the different places we went to," Red says. "He also had a great personality. People were drawn to him." As a result, doors opened for the Trotters and Generals. People wanted to be around the famous American sports ambassadors. This included movie stars, politicians, and even world leaders such as Juan and Evita Peron, several Popes, and years later, Nelson Mandela. For example, Red talks about a trip to Australia and a stop at a nightclub, where Gene Hudgins took the microphone from a member of the band and began to sing. "Gene was a great singer, almost as talented as he was as a basketball player. The people in the club loved it, and Gene just kept going. He loved it too. We didn't pay for drinks or food after that."

The Trotters' and Generals' "show must go on" reputation was hard-earned. Red loves to recount a tale from one of his first visits to the Middle East with the Generals: "We were ready to board an Air France plane following a game in Syria for a game the next night in Istanbul, Turkey. We used to call it 'Air Chance,' because aviation was pretty shaky overseas at the time. We were ready to take off and got word that the plane was overweight. It was too late to dump fuel. Abe ordered me and three other guys off the plane. There was a guy from my team and one from the Trotters. We needed to drive 100 miles across the desert to catch a different flight in Beirut, Lebanon."

What happened next astounded even the travel-savvy Klotz. "The Trotters' flight takes off, and we're standing there with our clothes bags when these Lebanese drivers pull up in a couple DeSotos. They don't speak English. In those days, there was a very prevalent black market, and you could get anything. I'm not sure these guys were brought in off the black market, but I had my suspicions. We get in the American cars and drive 100 miles through the desert until we reach the Syrian-Lebanon border."

There, the group was greeted by unsmiling, heavily-armed military personnel. "Syria was getting ready to attack Israel for the umpteenth time. Nobody speaks English, and I'm doing a pantomime of dribbling and shooting a basketball. The guards aren't buying it. They want identification, and I hand them the manifest from the plane. It has 41 names on it, and the first ones on the list are Jewish: Saperstein and Klotz. I'm thinking they want to know where the 37 bodies are buried."

Finally, somebody showed up who knew English, and a translation was provided as to Klotz' party's intended business. The guards relented, and the group was allowed to pass through. They caught their flight and arrived in Istanbul where they checked into a brand new Hilton hotel.

"At the front desk, I picked up Abe's mail," Red remembers. "We got up to his suite, and they are all relaxing with drinks and eating fruit. Abe was sitting there, eating grapes with Eddie Gottlieb, Dave Zinkoff, and a couple other people. I'm looking at all this luxury and thinking about the harrowing drive through the desert and our experience at the border. Abe looks at me and says, 'Red, what the hell happened? You know my policy. I want to know what's going on at all times. Why didn't you let me know?' I just looked at him and handed him the mail I picked up at the front desk. I said, 'of course I know your policy. Here's my cable. I didn't do too badly to get here before the cable was delivered.'"

While Red recounts the tale with a twinkle in his eye, he said there was a deeper side. Klotz was establishing a bond with Saperstein that would prove unbreakable for the rest of Abe's life. "One thing Abe knew was that he could depend on me. After you go through incidents with a person, you can't help but become closer. He was a great friend."

Abe loved his celebrity status. In another postcard, this one from Madrid, Spain, he wrote about an encounter with a famous band leader and his sultry torch singer. "Just a quick hello. On my way to dinner with Xavier Cugat and Abbe Lane – What a dish!"

Red enjoyed the star treatment as well, but it wasn't the thing he liked most about the tours. It was an additional facet of his great basketball odyssey and his charmed life. For Klotz, the real thrill of the tours was about the basketball and representing his country.

Red: "It was nice to be received the way we were. How many people can say they met so many foreign dignitaries and celebrities? The best was introducing a wonderful game to people and showing them how to enjoy it. As we did it, we were made them like us. We were *making* people like Americans. That wasn't such an easy thing to do in some of these places."

Many of the people they encountered were curious and had their own ideas about Americans before the Trotters' arrival, he said. "I guarantee you that we changed many of those ideas. Everyone loves to laugh and to be amazed. We were putting on shows the likes of which they'd never seen. We were making them laugh. Laughter cuts across every culture, every language."

By 1961-62, the Trotters had reached a new milestone, and along with it another new level of success. The "magicians of basketball" were celebrating their thirty-fifth season, and Abe's roster of countries visited had reached 80. Red had visited virtually all of the countries. Any European nations that he missed while in South America or playing stateside were made up on future tours. In 1960-61, following their triumph in the Soviet Union two years previous and a year following a first foray into Bulgaria, the Trotters sniffed haughtily at the height of the Cold War.

"Nobody was telling Abe any country was off limits. To an extent, I think Abe believed the more dangerous, the more politically volatile the country, the more he wanted to go there."

The twelfth annual European tour began in Finland, where Abe was hosted by the head of the national basketball federation, and triumphant return stops were made to Austria, West Berlin, and Belgium.

The tour brought the Trotters into such places as Poland, Hungary, Romania, and a return to Moscow in the USSR. Their reputation cemented during Wilt's appearance during their previous visit, the teams found public advertising posters around the country touting the Trotters' game alongside those promoting the biggest national hero at the time. Cosmonaut Yuri Gagarin was at the controls of the world's first manned spacecraft, launched two months before Alan Shepard became the first American in space. Gagarin's smiling image shared equal billing with pictures of the Trotters' game action.

Once again, the top American diplomats were on hand to be photographed with Abe and to thank him for helping to put America's best image forward in places Americans rarely were seen. The London-born Saperstein was keenly aware the United States had afforded him the opportunity to become a basketball tycoon, informal ambassador, and a national celebrity. He considered himself a citizen of the world, and as such, continued to break new ground.

The people responded to what Abe was offering. In Bucharest, Romania, over 120,000 fans turned out for three nights in Stadium Republic, packed with 40,000 for opening night, 10,000 above the listed capacity. In Hungary, three sold out games in Budapest also were broadcast on nationwide television, even though only a small handful of Hungarian homes had television then.

Poland especially was touching for Abe, who made sure to visit the ruins of the Auschwitz concentration camp, where millions of Jews died at the hand of the Nazis. At another point in the trip, he and members of the team were received by U.S. Ambassador Jacob Beam. Abe also made it a special point to drive more than 60 miles to visit the town of Lomza, birthplace of his parents.

A second unit traveled to several other exotic locales that year. The Trotters and Generals visited India, where fans jammed an outdoor cricket stadium in Bombay. In the "down under" nations of Australia and New Zealand, fans packed stadiums and arenas to see the American athletes. In Pakistan, martial law was in effect during the stop.

As always, Red took it all in with a mix of wonder and awe. He was most comfortable on the court. "Basketball is a wonderful game in terms of improvisation. Things happen out there you can read and be a part of and contribute to. If you know the game, and you know your teammates, you can react in situations to make everyone look better. That improves the show."

At this stage of Red Klotz' career (age 40), his overall game was beginning to take a backseat to his shooting ability. Oh, Red still could set up a teammate by drawing a double-team and getting the ball to the resulting open man. He also could reward a cutter with a pinpoint delivery for an easy two points. On nights the Generals needed him to score to keep it close, Red Klotz was known to fill it up in that situation. His 20-point nights were routine, and there is a documented high score of 37. Although not confirmed by a box score, a program scored by a fan in Chicago had Red going off for 52 points.

"There is no way that if Red Klotz came along today that he wouldn't have been in the NBA," Meadowlark Lemon said in an interview. Red also has called himself, "the best three-point shooter in the world," an interesting statement since the vast majority of his career was spent before the three-point line existed. In June of 1992, after his playing days already had ended, Red sank 21 straight from behind the NBA three-point arc in front of numerous witnesses at the Palace at Auburn Hills, in Michigan.

Red's neighbor Kelly Moscowitz tells an even more amazing tale from a game of "Around the World" at Red's favorite playground in Margate. "Red had already won the game. I was rebounding for him, and he just kept hitting three-pointers. After making 15 in a row, the other guy got disgusted and walked away. Red kept shooting, and I kept rebounding. He made 36 straight before he finally missed."

Once again, Abe could depend on Red: not just to get to the arena on time and in one piece, but to keep the Generals in the game and to keep the fans entertained. Red's other skill was his ability to help sell the reams and take heat off his own ballplayers. "I was never afraid to be the butt of their jokes, but some of my players just couldn't handle that part," he would say. "This is what made them great ballplayers, they were highly competitive. But that's not what our games are about. We can be competitive all the time, except during the Trotter routines. I always got that."

If it meant having the ball shoved under his jersey, getting in the way of the water bucket, or being the foil in the classic ream that involved carrying a female audience member's purse around the court, Red always was game. "All of the great comedy teams had the straight man. The Trotters got the laughs and the glory, but that was fine with me. If they were getting laughs, I was doing my job."

Between the accuracy of his three-point scoring and his central role in the comedy routines, Red now was becoming more of a household name and not just a known quantity to basketball purists. He developed great comedic timing, such as a double-take, which helped sell the reams, and the ability to improvise reams. "Sometimes the ones we made up on the fly worked the best. You might run into the stands at some point, or make a comment back after Meadowlark threw out a line."

The formula still was working for Abe. Give fans a great game and great entertainment, they will buy tickets. As the tours continued to break attendance records and expand to even more areas that had never seen a basketball before - "Just a big hello from gaucho land," Abe wrote from Uruguay in 1957 - Abe and Red continued to expand their horizons.

Though avowed "East Coast people," Red and Gloria visited Los Angeles and struck up friendships with Hollywood icons such as Johnny Mathis, (who made a guest appearance for the Generals), Pat Boone, and photographer to the stars, Wallace Seawell. "Wally" made portraits of Red and Gloria that still hang in the couple's bedroom, and some fun shots of a staged "wedding" more than 20 years after the actual fact. Red is wearing a top hat and tuxedo jacket over his Generals' uniform and Gloria's veil compliments a showgirl outfit finished off with fishnet stockings.

"My dad hates that photo," Ronee said with a laugh, "but he brags about how great my mom looks in it after having six kids (Jody came into the world in 1954 and Casey had been born in 1955.) Just look at those legs!"

When Abe visited Israel, he brought son Jerry for the trip. Occasionally, wife Sylvia went along, a rare occurrence that moved her to superlatives: "Hi group," she wrote to the Klotz clan. Can you believe Abe and I are together for a trip around the world? I'm feeling great." From Thailand, she wrote, "The trip so far has been one of interest and we are enjoying our own company. And also the comfort of the air conditioning. Really a hot period."

Abe's correspondence usually had to do with revelations of the road: "Ghosts of history are around every corner," he wrote from Brussels, Belgium. "Napoleon's Waterloo, (two) World Wars, very soon to be the capital of Europe's Common Market—and the largest strawberries in the whole world."

Saperstein continued his trademark letters and cards written in the native tongue. Red has cards written in Spanish, Bulgarian, and Italian, among others. *"Gelati. Casata, Spumoni, e Pellegrino molto vino chianti e lasagna Verdi!!! Yeah man,"* wrote Saperstein, extolling the virtues of the local cuisine and wine.

The combination of fast living, brutal schedules, and too much food was beginning to wear on Abe. "He never seemed to have time to take care of himself," Red said. "It was always a case of getting through the day's events and looking ahead to the next day. Everything was on the fly. Abe was a great promoter, but he wasn't the greatest businessman. He thought nothing of reaching into his pocket and peeling off bills to help a player with a sick relative or a sportswriter who couldn't make ends meet that month. He did a lot to help people that nobody knew about. He didn't make a big deal out of it. He just liked people and liked to help them. It cost him a lot of money sometimes, and that never bothered him. The operation was still growing, and I think he felt it could go on like that indefinitely."

Abe had a great advance man in Harry Hannin and a great organizer in Marie Linehan, who ran things back at the office in Chicago. The PR guy was Walter Kennedy, who would go on to become commissioner of the NBA. "Walter had an office in New York in the Empire State Building, where he did a great job of securing media coverage."

Along with commercial jet travel, which was becoming more routine, and the rise of television, Abe and Red and their teams were succeeding in helping to "shrink" the globe. "We got the world excited about basketball," Red said. "Abe was doing what he always did: investing in the team and the tours and the people who made it all work. Abe saw no reason why it shouldn't just keep growing, keep expanding. And why wouldn't it? It grew to the point that it did through Abe's genius."

As the 1960s progressed, things would change more rapidly. The changes would affect Red's and the Trotters' operations. Most of all, they would affect Abe Saperstein.

Red (#30) in a ream on the deck of the USS Enterprise. Red has been proud of his role in entertaining American troops throughout his career.

Comedian Bob Hope poses with Abe Saperstein at Cleveland Indians'
training camp. The Indians were owned by mutual friend, Bill Veeck.

Chapter 20

The Amazing Abe

For the first 35 years, Abe Saperstein's approach to running the Harlem Globetrotters worked like a charm. He grew the organization through hard work, networking, and implementing sports marketing principles he invented, many of which are still in use today. The momentum began slowly, and though it stalled at times, when Abe's efforts took hold, they finally paid off in a big way. After the Trotters won the 1941 World's Professional Invitational Tournament in Chicago, Saperstein managed to sustain the operation through World War II. He then proceeded on a career roll that forever would change basketball.

The Globetrotters' national acceptance began with consecutive wins over the mighty Minneapolis Lakers, appearances in the newsreels, and two successful feature films. Global acclaim would follow with world tours that proved to be diplomatic and financial triumphs. He followed that up with hugely successful tours of large U.S. ballparks, the signing of the game's brightest star, Wilt Chamberlain, and launching the immensely popular World Series of Basketball. Abe seemed to have the Midas touch. The media, heads of state, U.S. diplomats, and stars of entertainment were all eating out of his hand.

"He was a true genius as a promoter, though he never made a lot of money. He was always flying by the seat of his pants," said Red. "He was watching the house. He could look at a building and tell how many people were in it. Eddie Gottlieb could do that, too. But Abe wasn't watching every penny, and he sometimes made financial decisions that really weren't in his best interests. He made a lot of friends, though. He made personal friends, and he made lifelong friends of the game."

Despite the shoestring operation, Abe's run of success was unparalleled in basketball and a primary factor in its national and worldwide popularity. The so-called "major league" of the sport needed Abe's team from the outside to help draw big crowds. Heading into the 1960's, the NBA still took a backseat to the Globies.

The first crack in Abe's seemingly invulnerable veneer appeared in 1959 when old friend Gottlieb lured Wilt Chamberlain away from the Trotters and into the NBA. Both men had been friends for more than 30 years and had always done what they could to help each other's ventures. Abe held minority shares in Gotty's Philadelphia Warriors and both had promoted and held interests in baseball's Negro Leagues. Together with Eddie and another flamboyant Chicagoan, Bill Veeck, Abe unsuccessfully bid to buy the Philadelphia Phillies in 1942. Veeck did buy the Cleveland Indians in '48, and at Abe's urging, signed Negro Leagues legend Satchell Paige as a 48-year-old relief pitcher. To the astonishment of the entire sports world, Paige won six games down the stretch for Cleveland in 1948 and was a key piece in their American League pennant drive and World Series win over the Boston Braves. "Abe really delivered for me at that time," Veeck told Wendell Smith. "If he hadn't come through with Satchel Paige when he did, I doubt we would have won…"

Paige, who also would tour to make promotional appearances with the Trotters, "a wonderful guy" Red says, pointed to Abe's influence as the highlight of his long baseball career. With input from Abe and Eddie, Veeck also signed Larry Doby, a former Negro Leagues' star and the first African American to play in the American League.

Eddie's presence and guidance were staples on Trotter tours since the early 50s, but as the NBA began to gain in popularity, the relationship began to wane. The NBA finally was making inroads and finding a national fan base. Red Auerbach had built one of the great dynasties in any sport with his Boston Celtics. Wilt Chamberlain's move to the league, at a pay cut of his Globies' money by 50 percent, by some estimations, was leading the NBA to some long-sought-after crossover interest from fans of other sports, and with it, much larger gates. Magazines openly were asking the question, as one did in a headline, "Is the NBA Major League?" Now, at least, they were asking the question.

Around this time, Abe also had a falling out with the other NBA owners, many of whom who were by then attracting and signing the bulk of the great black players. In addition to Chamberlain, who was tearing up the league scoring records for Gotty's Warriors, point guard Guy Rodgers was getting him the ball. Wilt averaged 37.6 points per game and 27 rebounds as a rookie. On defense, he had innumerable blocked shots, which were not yet kept as a statistic. Wilt wasn't playing for laughs anymore, and he was dominating both ends of the floor. More importantly for Gotty and the league, Warriors' attendance was up more than 50 percent. Chamberlain led the Warriors to a second-place finish in the Eastern Division, and they made it to the Eastern finals against the Celtics, where they lost in six games.

There were other great black stars emerging as well. Bill Russell and K.C. Jones, both alumni of the national championship teams at the University of San Francisco, were key members of the NBA champion Celtics. The Cincinnati Royals' Oscar Robertson was the best all-around guard in the game. The Lakers' Elgin Baylor had Trotter-like moves that later would be compared to those of Julius Erving and Michael Jordan. Previously, black players of that magnitude had no real option other than to sign with the Trotters.

Abe stopped booking his team as part of doubleheaders involving NBA contests. The pro league's crowds slowly grew, despite the Trotters' absence. In Boston and Philly, where the Celtics-Warriors and Chamberlain-Russell rivalries heated up, the fans actually were lining up and filling Boston Garden and Convention Hall to watch Wilt and Big Bill go at it. In New York, a mecca of the sport where college ball previously ruled, the Knicks were becoming a hot ticket despite being a bad team. They largely stopped playing in small armories and gyms and began drawing big crowds to Madison Square Garden. The Lakers would move from Minneapolis to Los Angeles, with the Warriors to follow west in 1963 when Gotty sold them for $850,000. He would stay on as a consultant to the San Francisco Warriors.

While all appeared to be on the rise for the NBA, Wilt shocked the sports world in 1960 by announcing his retirement, and he said he meant it. "I'm done with the NBA," he said. "It's over." Some thought it a ploy, as Chamberlain was in the midst of salary negotiations with Gottlieb. However, Wilt expressed his dismay about the state of the league and his ambition to train to become a world-class track athlete. Reportedly, Eddie had offered his prize rookie a three-year deal worth $100,000. It then was revealed Wilt was considering an offer from Abe to return to the Trotters for the same figure, but for only one season.

Gotty was furious over the attempt of his longtime friend to sign Wilt, which he viewed as a betrayal that could have put the Warriors out of business. He fumed some more while Wilt joined the Globies' summer tour of Europe. "It's very upsetting." Gottlieb said. "If I knew he was only going to play one season, I wouldn't have gone after him."

Despite the deteriorating relationship with Gottlieb, Abe knew remaining stagnant would take the Trotters out of the public eye. His efforts to get Wilt under contract again were consistent with his longtime business model of putting his resources back into the product. Wilt was happy to spend his second summer in a row playing ball for fun with his friends while he saw more of Europe and let Eddie Gottlieb to stew and try to figure out how he might up the ante.

The rift became more pronounced when Abe announced plans to launch a rival major pro league, the American Basketball League, to begin play in the 1961-62 season. Abe believed the NBA had promised him the franchise in Los Angeles prior to approval of his longtime rivals, the Lakers, to move there. Abe placed one of his ABL teams, the Jets, in LA to go head-to-head against the Lakers. Saperstein awarded franchises in seven other cities that did not have NBA teams at the time (Chicago, Cleveland, Pittsburgh, and Washington in the Eastern Division, and Hawaii, San Francisco, Los Angeles, and Kansas City in the West). Not coincidentally, the NBA awarded an expansion franchise, the Packers, to Chicago, where they would compete directly with Abe's Chicago Majors. In addition to owning the Majors, Saperstein was his new league's commissioner.

Abe's bold move, disastrous as it would turn out to be, was not just about going up against the NBA. He felt the pros had abandoned defense and had taken the little man out of the game. In an effort to improve the pro game's on-court product, he added six seconds to the 24-second shot clock the established league was using and he awarded three points for field goals beyond a 25-foot arc. "(The game has been) taken over by behemoths" Abe said. "Even a fellow six-foot-five was becoming considered not tall enough." Saperstein also widened the foul lane to clear big men away from the basket.

One of Abe's ABL colleagues was a young shipping tycoon named George Steinbrenner, who headed the Cleveland Pipers. The coaching ranks included Pittsburgh's Neil Johnston, a former NBA scoring champ and member of Gottlieb's champion Warriors of 1956. Red's old Sphas' teammate Red Rocha (Hawaii) and ex-

Celtics' star Bill Sharman (Los Angeles) were other well-known names in the basketball community tapped to coach in the new league.

Steinbrenner's head coach in Cleveland was John McLendon, the first black man to lead a major pro team in any sport. Steinbrenner, showing the same aggressiveness as an owner that would later serve him well throughout his stewardship of the New York Yankees, signed three-time All-American Jerry Lucas from Ohio State to a $40,000 contract. Lucas had led the Buckeyes (with John Havlicek and a young reserve named Bobby Knight) to the 1959 NCAA championship. Lucas had briefly played AAU ball for McLendon, and the signing proved to be a good fit for the Pipers, who would go on to win the ABL championship. Connie Hawkins, a New York schoolyard legend who was banned from the NBA for alleged association with gamblers, was the star of the Pittsburgh Rens.

Lucas' signing shook pro basketball and gave Abe's new league instant credibility. The contact was only $15,000 less than the NBA's reported salary cap at the time per team. Here was an upstart league, headed by one of the game's most flamboyant and successful executives, giving a rookie more money than almost all of the NBA's established stars. Unfortunately for Abe, the momentum wouldn't last. Despite the Lucas deal, presence of known basketball names, Abe's innovations with the rules and hard work, and good crowds in Hawaii and Kansas City, there was simply not enough interest to sustain the venture.

The Los Angeles franchise did not last through the first season, and the league owners balked at the transportation costs associated with flying to Hawaii to play the Chiefs. The franchise relocated to Long Beach the following year, and the Washington Tapers moved to Philly, whose fans had been shocked by Gottlieb's sale and move of the Warriors. Red Klotz was reported to be part of an ownership group heading the Philadelphia team, and was rumored to be hired as a coach in the league. Red thought the better of it. He was more secure and content to provide the Globies' opposition and to embark on yet another successful world tour, with Thailand, New Zealand, and Australia among the places he was seeing for the first time.

"I was perfectly happy doing what I was doing and running my own operation," he said. "Abe had some great ideas for the ABL, particularly the three-point shot, which has changed the game forever and for the better. The problem was there wasn't enough interest in the pro game to support a new league."

To this day, among his memorabilia collection, Klotz keeps a lifetime pass to any game in the ABL, signed by Abe Saperstein. The card would be good for just a few months into the 1962-63 season. Hemorrhaging red ink, the league folded in December of 1962.

No one knows how much money Saperstein lost in the venture. If the ABL's demise was a blow to his reputation, the Trotters' boss didn't show it in correspondence to Red: "Hi! Here we go again: this time Rio, Uruguay, Argentina, Chile, Peru, Ecuador, Panama, Trinidad, Puerto Rico, and Cuba," Abe wrote. "*Hasta Luego.*" From Singapore, he sent a card with a picture of three topless young women: "Yes, it gets pretty damn hot here in the months of June, July and August. Regards, Abe."

By all accounts, Abe shook off the ABL's crash-and-burn and simply moved on. There were still new basketball worlds to conquer, more countries to explore, and new fans to be won over. Abe attempted to bounce back with a 1963-64 season that had numerous highlights. The Trotters were continuing to evolve from their competitive early background to a show team that relied more on comedy reams, fancy ball handling, and trick shots.

Abe sensed the change and aligned himself with other stars of the sports and entertainment world to keep the Trotters relevant and in the public eye. The Green Bay Packers were champions of the National Football League, and they fielded a pretty fair basketball squad to face the Globetrotters. More than 20,000 turned out at Chicago Stadium as Paul Hornung, Bart Starr, and other big names on the pro football championship team bowed to the Trotters, 83-52. Another big crowd saw the Globies prevail in a nine-point win a few nights later in Milwaukee.

Chicago Cubs' shortstop Ernie Banks traveled with the tour and served as master of ceremonies for the always-evolving half-time show. The new dance craze, the "Twist," was sweeping the nation, and Cab Calloway led selected fans down on the court to show off their moves. The gimmick attached the Trotters to the latest pop culture phenomenon and provided a showcase for their own routines and reams.

Lest anyone think the Globetrotters didn't retain their straight basketball roots, Abe's team thrashed the College All-Stars 14 games to one in their series, which by now was in its twelfth year. The Stars featured the likes of future NBAers Dave DeBusschere from Detroit University and LeRoy Ellis of St. Johns. The Trotters were led by Lemon, Gipson, Tex Harrison, Bobby Hall, Clarence Wilson, Hallie Bryant, and many others.

It would prove to be the final edition of the popular series. In yet another blow to his empire, the Amatuer Athletic Union ruled that the participants, college seniors, would lose their final semester's scholarships.

A passing of the torch seemed to be in play for Abe's roster as well. Sweetwater Clifton returned to the team after years in the NBA, and a new star, Hubert "Geese" Ausbie, the nation's third leading scorer in college behind Elgin Baylor and Oscar Robertson, joined the squad. Ausbie, an All-American at Philander Smith College in Arkansas, would go on to a long career as a Trotter scorer and dribbler. There was no doubt he was impressed with the 42-year-old star of the opposition's team.

"Red was already 'old' when I joined the tour," Geese said with a laugh. "The thing was, he didn't play old. People were coming out to see the Trotters. They were also coming to see Red. In many ways, Red was 'it.' You knew he was going to give you good basketball and help with the show every night. People loved to watch him, and he was as big a star and as big a name as many of the Trotters. All (of the Trotters) liked him as a person and respected him as a player and a coach and a manager."

At one point, Red left the tour to attend to matters at home, where a wry postcard awaited from one of his local Atlantic City–area players, Marv Becker. "Hi, everything is going great," Becker wrote. "The only trouble is we have not won a game since you left us in Berlin."

Things at home were looking up. Red Klotz Liquors and the bar were unqualified successes, mostly due to Gloria's tireless efforts. Red's wife immersed herself in the community, organizing youth softball and bowling teams, providing scholarships for deserving neighborhood kids, and just lending an ear and providing a solution when she could find one. The bar was a gathering spot in the gritty Uptown of Atlantic City. "We offered entertainment and low prices, and people appreciated they could go out for the night and not go broke," Gloria said.

Red remembers the risk they took. "Some Atlantic City people said the business would close in six weeks," he said. "Gloria truly cared. It wasn't just about coming in and making money, it was about getting to know people and being part of the neighborhood. If somebody needed a few dollars for food, she would give it to them. If they needed to run a tab at the bar, she allowed it. We were accepted and respected. That was mainly due to Gloria."

There were times when Red and Gloria did reap the rewards of their hard work. The annual trip to the West Coast was an opportunity to renew their friendship with photographer Wally Seawell and to socialize with Abe and Sylvia.

"We enjoyed Wally's company," said Red, "and you never knew who might be around him." Besides singer Johnny Mathis, and crooner Pat Boone, Red and Gloria also became friendly with Dodgers' owner Walter O'Malley and his family.

At a Hollywood party, Klotz ran into his old Atlantic City Senators' teammate Chuck Connors, who by then had given up his pro sports careers with the Celtics and Dodgers and parlayed his winning personality into TV stardom. Connors' show, "The Rifleman," was a major hit.

"Chuck looked at me and his eyes got big," Red recalls. "He couldn't believe I was still out there playing. He said, 'You're still doing this?' and we both had a good laugh about it. Little did either of us know I would keep going for 20 more years."

While Red and the Generals soldiered on against the Trotters, Abe continued to earn praise and awards for his diplomatic efforts. During another Cold War foray into the Soviet Union, Ambassador Lwellyn Thompson met with Abe and the team. "Perhaps we need more Globetrotters over here and fewer diplomats to ease the tension," Thompson said.

Abe recounted his meeting with Soviet dictator Nikita Khrushchev to Cobey Black of the Honolulu Star-Bulletin. It was the hottest day in July, and the only cool place in town was Lenin's tomb in the Kremlin, which Abe referred to as, "the ice box." Abe's party, including Gottlieb, was whisked past a long line by guards and taken into the tomb and out again, where the guards insisted they look at another attraction.

"They wouldn't let go of me," said Abe, who wanted to return to his hotel and take a nap before that night's scheduled game. The guards refused to budge. "I (was) captive in the Kremlin."

Suddenly, three large Russian-built cars pulled up, and out stepped Khrushchev, a man who three years previously had threatened the United States by saying, "We will bury you!" in a speech before the United Nations. This time, the Soviet strongman had a huge smile on his face as he immediately pointed out Abe among a group of tourists and, "(threw) his arms around my shoulders like a lost brother," Abe said. "Photographers appeared from nowhere and the group gathered around the dictator and everyone smiled for pictures that would appear in papers worldwide the next day. "The whole thing was planned," said Abe. "The Associated Press bureau chief said he had never seen pictures pass through the censors so fast."

Back in Chicago, Abe was honored by his hometown. Mayor Richard J. Daley awarded him officially recognized him with a certificate of merit for global achievements.

When the 1964 summer tour rolled around, something was different. Abe still posed at Idlewild Airport, smiling with his band of basketball ambassadors. This time, there was a glaring absence in the photo. Eddie Gottlieb opted to stay home in Philadelphia, and the two men would remain distant for the rest of Abe's life. Something else was different. Abe, at age 62, was beginning to show the strain of 37 basically year-round seasons at the helm of the Trotters.

Red Klotz in the mid-1960s.

Chapter 21

The Show Goes On

A be Saperstein traveled 60,000 miles, visited 31 nations, and, "(got) myself good and tired," during the 1965-66 season.

It was just a typical year for Abe, whom *Chicago Tribune* travel writer Estele Atwell dubbed the airlines, "Number 1 commercial air passenger." The title would be difficult to dispute. Chicago-based United Airlines issued the Globetrotters' founder a card certifying that he had four million air miles to his credit, a figure Abe said would reach five million by the end of the following year's schedule. Of course, prior to the jet age, Abe had done a pretty fair share of transporting himself, the team, and its equipment by bus, train, boat, and that battered old Ford Model T.

All of the travel, combined with a poor diet and the stress brought on by the business side of the Trotter empire, took its toll, and Abe's health began to deteriorate. "Abe never really took care of himself. He was too busy running the organization and having fun doing it," Red said. "It all finally began to wear on him."

Abe considered himself a gourmet, and always sampled the local delicacies. He may not have splurged on himself as a rule, but he made an exception when it came to fine dining. His favorite food was liver, and extolled the virtues of, "chopped liver par excellence," at Iso's in London, and a soup from Capprico's in Rome with the main ingredients of rice and chicken liver. Press photos depict Abe cutting a massive steak at Toots Shor's in New York, while the famed proprietor beams his approval. He also is pictured ordering chocolate-dipped strawberries in Belgium. An article in a Trotters' program runs down each course of a massive meal, with Abe's favorites listed in each category. "Now we're down to dessert, and Abe is sort of stumped: He likes so many of these he's run across."

"The strawberries must have been from Antwerp," said Gloria. "I was along once, and it was the first thing he had to do when he got off the plane. Had to find those strawberries."

For a man whose business empire began so humbly, Saperstein's love of the finer things, at least when it came to lodging and dining, was understandable. This was a guy who had endured temperatures below zero and above 100 degrees, lunchmeat sandwiches, and catnaps in the car. Abe had originated the Trotters concept and built the team to household name status all through hard work. Nobody blamed him for enjoying a great meal.

Interestingly, "Abe really did not have a flashy lifestyle," Red said. "He lived most of his life in a small, plain house in Chicago. Of course, he was hardly ever there."

One other rare splurge would be an annual fishing trip to an exotic location, which Klotz, who also enjoyed fishing, usually was invited to attend. The other standard invitee was Inman Jackson, one of his original players and a Trotters' coach in the final years of Abe's life.

"Jackson was more like a brother to Abe than an employee," said Gloria. Abe, Red and Jackson sometimes would travel to a remote spot in Northern Canada to fish. Aside from the fishing trips and the dinners, Abe allowed himself very few luxuries. He knew what it took to grow the Trotters to that point and would rather invest in his business interests than pamper himself. The formula always had worked, but as things grew and times changed, the mechanics of keeping everything moving became more complicated. The top players were harder to come by; they wanted more money and had larger egos. He could no longer operate "on the fly." There were too many implications to each business move.

Abe's failed ABL venture was not his only business flop. He helped to back an ice show's foray into Europe, which lost money and ended after a few months. Adding to the misery was the end of the summer ballpark tour, which had slipped in popularity in recent years, and the College All-Star series, which had taken a backseat to the NIT and NCAA postseason tournaments and the AAU ruling.

However, Abe was Abe, and his business instincts still brought great successes. Among these were signing the great Connie Hawkins following the collapse of the ABL; planning a publicity-fueled return to Hinckley, Illinois, site of the Trotters' very first game; and the best move of all: putting the Globetrotters on television as much as possible.

Television was the nation's dominant medium by this point, and Trotter appearances took their popularity to even greater heights. Abe and team members appeared on the "What's My Line" game show, and numerous times on "The Ed Sullivan Show," the most-viewed program on Sunday nights. It was Abe's visionary contract with CBS to showcase the Trotters and Generals on the "CBS Sports Spectacular" that once again put the Trotters in the national limelight's brightest glare.

The CBS specials, for which Abe was paid a reported $150,000 per year, displayed the power of TV to one Louis "Red" Klotz. The foil of so many reams, Red did not let his straight man role get in the way of basketball. The old two-hander never failed him, and the Generals always stayed competitive with their more famous foes. He also showed off his skills "chasing the dribbler," who by now was Curly Neal. Red's name recognition soon would match that of any of the Trotters.

Curly, a Greensboro, North Carolina native, was a 23-points-per-game scorer at Johnson C. Smith University in Charlotte. It was Neal's ball-handling skills that made him a Trotters star with popularity approaching that of Meadowlark. Although not quite the equal of Marques Hanes as a dribbler, Neal was dazzling nonetheless, and his trademark shaved bald pate and huge smile made him instantly recognizable. Just as Lemon's TV exposure made him more famous than his predecessor Tatum, Neal's mass appeal would dwarf that of Haynes.

The same held true for Klotz. Television audiences took note as that funny "old" guy Klotz stayed right with Curly as he dribbled in circles and figure eights, adding to the comedic value of the show. Klotz long ago had mastered the double and triple take when he was victimized by the ball-up-the-jersey trick and other reams. This translated well to TV. It was impossible for fans and non-fans alike to watch the televised specials and not notice who Red Klotz was.

"We used to watch the Trotters and then go out and play pickup ball," said Bill Schmidt of Collingswood, New Jersey, who was typical of the kids of that generation. "The Trotters would get us working on ball handling, and we always fooled around with trick shots for fun. There were always arguments about who would be Meadowlark. And somebody was always Red Klotz. Usually the guy who considered himself to be the best shooter."

The CBS shows put the Trotters into millions of homes and probably benefitted Meadowlark Lemon the most. Already an international comedy star, Lemon's distinctive name, showmanship, and hook shot would turn him into one of the nation's most popular sports personalities. Fitted with a microphone that allowed the audience at home to share in his antics, Meadowlark took center stage. He had very talented and entertaining teammates in Neal, Hawkins, and Ausbie, but they all took a backseat to Meadow.

For the first time ever, fans gained access to the Trotters' rap that went with the reams. The baby boomer generation grew up looking forward to the Trotters' annual appearance on nationwide TV. Now, the Globetrotters (and to an increasing extent, the Generals) were not just sports and entertainment entities, they were major figures in pop culture. At this point, the Generals began to adopt their persona as lovable losers. As was the case with their coach-owner, the Generals' franchise had been on tour long enough to have an instantly recognizable name.

"It was unbelievable," Red would say about the televised games. "To this day, people come up to me and tell me about how they got into basketball by watching us play the Trotters on TV." Upon meeting him, one confused man asked, "Are you the *original* Red Klotz?"

Abe was a fixture during the telecasts as well, coaching his team from the sidelines and participating in numerous interviews. However, the Trotters' boss was conspicuously absent in 1966 when the Trotters-Generals game aired in January. He had developed a heart condition and was hospitalized for an extended period of time.

"The problem was Abe refused to slow down," said Klotz. "He was always too busy to do what the doctors asked him to do. As soon as he would leave the hospital, he would get on a plane and re-join the tour. Sometimes, if his kids were along, I would be called upon to babysit Jerry and Eloise at night. Abe knew I wasn't going to be out partying with the boys."

Abe still kept going, despite his heart disease. "He knew what he was doing to himself. One time he looked at me and said, 'Red I'm too busy to die.'"

There was another instance, Red said, when Abe checked into a hospital and left the tour in the hands of PR man Walter Kennedy. "You knew he was sick for him to do that. We had never seen him walk away from the tour."

Bouncing back like a rebound off the glass, Abe soon got back in the saddle and joined one of his most ambitious journeys yet.

In 1965, a four-month marathon began in England and continued on through Turkey, India, and the Far East, Australia and New Zealand, and wrapped up in Hawaii.

The Trotters were celebrating their fortieth anniversary season, and Abe still had goals, Red said. He hoped to be around for the fiftieth, and he wanted to travel to 100 countries. It was almost as if the game's greatest promoter was challenging himself to see if he still could pull it off the nearly impossible.

"It was too much, even if he had been healthy." Red said of Abe's last worldwide jaunt. "At one point, I brought him some soup up in his hotel room. He looked terrible. All he would admit to was being tired, but I knew that he just wasn't right. He ate some of the soup. He was in bad shape. I knew he was dying, and Abe knew it, too."

Not that he would ever acknowledge it. In the last postcard from Abe, attributed to the French stop on the last march through Europe the message was shorter than usual, but still upbeat. It featured a picture of an attractive young woman. "French lass with lots of class says hello to you and to me too," Abe wrote breezily. The tone belied the gravity of the situation.

Saperstein returned home to Chicago on another grueling flight, and it was later discovered, Red said, that Abe had suffered a heart attack. He spent weeks recuperating and still felt the need to go to his Chicago office and keep his hand in things. He did rent an apartment in Hollywood, which he escaped to with Sylvia, away from the harsh Chicago winter. It didn't help, as he again wound up in a Los Angeles hospital. This time, tests revealed he needed prostate surgery. He returned home once again and scheduled the surgery.

While prepping for the operation at Weiss Memorial Hospital in his hometown, Abe suffered another heart attack. He passed away on March 15, 1966, a few days after his admission to the hospital.

Red was playing in Greensboro, North Carolina when the Trotters' tour manager, Parnell Woods, delivered the news. Klotz bowed his head and walked off the court.

Red: "The show must go on. The Trotters put on a brave face and kept going because that's what Abe would have wanted. My team finished the game, too. But I just couldn't go. Abe's death was not unexpected, but it was still a tremendous shock. He was only 63, much too young. This was a man who built one of the greatest organizations in sports and who gave me my big chance. Next to my own family, I owed the most gratitude of my life to Abe. I remembered thinking to myself that this will change everything."

For Red personally, the sense of loss was overwhelming. "I had spent so much time on the road with him; we had become very close. He became one of my very best friends, and I like to think I was one of his closest friends. When I received the news of Abe's passing, it was hard to imagine that he was really gone. He seemed so much larger than the tour and the organization. To me and to many people, Abe *was* the Globetrotters."

Immediately, the tributes poured in. "Saperstein could have served as a model for the United Nations," an Associated Press reporter wrote in the obituary that was picked up worldwide. "He was one of a Jewish family of 10 born in London who organized a Negro team…and found the welcome mat out in the Vatican as well as behind the Iron Curtain."

His funeral, some said fittingly, took place on St. Patrick's Day, one of Chicago's most festive occasions that included a raucous parade. "Abe was a showman to the end," one article said. "He was born on the Fourth of July and buried on St. Patrick's Day."

Bill Veeck's reaction was more thoughtful. "There were months when we didn't see him, but he was never very far away," wrote Veeck, a friend for 30 years. "There would be a cablegram from London, 'See you tonight,' or a clipping from Pravda…a call from Prague: 'Don't forget to watch the Ed Sullivan Show Sunday.'"

Veeck, a promoter with skills rivaling Saperstein's, said that Abe sold a product: laughs. It was a product that knew neither boundaries nor class distinctions. "Abe moved among the big and the little and was accepted by both. (I) never ceased to marvel that a dictator, a sheik, a prince, or a pauper were equally approachable by the immigrant tailor's son from Chicago..."

At the time of his passing, Abe's list of accomplishments was staggering. He was the first to take a basketball team around the world (1952), had attracted the two largest basketball crowds in history (Berlin and Rio de Janiero, 1951), had audiences with four Popes, completed 17 European tours, did "command performances" in Europe and in Algeria for the French Foreign Legion, and entertained thousands of United States troops stationed abroad. Playing in bull rings and soccer stadiums had become routine, but there were also games on a court laid atop dozens of beer kegs (to avert a muddy soccer field), at the bottom of a drained swimming pool, and in a Philippine leper colony. The Trotters' forays into the Soviet Union and behind the Iron Curtain, at the height of the Cold War, presented an alternating view of a repressed African American.

The win-loss record, more important in the early days, but still recorded at the time of Abe's death, stood at 8,680 wins and 322 defeats. Several of the losses were inflicted (and would be again) by teams on which Red Klotz plied his trade of two-hand shooting, pinpoint passing, and the occasional steal to keep the dribbler honest.

Few if any contemporaries could provide a more intimate view of Abe over such a long stretch of time. Red would often talk of the less publicized but equally important aspect of Abe's career: his charity work. In addition to the unpaid performances for the troops in North Africa, Alaska, and the Azores among other places, Abe's first visit to Israel in 1955 resulted in free passes to Israeli military and the donation of all of the tour's proceeds to help in the construction of youth centers. In 1963 in England, he gave the game proceeds to the royals' pet charity at the time, Playfields of Great Britain, and personally was served champagne at halftime by Queen Elizabeth's husband, Prince Philip, joining the comedy routine in a waiter's uniform. He staged dozens of clinics in countries where the game was new, leaving behind legions of basketball converts.

"Abe was truly a pioneer of the game," Red said. "The NBA wants to talk about taking the game international. During the Olympics, you hear about the 'Dream Team,' and they were great. The NBA certainly took things farther along internationally. But we were there first, and we paved the way for the international appeal of the game. The NBA would not have been so well received if the people hadn't already been introduced to the game. That was solely due to Abe Saperstein's foresight."

Meadowlark Lemon made similar statements. "I jumped at the opportunity Mr. Saperstein gave me…Who knows how my life would have turned out if I hadn't practiced for a tryout with the Globetrotters."

Abe's family wanted his legacy to continue, and to that end Abe's attorney Allan Bloch and a Chicago bank, incorporated the team as Abe Saperstein Enterprises, Inc. According to an article by William G. Margolis, most of the team was left to Sylvia, Eloise, and Jerry. A board of directors was established to run the finances.

Saperstein had left the operation in fine shape to continue. Coach Inman Jackson had Meadowlark, Curley, Geese, Gipson, Hillard, Showboat Hall, Hallie Bryant (a former "Mr. Basketball" in the hoops-crazed state of Indiana), Jackie Jackson, and Bobby Joe Mason, among others.

Despite the glaring void Abe left behind, the tour and other activities played on in the two months following his passing. The annual sportswriters' banquet in Chicago still took place, where the outgoing president of the organization received a plaque for his service, renamed the "Abe Saperstein Memorial" award.

Red posed next to the plane with his team and the Trotters upon his arrival in San Juan Puerto Rico. This traditional photo op seemed forced this time without an appearance of the "Skipper." A huge cake marking the fortieth anniversary was presented in Honolulu, followed by the visit to Hinckley. Abe would have been proud as the PR team assembled a group of older residents who were said to have attended the first game, and the Globies made appearances around town. The wires dutifully picked it all up. Son Jerry was seated courtside in a spot not far from where his father would have been. Sylvia was on hand as well.

Red knew that Abe had built something bigger than himself. All the way back in 1926, Wallace Morgan of the Winona, Minnesota *News* seemed to know it too when he typed an article that today would be considered politically-incorrect. Nevertheless, it bears mention as one of the first documented references to Saperstein's new "brand."

"Colored Boys Defeat Arcadia Police," the headline announced, and the main article was worded similarly: "Four clean-limbed young colored men and a squat, bandy-legged chap of Jewish extraction furnished local basketball devotees some exceptional diversion Saturday night when these five, styled the Harlem Globe Trotters, beat the Arcadia Police quint, 29 to 18." After getting the racial and religious affiliations out of the way, the article got down to basketball: "the (Trotters) presented a mixture of tomfoolery and downright skill which kept the crowd alternately laughing and exclaiming in surprise at their tricks. It was soon evident that (the local team) was no match for them…"

Similar articles, many of which were set up by Abe's diligent advance work, would continue for the next four decades, much to the delight of the fans and keepers of the game. Basketball became an Olympic sport, and the next generation of players would include international players at the highest levels of play. "Abe planted those seeds," Red said. "He gave more to the game than he received from it."

Over the next few years, the Trotters would take their next evolutionary steps for the first time without their founder, leader, nurturer, and public face. Abe was gone. Red's rueful thought as he stared at the hardwood as he exited the court that sad night in Greensboro: The Harlem Globetrotters forever would be changed.

Abe Saperstein, truly the original Globetrotter, shown
in one of his favorite publicity shots.

Curly Neal launches a jumper as Red Klotz defends.

Chapter 22

Re-Evolution

By 1967, pro basketball had embarked on yet another stage of its development. The NBA finally was accepted by the mainstream as a major sports league, and it had a national TV contract showcasing the best players on earth. Following at the heels of the newfound success came another rival start-up league, the American Basketball Association. Although Abe Saperstein had passed from the scene, his legacy of a three-point field goal was incorporated by the ABA and eventually would be adopted internationally and in the NBA, college, and high schools.

"Abe would have loved it," said Red with a rueful smile. "The three-point field goal, really, changed everything about the way the game was played. Can you imagine what kind of scoring damage I could have done? I probably hit a couple thousand threes that only counted as two."

As Red continued playing major minutes and in most every game well into his forties, fifties, and sixties, he was relying more on his perimeter shooting, which hadn't suffered at all, and even may have gotten better with age. As of the 1979-80 season, those shots were worth three points in the NBA.

At age 59, Red Klotz could keep the Generals close in games with less effort. The "point" was not lost Eddie Gottlieb, who, from his new perch as NBA elder statesman and schedule-maker, praised the man whose services he had passed by for his Philadelphia Warriors at the league's inception.

"I know who I would sign if I were an owner: Red Klotz!" Gotty told a basketball magazine reporter just prior to the three-pointer's introduction in the NBA. Though his tongue firmly was planted in-cheek, Gotty wasn't kidding about the three-pointer as a weapon or about Red's deadeye sniping. This was an example to which basketball people and fans could relate. "If I had a shooter like him, I would be able to make up a large point differential in a very short amount of time."

Red's neighbor in Margate, fellow ex-Villanova player Chris Ford, would be the first to nail a three-pointer in NBA history. Ford would finish second in the league (behind Seattle's "Downtown" Freddie Brown) in three-point shooting percentage that year. Ford clearly understood what Gotty was saying. "Red was ahead of the times, as far as the three-point shot," Ford said. "I've seen Red get in a rhythm where a distance shot for him was almost like a free throw."

Indeed, the more Red shot, the more comfortable he would become. None of his teammates ever accused Red of being a "gunner," because he never got into a cold streak. He was always "Red hot." "They didn't keep track of his shooting percentage, which is a real shame, because it had to have been unbelievable," Sam Sawyer said. "All I know is we were shocked when he did miss, and we weren't shocked much."

The ABA's birth and nine-year lifespan put new pressure on the NBA. The new league's commissioner was none other than Red's old tour buddy and Globetrotter nemesis, George Mikan. Its owners created a bidding war for some of the top stars in the game, and they won a few of the major battles. Former NBA Rookie of the Year and scoring champ Rick Barry was the first big name to bolt, signing with the Oakland Oaks. Due to a contract dispute, Barry was forced to sit out that first year. However, his signing sent shockwaves throughout the basketball world. If Rick Barry could cast his lot with a new, unproven enterprise, pretty much any player could. The players who stayed in the NBA now had an extra bargaining chip come contract time.

The Oaks were coached by Alex Hannum, the only coach to interrupt the Celtics' string of championships in the 50s and 60s with two different teams (the St. Louis Hawks and the Philadelphia 76ers). Their roster included a young point guard, Larry Brown, who would go on to a Hall of Fame coaching career himself. The Philadelphia 76ers' star forward Billy Cunningham, and the St. Louis-Atlanta Hawks' center Zelmo Beaty were among the other marquee NBA players to switch leagues.

The ABA also would spawn a number of stars drafted out of college or signed early before their class graduated. The most prominent among them was one Julius Winfield Erving. Moses Malone, who later would team with "Dr. J" for an NBA championship in Philadelphia, longtime player and Coach Dan Issel, scoring machine George Gervin, and defensive stalwart Bobby Jones (another ex-ABAer on the Sixers' title team) were just a few of the new league's homegrown stars.

Connie Hawkins, still banned from the NBA, left the Trotters and joined the Pittsburgh Pipers. All he did was lead the league in scoring with a 26-points-per-game average, take the Pipers to Eastern Division and ABA championships, and win the league's first MVP award. "I was really happy for Connie Hawkins," Red said. "He had been banned from the NBA, even though he had done nothing wrong. He was 25 years old and had already lost a few years of income and his early prime. Anyone who saw him play with such intensity in the ABA and the ABL before that knew what a talent he was."

The ABA lacked a national TV contract and did not play in major markets. Nevertheless, the upstart league proved to be a constant thorn in the side of the NBA, either by raiding talent or grabbing headlines. It was also the first of the pro leagues to embrace a style of play much closer to what the Globetrotters had employed. Behind-the-back passes, blind passes, and between-the-legs dribbles rarely were seen in the established league, but were commonplace in the ABA. The league was "borrowing" much of what the Trotters had been doing for years.

"Before this time, fans weren't seeing that stuff," Red said. "The only place to see this type of play had been at a Trotters' game. Now, they were seeing it every night in 'straight' basketball."

The ABA didn't stop at raiding on-court innovations. Most of the teams had flashy uniforms, up-tempo offenses loose "d," and halftime entertainment. They played with a red, white, and blue basketball, termed the "beach ball" by players and purists. The league also provided jobs to dozens of the top African American players who previously had the NBA and the Trotters as their only higher-paying professional options.

The ABA also was the first basketball enterprise to mine the riches of lesser-known hotbeds of the game. Indiana, Houston, San Antonio, and Miami are all thriving NBA markets first exploited by the ABA and thought to be "minor" at the time by the established league.

The Trotters took a big hit when the ABA came along. Besides increased competition in player acquisition and development, the Trotters had to deal with the many aspects of transitioning into the post-Abe years. At first, Abe's family continued to own the team under the name Abe Saperstein Enterprises, and eventually sold it in 1967 to the three-man partnership of Potter Palmer, John O'Neil, and George Gillett, Jr.

While all this was going on in the pro basketball universe, the United States was entering one of its most turbulent periods. Discussions on race relations were more frequent and open than ever, and racial divides culminated in big city rioting. At the same time, a national debate was raging over the unpopular war in Vietnam.

The Trotters' and Generals' popularity continued on unabated, probably due to the strength of the brand Abe had built and the quality of the show. In 1970, Abe was inducted posthumously into the Basketball Hall of Fame. Meadowlark and Curly remained the stalwarts on the court, while Red and the Generals enhanced their image as lovable losers. Pop culture references became more frequent, and the name Red Klotz became synonymous with losing.

Red did better than take it in stride, he became philosophical about it. By the time the 1970s dawned, he was approaching the 5,000-loss plateau. "Most of us are losers," Red told reporter Jack Etkin. "There's only one champion team in a division. You're not really a loser if you're a great athlete and you love to play the game."

The message seemed to have a calming influence in a tumultuous time. There was no way an exhibition basketball tour would quiet the nation's collective restlessness, of course. However, it certainly provided a needed respite from more serious matters.

It also helped that the Trotters and Generals continued their longstanding support of the United States military and interests abroad. For their CBS Sports Spectacular appearance in 1967, they played on the flight deck of the aircraft carrier *U.S.S. Enterprise,* docked in Oakland, California. Red played a prominent role and was distinctive on TV, wearing dark sunglasses.

"The glare on that deck was unbelievable," he recalled. "Some of the guys made fun of me for wearing them. They sure changed their tune when they saw how bright it was and how I was seeing things better than everyone else. Believe me, that was a change," he said, making fun of his lifelong battle with nearsightedness.

Three years later, the Trotters celebrated the 10,000 game in their history, shading the Generals 83-74 in Miami Beach. "That was just one more piece of history," Red recalled. By now, the numbers were becoming staggering. In 1977, the Trotters celebrated a half-century as a team and continued to add to their roster of countries visited. An historic tour of Africa took place in 1978 and raised the number of total countries visited to 97.

With Red's children grown by now, Gloria became a more frequent traveling partner. She would sit behind the Generals' bench and keep score. "The most annoying thing was when the Trotters went on a scoring run and I would feel a tap on the shoulder," Red remembers. "It would be Gloria saying, 'Hey Coach, I think you could use a time-out.'"

He joked, yet in reality, Red was delighted to have Gloria at his side. "This was a great period in both of our lives," he said. "There had been so many years that I was away and she did everything else."

Gloria also cut a glamorous figure in the stands. She always was fashionably dressed, well-coiffed, and just looking fabulous overall. "My mother looks like that all the time," says Ronee. You could visit her at 8 a.m. on a Saturday and she would be done up to perfection." She would keep score until late in the game, and when the outcome was assured for the Trotters, the scorebook would give way to one of her passions: crossword puzzles and/or knitting.

Red loved having his wife on the road and even had an official Generals' warm-up jacket made up for her with "Gloria" stitched on the back. Why not? She was officially part of the team.

Red: "Her official title was 'Tour Secretary.' If a problem came up on the road, she was a go-to person. It was also nice to run things by her. We could have a very long day of trying to figure things out. Then, I would catch up with Gloria at the hotel or on the bus, and she would give me a really good common-sense suggestion. She was right, too, almost all of the time. It made me wonder how I survived all those years on the road without having her there as a resource. I guess I was lucky."

Together, Red and Gloria embarked on the world and U.S. tours that were part basketball, part-second honeymoon. When the games weren't going on, Gloria would shop for holiday gifts for family members and items for the house in Margate. They would visit tourist destinations together and share romantic dinners. The couple's home is decorated with dozens of mementos from their world travels.

"These are two special best friends who happen to be husband and wife," Ronee observed. "They always worked hard and worked as a team. And they have been doing it for so long that it became second nature. It is really quite remarkable to see how they are together and how they take what they have accomplished in stride. And they always look ahead, not back. This is what keeps them going. There is always another plan or a new project."

While the NBA and ABA were slugging it out, the Trotters were staying relevant in their fortieth anniversary season. The World Series of Basketball was a thing of the past. However, the Trotters played a memorable game against a college all-star team featuring Michigan All-American Cazzie Russell. More than 9,000 packed an arena in Kalamazoo to watch the Globetrotters humble the home state hero and his mates, 99-88. Cazzie then accepted the Abe Saperstein Memorial Award as the top player in college at the annual Chicago Sportswriters' Association dinner.

Wire photos of Meadowlark and his teammates surrounding a birthday cake made up to look like a basketball court went around the world when the Trotters and Generals made their stop in Honolulu. However, all that paled to the Trotters' and Generals' visit to Hinckley, Illinois, site of the Trotters' first game in 1926. Meadowlark and Geese Ausbie posed with C.L. Grimm, a longtime resident who attended that first game, and the hometown Hinckley *Review* made the Trotters' return appearance front-page news.

The world tour continued to generate publicity, interest, and huge crowds as well. Curly, Geese, and Meadow met with Philadelphia-born comedian Bill Cosby on a movie set in Rome. Cosby was the first African American to star in a hit television series, "I Spy," and would suit up with the Globetrotters on several occasions.

In Moscow, the Cold War showed no signs of thaw, according to the account of Stefano Susi an Italian sportswriter representing *Lo Speccro* of Rome. "The Muscovites' reaction was a strange one," Susi wrote. "At first they were indifferent, icy, and almost hostile to the theatrical buffoonery with which these basketball experts filled their exhibition. Then they broke into an unrestrainable enthusiasm…as the team abandoned their joking to give themselves over to an essentially perfect demonstration of real basketball, the best in the world."

President Lyndon Johnson praised the Trotters' milestone in a congratulatory telegram stating, "This team, unique in the world, has brought joy and amusement to millions of people in every corner of the world. I am certain that everywhere it exhibited, it has contributed to a better image of America."

Although Abe had passed, his presence was felt in these special moments brought about thanks to marketing and the special events techniques he perfected. "It just wasn't the same without Abe there to revel and be a part of such success," Red said. "There's no doubt he would have been proud of how his traditions endured and carried on."

In addition to the photo ops, media availabilities, and TV appearances, the team performed its signature charity work (a sold-out game in support of the Milk Fund in Michigan and basketball clinics abroad) and continued appearances in supporting U.S. troops overseas.

It continued that way throughout the remainder of the 60s and into the 1970s. Then, in 1971, the unthinkable happened.

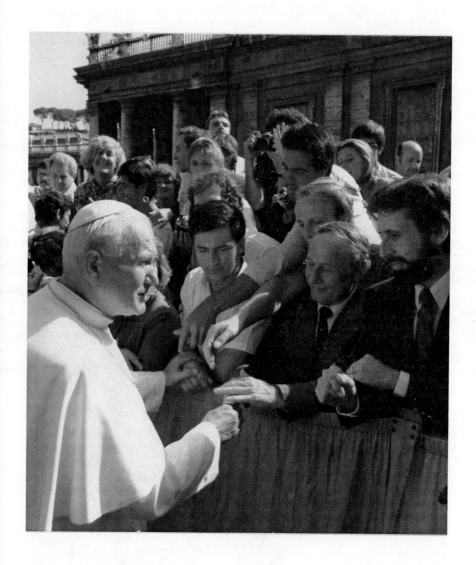

Red and son-in-law John Ferrari, the Generals' general manager during an audience at the Vatican with Pope John Paul II.

Red at Age 51, with the Jersey Reds

Chapter 23

Tennessee Lightning

Red called it "just another one-night stand." Chuck Klotz, then in his fifth year as the Globetrotters' public address announcer, and on this night also the clock operator, thought differently. "I don't know where (the Globies) were that night. They surely weren't out there on the court."

That's exactly where the Trotters were, of course. The same place they had been almost 300 times a year since Abe ramped up the schedule in the early 1950s: a 4,700-square-foot expanse of hardwood. This one happened to be in the relatively obscure location of Martin, Tennessee.

Neither Red, Chuck, nor any of the players interviewed said there was anything unusual leading up to that night's game. Red was too busy tending to the details of the tour. "You get all that small stuff taken care of, and the game should take care of itself. The Trotters know what they have to do and so do we."

However, something would be entirely different on this Tuesday night in January, 1971.

Martin was and still is largely a college town, home of the University of Tennessee at Martin. That night's show would take place in the then two-year-old basketball arena, which is still in use and currently named Skyhawk Field House. Most references to it back in the day were simply, "the gym." It seated approximately 3,000 for basketball, and the game was a sellout, as Chuck Klotz recalls.

"They were pretty much all packed houses around that time, and we were received quite warmly throughout Tennessee. I remember meeting a high-ranking state elected official. The guy shook my hand and said, 'I can't tell you a damn thing about East Tennessee or what is going on in West Tennessee, but ask me anything you want to about Middle Tennessee.' And he was proud of it."

The burg of Martin was tucked away in a mostly rural area in the northwest region, parts unknown to the public servant with whom Chuck spoke. The college enrollment of about 8,000 exceeded the number of residents by nearly 40 percent. The UT-Martin sports teams were then known as the Pacers, and it was not clear if a certain member of the varsity women's basketball team was on hand for the game, but it's a pretty good bet that Pat Head was there. After all, the future Pat Summit often said her life had revolved around basketball since she was a very young player. Unless the Lady Pacers were playing a road game that night, it is highly likely that the future winningest coach in the college game, male or female, would have been in the house to watch the world's losingest coach take on the world-famous Globetrotters.

On this night, the Generals were playing as the Jersey Reds, a team nickname beloved by their star player-coach-owner. "I liked the Boston Shamrocks more, because I always liked the Celtics. The uniforms were green and had shamrocks on them and reminded me of my time with Honey Russell, Chuck Connors, and that bunch. But I liked the Jersey Reds, too."

At that stage of their existence, The Generals' name rotated with that of the Shamrocks, Reds, Baltimore Rockets (a nod to Red's actual NBA team), and in a sentimental gesture to his adopted hometown that also boosted its visibility, the Atlantic City Seagulls. Red has a wonderful photo of himself from this era. He is pictured sporting the Seagulls' uniform with old friend Dave Zinkoff at the now-demolished Spectrum in South Philly. Both men are wearing the ear-to-ear grins one might expect at such a reunion. Zinkoff was a buddy who had been there from Red's days with the Sphas, and had written articles documenting the early European and South American tours. He since had achieved cult hero status as the Philadelphia 76ers' public address announcer and would have a street in the sports complex named in his honor after his death.

Klotz and his players would don the different uniforms and a new identity each night. The idea was to give the impression the Trotters were in a league and playing more than one squad. In reality, the opposition was the same old Washington Generals every night; they simply were rotating laundry. For this particular game, it was quite fitting that the team would don the threads honoring their namesake. The red jerseys and pants bearing the name "Jersey Reds" paid homage to the most famous "loser" in the game.

It didn't take long after tip-off for people to notice something was amiss. The Trotters were sluggish, which sometimes happened. And while Harlem seemed to be running in cement sneakers, the Jersey Reds were as fresh as the Rolling Stones' new hit single, "Brown Sugar."

"We were popping them in from everywhere. Inside and out," Red says with pride, "and I was probably hotter than anybody that night. (The Trotters) knew if they gave me an opening, I was gonna take it. They knew if they got careless with the ball, we were going to steal it. And they knew that if we got open, we were going to shoot the hell out of it."

Gerry Carpenter, the current UT-Martin golf coach, was in attendance and confirms Red's recollection. "I came to see the Globetrotters. I watched them on TV as a kid and I loved Meadowlark Lemon. He was my favorite," Carpenter said. "But Red Klotz was the best player on the court that night."

The Globetrotters couldn't seem to do anything right. "They were missing everything," Chuck Klotz remembers. "Inside and out. They were turning the ball over. Meadowlark's famous hook shot had deserted him."

Red, who is in possession of hundreds of box scores, score-books, and newspaper articles, has no record of the game. He can't recall who was out on the court with him that night, other than Atlantic City homeboy Sam Sawyer. There was no game coverage by the lone newspaper covering Martin, the *Weakley County Press.* Although legend of the game is known generally by basketball insiders, most fans are not aware of it. When contacted, an assistant sports information director didn't know that one of the biggest upsets in sports history had happened on the UT-Martin campus.

Articles written about the game years later vary in their accounts. Some claim the game went into overtime, although that is unlikely. "It came down to the end of regulation," is the way Red remembers it.

Sawyer, who would go on to play 14 years for Red, the longest tenure of any Washington Generals' player ever, concurred. "I remember a lot from that game, but I don't remember an extra period."

Sam, who had his work cut out for him that night, was doing what he always did best: "guard" Meadowlark Lemon in a way that facilitated the show. It was particularly difficult if Meadow was having a bad game.

"Meadow would hold out the ball, and I would swipe at it. He'd put the ball on the floor, and I'd reach for it. I made his reams look better, and he appreciated me for that. I enjoyed it too. When you are doing your part to make the show better, it makes you feel good, because you're putting smiles on people's faces. On this night, there was no saving the show. (The Trotters) were performing terribly."

It wasn't the first time the Jersey Reds had given the Trotters a run for their money during the 1970-71 season. That year, the owner-coach-51-year-old star player especially was pleased with the on-court product. "Once again, the Trotters' roster was loaded...*loaded*...," Red would say with reverence of the unit of Lemon, Neal, Ausbie, Hillard, Hall, Bobby Hunter, and Bobby Joe Mason, among others. "But we were a pretty damn good team, too." In addition to Sawyer, who was in his seventh season on the tour, Red's squad included crafty guard Chet Hildebrandt, six-foot-ten center Chuck Lightcap, and forward Paul Favorite. It subsequently has been reported that Roy Kieval was there, and it has been confirmed that Paul Favorite was at Martin that night.

This was still an era in which, despite an impressive array of well-practiced reams, the Trotters' show still largely was improvised and included lots of real basketball. Both squads had plenty of real basketball players.

"During the basketball part of it, things got pretty heated sometimes," Favorite recalled. "Red Klotz is a proud man when it comes to the game. If you weren't a fundamentally sound player and a smart player, you weren't going to last very long with Red. The Trotters sometimes relied on the tricks and the fact that they had superior talent. But that didn't mean we couldn't play them and play them hard."

Red took it a step further: "I always took it personal," he said. "I always told my guys, 'You are good players. Make them respect you.' If a guy was intimidated, if he couldn't keep his head in the game and help us play as a team, there was no option but to send him home. We never got in the way of what they were doing with the show. But we never stopped playing hard or playing smart."

That year's edition of the Generals/Reds certainly heard their coach. A Cleveland newspaper account from earlier in the season details a contest in which the Reds took the Globies into overtime. Playing before 10,526 fans at the Cleveland Arena, Harlem rolled up a 51-32 halftime lead. In the second half, they put on the show to, "the delight of the spectators." The Reds then mounted a furious comeback, resulting in an 82-all deadlock at the end of regulation.

Late in the three-minute extra period, "The Reds had the Trotters on the brink of a rare defeat when player-coach Louis (Red) Klotz sank a 40-footer to give the New Jersey foes a 96-95 margin with seven seconds to go," sportswriter Rich Passon chronicled. The Trotters prevailed on the last shot of the game by Curly Neal.

Another time that season in White Plains, New York, the Trotters won 120-119 in regulation. Again on the final shot.

But something was different that night in Tennessee. More than four decades later, actual details of the game are very hard to come by, even by the memory of those who were there. Confirmed facts are almost nonexistent. Certain recollections stand the test of time however, and when pieced together, a fuzzy picture becomes a little more focused.

"It was almost magical," Chuck Klotz said. "(The Reds) couldn't miss. It was a beautiful thing to behold. I knew all those guys (on the Trotters), and it was funny to see them frustrated for a change."

"It seemed," Red Klotz recalled, "like the rim was the size of a trash can lid for us and a thimble for them. Everything we were throwing into the general area of the basket was going in. We were getting every rebound, and we were stopping them defensively."

Sawyer was having a different result with his "matador" defense. On this night, it actually was working. Lemon had improved tremendously as a player during his Globetrotters' career. He could drain his signature hook shot from half-court with amazing regularity. On this night in Martin, Meadow "couldn't make a hook, a dunk or a layup," is the way Sam put it.

The fans "were getting restless at times," according to Chuck Klotz. "Not because they weren't seeing the Globetrotters' show... because they weren't seeing the Globetrotters the superstar basketballers. Remember, these were serious basketball fans."

A rumor circulated years later that there may have been an off-court dispute of some kind that triggered the Trotters' off-night, or may have fired up the Reds. Red Klotz strongly disputed that notion. "It was just one of those things. When you play so many games a season, you aren't going to be on your game each and every time. It just so happened they picked the wrong night to be off their game."

Part of Red's formula for success was to tell his guys to go all-out all the time. He knew that if things got too close on the scoreboard, the Trotters always could revert back to a ream that would guarantee them points. By playing hard and smart, the Generals added to the show. Their professionalism in the face of constant losing added more credibility to the Trotters' talent. It also sold the "games" as looking more real, even to a serious hoops fan.

"That is the thing about watching a Trotters' game, I always gravitated toward watching the Generals more closely," said longtime fan Chris Unger. A former high school star in New Jersey and former college player, Unger knows the game. He also knows the Trotters' reams from his childhood and finds different things to look for in the Generals-Trotters matchup. "As good as the Trotters are, you expect it. The Generals stand around and get 'victimized' by the tricks, and then run down the court on offense and execute a pick and roll as well as you'll ever see it run. The Trotters are trying to stop them, but you can see how well coached and disciplined the Generals are. To me, that is a big part of the entertainment."

On that night in Martin, there was a disproportionate share of what Unger was describing. The Jersey Reds were doing something Red Klotz built a career around *not* doing: upstaging the Globetrotters. In the absence of a scorebook, box score, or official account of the game, it is impossible to know which Trotters besides Lemon were part of that infamous night. Lemon confirmed it in his own book. It is known that Curley Neal was *not* there. His absence may have made a difference in the final outcome, as there would have been specific reams built around Curley's dribbling talents, most of which ended with a dunk or uncontested layup. However, Neal was not so sure about that.

"Sometimes (a win) just isn't in the cards," he said. "Who knows what might have happened had I been there? If you start with the 'what-ifs,' you could go on forever."

What if Red and the Generals hadn't been so hot offensively? What if the Trotters hadn't been so sluggish? What if the Trotters had snapped out of their funk?

The latter scenario actually is what happened, albeit too late to make a difference. Down 12 points with two minutes left, according to one account, Harlem finally mounted a comeback. The Reds unfurled their loose show "defense," and Chuck Klotz cooperated with his finger off the clock switch to give Harlem extra time to catch up.

"If you think the last two minutes of an NBA game is an eternity, you weren't watching this game," Red's son said, laughing. "(The Reds) were doing everything they could to get the outcome where it was supposed to be. I was doing everything I could do. And it looked like - just like most nights when the score was close - that it was going to work out."

Having finally responded to their wakeup call, the Trotters went into fast motion and closed the gap. They came all the way back to take a 99-98 lead on a basket by Lemon, as Red remembers it. Klotz then called a time-out with seven ticks showing on the clock.

What happened next stunned everyone in attendance.

"During the time-out, I told my guys to get me the ball."

There has been speculation that Klotz did not want any of his players to be in a position to miss on purpose, a violation of Red's longstanding "try to win" edict. It also has been said that Red did not want one of his guys to be the one to hit the shot to beat the Trotters. Klotz disputes the notion. "It was just a basketball thing," he said.

Red: "This was no different than a pickup game in the school-yard. I want the ball in my hands at the end. If my team has a chance to win, I want to take it. Some guys shy away from the ball in that situation. I am always going to want the ball. If they can't beat us with all that talent, with all those show plays, with the referees calling it their way, with the support of the fans, well, then it's not our fault if they lose, is it?"

Red thinks he took the inbound pass directly. None of those interviewed remember exactly where on the perimeter he was positioned, but all agreed the shot he would take was a long one. "It was at least a step outside the NBA three-point arc," Sam Sawyer said.

Red shrugged. "I was out there pretty far, but that never bothered me. I got a nice clean look at the basket."

Klotz squared up his body and immediately let fly. Just like his final shot at Villanova, and like hundreds of times at dozens of gyms and playgrounds, he knew the shot was going in.

SWISH!

With that, Chuck Klotz hit the clock's toggle switch one last time. Three seconds remained with the Reds up 100-99. The fans were going nuts. "It was set up perfectly for a great ending, and the fans were roaring. There was not going to be defensive resistance. All they had to do was dunk the ball."

Instead, the ball was inbounded to Lemon, who launched a hook. It bounced off the rim with a clang. Chuck reached for the clock controls instinctively as the buzzer sounded. The game was over. The Reds had won. The immediate reaction was silence.

"It was as if the collective air had been taken out of the entire building," Chuck Klotz said.

"Nobody knew what to do. Everybody was stunned," Sam Sawyer said.

Red repeated his oft-quoted reaction: "It was like we had just killed Santa Claus."

The confused quiet soon turned to boos and jeers. Red totally understood. "These people paid good money to see the Globetrotters' show, and that is supposed to mean a Globetrotter victory. They didn't get what they had come to see. What they paid to see. I couldn't blame them."

Spectator Gerry Carpenter, then in the third year of his 45-year employment tenure at UT-Martin, sensed he had witnessed something special. "I remember thinking, 'This is kinda neat, I saw one of their rare losses.' But I had no idea at the time just how rare it was."

The Reds certainly were happy. "We looked up at the stands, and people were cursing and booing, and some were even throwing things," Sam Sawyer remembered. "Boos never felt so sweet."

Red's team retreated to their locker room. If ever there was an occasion to spray champagne around, this was it. Understandably, the Washington Generals do not travel with the bubbly. "We settled for what was on hand: orange soda," said Paul Favorite.

The available beverage could not have been more appropriate, as its artificial color nearly matched the color of Red's hair, now flecked with gray. The Reds dumped the contents all over the head of their owner-coach-teammate. A stunned Lemon visited his longtime opponents' locker room to offer his congratulations. It was a very classy gesture, all agreed.

Red then addressed his team. They had been part of history, he said, and he was proud of them and they deserved to win. He told them to enjoy the victory and go out there the next time and try to start a winning streak. He also had praise for Meadowlark Lemon: "Wasn't that nice of him to come in here and wish us well?" Red told his guys. "It was nice, but he really didn't mean it!"

NEW JERSEY REDS - 1970-1971

Back Row (L to R): Ed Maher, Louis "Red" Klotz, Sam Sawyer, John Healey, John McAndrew.
Front Tow (L to R): Dennis Witkowski, Paul Favorite, Matt Spinella, Charles Melvin.

The Jersey Reds in 1971.

Red Klotz, shown here in his 60s, guards Meadowlark Lemon. Although Red is quoted as saying he retired from playing at 62, published accounts have him appearing as a player up to the age of 68.

Chapter 24

Elder Statesman

In the eyes of some, it took a victory for the "lovable loser" to be legit. For years, reporters and fans scoffed when Red Klotz insisted he was playing to win against the Trotters. When he finally did it, the same words seemed to take on new meaning. To those who continued to doubt, Red could always point to that magical night in Martin, Tennessee.

And he has done just that for more than 40 years now. "It's basketball," he said. My teams are going to come to play and play hard. If (the Globetrotters) aren't ready to play their best, things might not work out so well for them. Nobody ever asked me to take a dive and I never would do that anyway." The words rang not so hollow now that Red's team had finally put a game in the "W" column.

The Generals' triumph was a giant embarrassment to the Trotters. Soon after Meadowlark congratulated his longtime rivals, the blame game began. Reportedly, Lemon was furious and wanted some members of Red's team and the sideline crew fired. Klotz would have none of it.

"They had every opportunity to win," he said. "It just shows you that nobody is infallible. The next night they came out and played the way the Harlem Globetrotters are supposed to play: they beat the living daylights out of us."

Initially, the Trotters organization and then-president George Gillett would not acknowledge the defeat. Gillett was said to have met his team at the next game and read them the riot act for messing up. But soon, Trotters management realized the value in admitting what had happened. Both the Trotters and Generals basketball credibility had been enhanced. The show aspects had eclipsed those of the competition and the fans were expecting reams. Instead they got mostly basketball and a nearly unheard of Trotter loss.

In a Syracuse *Post-Standard* interview in 1978, Klotz said "(Trotters management) was upset with me for weeks. But then they decided it was the best thing that could have happened. After all, anyone can get beat."

The earliest media reference to Red's win may have been from an interview Klotz gave Oakland Tribune sports columnist Ed Levitt in January, 1972. The Trotters' loss was still such a secret that Levitt could not or would not confirm it. He simply attributed the claim to Red. "Last season, (Klotz) says, he ended his club's losing streak at 10. That is, 10 years."

Soon after the historic victory, Red decided to retire the Jersey Reds' uniforms and their name. "I was so touched by (the victory) I decided to hang all the uniforms in the Red Klotz Hall of Fame."

As much as Red enjoys talking about that game, he tends to focus more on the immediate aftermath the following night, when things returned to normal.

"We had won a game against them…finally…and that felt good. But our job wasn't to beat the Trotters. Our job was to push them. The next night we're getting clobbered and I remember looking around the gym and all the happy faces and smiles in the crowd. That's when I realized it… we had won again."

At this point in his career, Red was being noticed more and more for his age. That an undersized, middle-aged man wielding a two-hand set shot was performing at a higher level than superbly conditioned athletes half his age was beginning to capture the imagination of the public. A post-Martin newspaper article describes Klotz as "a peppery guy of 51 whose hair is thinning but still as orange as the flame from a wood fire."

Never a shrinking violet with sportswriters, Red embraced the image. "I'm still playing half or three quarters of every game," he said in the Levitt article. "And I'm having one of my best seasons. If I play a half I'll usually get between 10 and 17 points. What other 50-year-old could do it?"

The writers were starting to ask why Red continued to suit up and play night after night, and the answer basically was "because I can." Red didn't have to worry about getting fired because he was the owner of his team. And as coach, he would be sure to receive all the minutes he wanted. There was not and never would be another owner-coach-player.

"I know my basketball. I could have (had other coaching jobs)," he said in the interview. "I enjoy playing basketball. I'd rather play than just sit and coach."

With Gloria still touring with him at times, Red continued to do just that. Who would have known how much more he would still have left in the tank? He simply kept rolling through the 70s and emerged intact, which you couldn't say for disco music, platform shoes or Richard M. Nixon.

"Red was amazing," Sam Sawyer said of his play during this period. "He was such a smart player, he knew how to conserve energy. He didn't waste motion. Red knew where the ball was going and where the players were going. To see him get up and down the court, if you didn't know what you were watching you might think he was taking it easy. That would be a mistake because the next thing you knew, the ball was in his hands and he was whipping off a perfect pass or getting off his shot. It was like he measured the shot before he got to where he caught the ball. Lots of times we'd just start back the other way when he shot it. We all knew it was going in."

When Klotz shelved the Jersey Reds, the Boston Shamrocks were soon born. Ever since Red was a kid, people who didn't know his name would look at his freckles and flaming locks and assume he was Irish. His daughter Ronee said "if he's not part Irish, he is at least part leprechaun." The Shamrocks reflected his love of all things green and Irish. For the duration of this project, Red called the writer every March 17th to wish a "happy St. Patty's Day." Red even named one of his dogs Shamrock.

Although he was the last man cut in 1947, Red always held a certain fondness for the Boston Celtics franchise, especially after its unparalleled run of success under another coach named Red, one Arnold "Red" Auerbach.

"How could you not admire what he did?" Klotz inquired of the late Hall of Fame coach. Sure he had some great players. But this was a guy who knew how to put all the pieces together and win year after year."

Klotz put "Boston" on the front of the jerseys and a prominent shamrock on the shorts. Naturally, the uniforms were Kelly green. Clearly, the Shamrocks were a tribute to the mighty Celts. Red liked to run his teams the same way the Celtics did, at least on the offensive end: clever passing, fast break when the opportunity to push the ball was there, and work the ball around for a high percentage shot in the half court game. It all made it that much funnier that Red's team played it so deadpan and looked so efficient.

"These are guys who know how to play," Curly Neal said. "It wouldn't be the least bit entertaining if we had an easy time with them"

Not only was the on-court product still strong, the Trotters continued doing well at the box office with sellouts most nights on the US tour, including the newer and larger NBA arenas. Outside the states, huge crowds and rave reviews were the norm. by 1975, the Trotters were celebrating their 25th anniversary of international tours and had expanded the number of nations visited to 94.

The presence of the Globetrotters on television was expanding as well. They switched networks from the previous CBS sports specials to appearances on ABC's highly rated "Wide World of Sports." The play-by-play and commentary was provided by Howard Cosell and Don Meredith, who were at the height of their popularity with Monday Night Football. Celebrities such as talk show host Dick Cavett and songwriter Burt Bacharach made guest appearances as players with the Generals. The CBS network rolled out an animated Globetrotters cartoon show which became the highest rated Saturday morning show, according to Globetrotters publicity materials. The show would run for several years and become syndicated worldwide.

The team appeared on public TV's award-winning children's show "Sesame Street." They also had their own comedy-variety show called "The Harlem Globetrotters' Popcorn Machine." The show featured team members in zany skits and song-and-dance routines. On Saturday mornings, the animated Trotters even showed up to help solve mysteries in the hugely popular "Scooby Doo" cartoon series.

Red and the Generals were not officially part of these Trotters' side projects. Nevertheless, the organization benefited from their association with such a hot commodity. For instance, Cosell seemed to delight in Red's abilities on the court and he sang his praises constantly during the "Wide World of Sports" appearances. The good words from "Humble Howard," the top sports broadcaster of that period, boosted Red's name recognition even more, and drew attention to the Trotters' skills. Harlem still had bankable attractions in Meadow, Geese, Curly, Jackie Jackson and Bobby Joe Mason. Marques Haynes was also back with the team for a second stint after touring for a number of years with his own squad.

The Generals were still attracting top players in their own right. Bill Campion, a 6-9 center out of Manhattan College was drafted by the Milwaukee Bucks of the NBA and the Virginia

Squires of the ABA. He still holds the Jaspers' single game rebounding record with 30. Campion opted to play a year in Italy and eventually joined the Generals in 1978. He played for Red's team for eight seasons and was a favorite foil of Meadowlark. Bill was a pro at going along with the gags and also knew the style of play Klotz was looking for during the basketball portion of the show.

"Bill played some great ball for me for a lot of years," Red said. "He was the type of guy I was always looking for. He was somebody who enjoyed playing and playing at a high level. He was also the kind of guy who didn't get in the way of the show and enhanced it.

"Red Klotz said that he would never tolerate anybody purposely trying to lose a game," Campion said in a newspaper interview. "I always felt the harder the Washington Generals played, you could see the best come out of the Globetrotters as well."

Charlie Criss came to the Generals from the Continental League, a minor pro loop of the era that attracted NBA prospects. Criss, a 5-8 guard, played the 1978 season with the Generals and finally caught on with the Atlanta Hawks. Criss would play for eight years in the NBA. "Charlie was a solid player and I don't think it is a coincidence he became noticed by the NBA after he began playing with us," Red said.

Greg "Kid" Kohls was another marquee name for the Generals, who signed with Red after his 1972 graduation from Syracuse. At that time Kohls was the fifth all-time leading scorer for the Orangemen. His 748 points as a senior was second only to Dave Bing for a single season at that time. He would put up big scoring numbers for the Generals in his four years touring with Red and company.

As for Klotz, it was business as usual, albeit a tad slower. He was still keeping himself busy managing the tour and conservatively, still playing in at least 100 games a year. There was foreshadowing of the Generals' future when Red's youngest daughter Jody joined the then 58-year-old on the 1978 European tour.

A former stellar athlete herself, Jody made history as the first female member of the cross country and track and field teams at Atlantic County (NJ) Community College. On tour, she began taking some of the road duties off her dad's plate, which allowed Red to concentrate more on playing the games.

Having Jody on tour was a luxury for Red. She was so well organized and efficient that Red was finding life on the road much more enjoyable. "The basketball part was always the icing on the cake," he said, and suddenly there was much more icing. In a 1978 post card from Barcelona, Spain, sent to Ronee and her husband Ron, Red wrote: "Jody is a great help on the tour. She keeps an honest score and helped with schedules, passports, etc. Could be a good manager. Acts (tour entertainment), players, manager and Meadow have all accepted her."

One of the Globetrotters road managers, John Ferrari, more than accepted her. He began seeing Jody, the couple fell in love and would marry. A detail-oriented, Ivy League (Cornell) educated and refined gentleman, Ferrari would later leave the Trotters and become fulltime manager of the Generals.

"Jody was all business on the road," Red remembered. "She was a tough manager. John is a brilliant guy and very sophisticated. They hit it off immediately and made a great team."

Sam Sawyer soldiered on as a Generals' mainstay during this era. Red's Atlantic City neighbor not only proved to be a favorite foil of Meadow and Curly, he was one of the Generals main offensive forces underneath the basket.

"Sam was dependable and a very hard worker," Red said of his old friend. "You could always count on Sam to play well and to do the right things off the court." In the off-season, Sam worked at Red's liquor store and bar and even appeared in print ads for the business in the *The Press of Atlantic City*.

As hard as Sam worked on the court and at Red's bar, he still managed to find time to have fun on the road. In 1981, the Generals and Trotters were in Italy when Generals teammate Tim Hirten invited him to go along on a tour of the Vatican. Hirten would go on to the Catholic priesthood and a high ranking Chaplain Major in the U.S. Air Force following his days with the team.

"Tim was the most religious guy I ever met," said Sam. "I wasn't one for doing much of the tourist stuff on the road, but when Tim Hirten invites you to go to the Vatican with him, you go. He had been there so many times before. He is going to know about things and places the tour guides don't even know about."

Once inside the Vatican, it wasn't long before Hirten took Sam off to the side and they had separated from the regular tour group. "Tim knew where he was going. He seemed to know everybody and even the guards were warm to us. Nobody told us to leave or to return to the group."

At one point, Sam came upon a man dressed in clerical robes who seemed to be different. "His robes were trimmed in velvet and his shoes were shined to the point you could almost see your reflection. This was the cleanest priest I ever saw in my life," Sam recalled.

The two struck up a conversation and Sam realized who he was talking to: "It was Father Guido Sarducci!" A fictional character made famous by Ohio-born television writer and comedian Don Novello, "Sarducci" was a recurring character on NBC's hugely popular "Saturday Night Live" program. Sawyer and Hirten chatted with him for a while and finally introduced themselves as Washington Generals. Novello indicated he would love to go to the game that night and Sawyer said he would leave tickets.

"We got back to the hotel and told the story and none of the guys would believe that we had met Father Guido Sarducci at the Vatican," said Sam. "It did seem (preposterous) and I just kept saying 'wait and see, he is coming to the game.' Then he didn't show up and everyone said I was full of crap. There was nothing I could do to convince them what had happened at the Vatican was true. It kind of bothered me because (Novello) didn't strike me as the kind of guy who would blow us off like that."

The next morning, Sam picked up a newspaper and there was Novello's picture splashed across the front page. "He didn't show for the game because he was in jail. Guido Sarducci was arrested at the Vatican for impersonating a priest."

Red "agonizes" after yet another loss to the Globetrotters.

Gloria, Red, and Shane in their Margate, NJ home, 2006.

Chapter 25

Overtime

The Trotters were always looking for new innovations. As the 1980s progressed, that meant experimenting with female players.

The women's game had made huge strides in the United States and internationally, and signing Lynette Woodard as the first woman to wear the red white and blue worked from both the business and entertainment standpoints. Woodard, who happened to be a cousin of Geese Ausbie, certainly knew what the Trotters were all about. She had the credibility of a four-year, All-American career at the University of Kansas and the stature of being a key member on the United States' gold medal winning team in the 1984 Los Angeles Olympic games. Sports fans of either gender knew the name Lynette Woodard.

In 1985, Geese retired following a 21-year career and the Trotters, at this time owned by the corporate conglomerate Metromedia, signed Woodard as the first female member of the squad. Woodard's skills were strong (she is still the alltime women's college scoring champion despite playing before the three-point era) and her new team enjoyed a new wave of international publicity.

The Trotters' roster was in transition and they surely appreciated the popularity bump. In addition to the departure of Geese, Meadowlark had left the team and Curly Neal retired. "Sweet Lou"

Dunbar was the new top showman and the mainstays were "Twiggy" Sanders and Billy Ray Hobley. Very good players, but not the household names their predecessors had been. Red, playing for the opposition, was one of the lone remaining ties to the original glory days and without question the best-known player on the floor.

In a 1986 Philadelphia Inquirer profile, Red said he was still playing in about 50 of the Generals 230 games, and was quick to add "not bad for someone 61 years old." At the slowed-down pace, Red was still playing 20 more games than college players. In the article he confessed to writer Pat Pfeiffer, "I used to roll into the stands and come rolling out again. I don't roll so good anymore."

But what he could still do better than anyone, was shoot. The three-point shot had been adopted by colleges and high schools by 1987, and the Trotters and Generals had already been employing it for a few years. "I can shoot that shot better than anybody, any-where," he said. I can go around (the perimeter of the court) and shoot it. In fact, I can shoot from 35 feet, so 23 is nothing for me."

The Trotters, buoyed by Woodard's popularity, added several other women into the mix in the next two years, including one Nancy Lieberman, generally regarded as the best woman player of the era. Lieberman had gained fame as the youngest-ever member of the U.S. national team and was a member of the silver medal winning 1976 Olympic team. The Brooklyn-born guard's flashy style would earn her the nickname "Lady Magic." In college, Lieberman broke numerous women's scoring records and won two national championships at Old Dominion. Following brief stints in a womens' professional league and in the mens' Continental League, she signed with the Trotters. According to one news arti-cle, she "did not catch on" with the team and instead joined the Washington Generals as their first female player. According to a Trotters media guide, Red signed her to a contract in 1987.

Ever the liberal when it came to women's rights and always a promoter, Red was open to having Nancy on the squad. But when it came to dealing out minutes, he was as old-school as they come. "If she wants to play with the men, she has to play by the same rules," he said. "If you want to be out there, you have to earn your playing time." He said that Nancy felt she should be playing more. The playing time disputes sometimes led to friction between the two, but there was mutual respect and mutual love of the game.

Lieberman played the entire 1987-88 season for the Washington Generals and wound up marrying her teammate, center Tim Cline, with whom she had a child and later divorced. Red remembers that season as somewhat bumpy, but one that resulted in much publicity and on-court success. Both Woodard and Lieberman would eventually be named for enshrinement in the Naismith Basketball Hall of Fame.

Red's playing days and time continued to dwindle. Eventually he stopped playing altogether but continued to tour and coach. There was no "last game" or farewell tour that he or anyone else could remember. The last article found documenting his playing career is from 1988, when Red was 68 years old. Marques Haynes claims to have played professionally into his 70s and Red's not so sure he didn't see some brief action in his 70s as well.

"I can't be sure, but what I do know is I always packed a uniform."

In a 1987 article, Ron Cook of the Pittsburgh Press said the best part of the Globetrotters game was a few hours before it started when Red warmed up, popping in about a dozen long two-handers. Around this time he challenged the Boston Celtics' Larry Bird, who had just won the NBA's first three-point shootout at the All Star game, to a contest. The challenge went unanswered.

"He won 10 grand in that contest," he told Cook, "I made 14 shots in a row, he must have made eight. He got the check and I got nothing. When you get as old as I am, all you have left is your ego."

Generals forward Gerald Hooks backed up his owner-coach-teammate. "Red has challenged lots of people, but everyone turns him down. They save themselves a lot of embarrassment. I'll bet he makes 19 out of 20 shots." Clyde "The Glide" Austin of the Trotters piped up, "Not too bad for a guy who's older than Noah, huh?"

In a Knoxville, Tennessee, *News-Sentinel* interview around the same time, Klotz talked about going into an arena before the doors opened to the public. "I took my shoes off and shot three-point goals in my socks. I made 11 in a row from one corner and six in a row from the other. I made 17 of 17. Larry Bird can't do that."

Bird, now president of the Indiana Pacers, declined comment through a Pacers spokesman.

In 1982, Red hit a personal milestone—one that Abe Saperstein hadn't lived long enough to achieve—when Red suited up and played in Reykjavik, Iceland. Red Klotz had now played basketball in exactly 100 countries!

At home around this time, Red purchased a bar and lounge in Margate and eventually sold his Atlantic City operation. Son Glenn became the manager of "Red's" a new wave/80s music club and bar that featured Trotter memorabilia on the walls. There was even an action shot of George Sutor playing for the Generals, despite the fact Sutor was tending bar at a rival establishment, Maloney's, just down the street.

"Red's was like home to the local kids, especially in the off-season when the summer tourists weren't around," said Ann Edmonds, a regular there. "I owe my college degree to that place. I used to go in there and do my homework while the music was blaring. Glenn was like our cool cousin or uncle. You knew you could go in there and be safe."

An entire generation of locals felt the same way. After the place closed in the early 90s, the regulars stayed in touch. There is a "Friends of Red's" Facebook page and regular reunions take place in Atlantic City.

While Red's nightclub was perking along, his basketball playing career was reaching the finish line. Although it can't be pinned down precisely when Red stopped playing, there was no secret as to why he stopped. A proud and accomplished athlete, it became evident he couldn't get up and down the court the way he used to, except for very short stretches.

The time had come. The pregame warm-ups he'd still take with the team occasionally, and the half court pickup games at Jerome Avenue in Margate now would be the only places left to see Red Klotz play the game he loved so much. The uniform was still being packed just in case, but the green and gold silks had finally given way to the standard coaching uniform of a suit and tie. Lest anyone feel sorry for him, Klotz would have none of it.

"I was probably the oldest active professional athlete in the world," he said. "Basketball gave me more adventures and good times than most people would ever have in their lifetime. That is something I'm very fortunate to have taken part in. And its something I'm proud of."

Around this time, Red's grandson, Morgan (Mo) Klotz, Chuck's son, joined the Generals and became an expert at Red's old role of chasing the Trotters' dribbling specialist.

A former star high school and college athlete, Mo treasures his years playing for and traveling with the team.

"How many guys in their 20s get to play basketball and fill up three passports while they are doing it?"

Following his retirement, Red didn't have much time to reflect because the touring rolled on. Klotz was still one of the best ambassadors for the Globetrotters and had become the team's institutional memory. When a sportswriter or electronic journalist wanted to ask questions about the team history, they went to Red Klotz. Whenever a pro team in any sport was on a losing streak, sportswriters would call. Red would always have encouragement for the unfortunate team or coach. "Its not about the losing, its about getting up and trying again," he said. "As long as you pick yourself up, you haven't lost."

Red was also a go-to media source for questions on Globetrotter or basketball history. "I am the last of the Mohicans," Red said, proudly. "People would call the Trotters office and ask questions and nobody ahd been around long enough to know the answers. The staff members would send them to me."

In 1992, *Sports Illustrated's* Tim Crothers followed Red and the Generals around on the road and wrote a cover story on Klotz, then 72. The cover itself was bumped when the article was scheduled to run in the famous swimsuit edition. But the story, "The General Whose Army Never Wins" gave new life to the Trotters and Generals. Many of Red's road experiences were related in the piece, but what Crothers captured the most was Red's love of Gloria and his family, the game of basketball, his devotion to making the Trotters show better and his understanding of his role in the operation.

The article also raised the question nationally as to why Red Klotz had not yet been inducted into the Naismith Basketball Hall of Fame. The Hall, which tabbed Abe, Meadowlark, and Marques Haynes among its inductees, never saw fit to name him among the finalists. This, despite a thick nomination file.

The year after Crothers' story ran in *Sports Illustrated*, former Trotter Mannie Jackson, who played for them in the early 60s, purchased the team from Nat West Bank. Jackson was a successful businessman for 25 years at Honeywell Corporation, where he rose to a senior-level vice president's position, handling a $2.3 billion business unit, according to author Ben Green's *Spinning the Globe.*

Jackson overhauled much of the Trotter organization with an eye toward promotion and ticket sales. The Generals, as with all the previous owners dating back to Abe, remained independent and renewed their ties as the main opposition. There was one big change, however. Jackson asked Red to "retire" the Generals name in favor of first, the International All-Stars, and then the New York Nationals. Red was not happy to see the Generals go out to pasture at this stage of his career, but it was hardly the end of the world.

"We're still here and we're still pressing them to play their best," Red would say at the time. The blow may have been softened due to the fact that the New York Nationals name had been used by Red's organization before. In one of the most famous picture of Red Klotz in action, he is seen wearing sunglasses and a New York Nationals jersey in the historic game played on the flight deck of the USS Enterprise aircraft carrier, a contest televised during the Trotters' run on the CBS Sports Spectacular.

There were whispers among some in the Trotters' camp that Jackson had called for the name change because he was upset at all the publicity focused on Red and his team in the *Sports Illustrated* article. The premise went that Jackson wanted Harlem to go back to its competitive roots and that attention drawn to the touring foils took away from promoting the main attraction.

The public was slow on the uptake with the switch to the Nationals. It was routine for Red's team to appear in a town and see "Globetrotters vs. Generals" on the building marquee. Pop culture references to Red's team still called them the Generals, and the Trotters themselves sold commemorative Generals T-shirts during games, long after the name had been shelved.

Red's role during this period was to be the face of the Generals and the memory of the Trotters' history. He continued to grant every interview request, and these were showing no signs of slowing down. He also continued to receive fan mail and autograph requests. He answered every letter and signed every piece of paper presented.

Although Red cut back on his travel schedule and appearances, he always hit places he felt were important for him to be there: New York, Philly, Chicago and L.A. the most prominent among them.

John Ferrari was doing a great job of running the organization and tending to the tour details, as he had on an increasing basis, since the 1980s.

"I had the luxury of John taking care of everything," Red said.

"The reporters called me, but they had no idea of all the work John was doing to make us look good and make the Trotters look good. The man is a professional doing an outstanding job. I am grateful to him."

During the era of the New York Nationals, which lasted 12 seasons, there were some outstanding highlights. The five-foot-nine inch guard Shawn Faust became the next famous Trotter opponent, known for his shaggy hairdo and hustling play. Faust was also a strong organization man and coached one of the Nationals' units for a period. Doug Stewart, a former star at Brown University played from 1994-1998 and went on to coaching success in college. He is currently Associate Head Coach at Oregon State University under Craig Robinson, the brother of first lady Michelle Obama.

In 2007, the Globetrotters inducted Red into their Legends Ring, the team's version of a Hall of Fame. He joined the ranks of Goose, Curly, Wilt and Abe, and was the first non-Trotter so honored. The award was made at halftime of a game at Temple University's Liacouras Center during the Globies' annual visit to Philadelphia. Surrounded by friends, family members, former teammates and former Globetrotter opponents, Jackson presented the championship-style ring to a beaming Klotz.

Later that year, after Jackson sold the Trotters to Shamrock entertainment, one of the first things new Trotter President Kurt Schneider did was bring back the Washington Generals. "The Generals history is intertwined with the Trotters," he said at the time. "Any recognition (the Generals) get rubbed off on the Trotters."

Red received another major honor in 2009 when the Philadelphia Sportswriters Association named him their "Living Legends Award" winner. Red joined the ranks of such Philly icons as Robin Roberts, Chuck Bednarik and Bernie Parent, among others.

Also in 2009, the Trotters retired Red's number 3 jersey and hoisted it to the rafters of the Wells Fargo Center in Philadelphia. A crowd of about 13,000 (four thousand more than at the Sixers game the previous night) looked on. The fans gave a standing ovation following a video tribute on the scoreboard.

Ex-foes Curly Neal and Govonor Vaughn were there, as was longtime teammate Sam Sawyer. "Nobody is more deserving of this honor," Curly said. "I love this guy and so did the fans," was Vaughn's take. "Of course he deserves it."

The Trotters' announcement again rekindled more of the Hall of Fame talk.

"He definitely belongs in the Hall," former player Marshall Brown said. "He gave of himself and represented the game in a respectful way and always put the game and the Globetrotters ahead of himself."

For reasons unknown, the powers that be at the privately-owned and operated Hall see things differently. His nomination file dates back (at least) to 1977. "Red has been a contributor to the basketball field for a good many years and has done an excellent job in the pro league of his day. Despite his size he was one of the outstanding two handed set shots of his time," wrote the late Hall of Fame coach Red Holzman. "I think more importantly he has been a contributor to basketball in general, being one of the pioneers of the game. His efforts led to an expansion of the game, sale of tickets and promotion of the game he loves. Having known Red a good number of years I can safely say he was always respected and admired for his professionalism. I am sure there are many more accomplishments to be credited to this great basketball man…"

Chris Ford, former Celtics and 76ers coach and the first man in NBA history to hit a three-point shot, put it this way. "The man has dedicated his entire life to the sport. If he's being denied because his teams 'lost' to the Globetrotters, they are missing the point completely. It should be about what he has meant to the game. It should be about how his efforts introduced the game to thousands and thousands of people all over the world."

Combine Red's numbers with the Generals (the Trotters website estimated he has been involved in more than 17,000 games at the time of his legends ring induction) with his pre-Generals resume and it is hard to find anyone in the Hall more qualified: championships in high school, an undefeated college freshman team, championships in two different professional leagues and one of the shortest men to ever play in the NBA, it is hard to deny the case.

Daughter Ronee says a Hall of Fame induction is the last remaining un-done matter of business for her father.

"Many of the people in there are his friends, and he belongs with his friends," she says. "He's more qualified to be there than most people who are already in there."

As far as Red is concerned, he's not losing any sleep over the slight.

"They (the Hall of Fame) are a private group, they are going to do what they want. I can't control it so why worry about it?"

Instead, Red spent his retirement years doing something he hadn't done in a half century: hang out with Gloria on a consistent basis. The man who traveled around the world more than a dozen times now considered his world to be Margate, New Jersey. A walk on the beach, a drive to Jerome Avenue for three-times-a-week pickup games and running local errands became the new extent of his travels.

"Its all out of my system. To me it's a big day to go to (the local supermarket) and then tend to my garden."

That was a bit of an overstatement. Red still wasn't done. In 2004, Margate city officials announced plans to demolish Red's beloved Jerome Avenue courts and replace them with a skateboard park. He mobilized about 60 players and concerned citizens, who inundated the next city council meeting.

"Can you imagine replacing these courts, the greatest game in the world all because of a skateboard park?" Red's comments were met with applause, picked up in local newspapers, and the courts were spared. In 2009 they were resurfaced and new-state-of-the-art goals were installed.

"They really should rename them the Red Klotz Courts," Sam Sawyer said.

One of his recent "hit" performances was an interview on a documentary, "the Team that Changed the World" about the Trotters' history. A youthful Barack Obama appears in the film during his pre-presidential days, as does former Temple coach John Chaney and Hall of Famer Bob Cousy. But it is Red Klotz who steals the show, regaling views with tales of how the Trotters took their own equipment into remote outposts that had been completely unfamiliar with the game.

Red Klotz remains the main face of the Washington Generals. Recently, he received worldwide attention when the Lakers Kobe Bryant, following the fourth loss in five games said "I think we need to schedule the Washington Generals, just so we could get a win."

Ever the promoter on the eve of the 2013 U.S. and world tours, Red told anyone who would listen: "I'd like to play the Lakers and I think we could squeeze them into our schedule before we leave for the tour, if they are up to the challenge."

On a recent spring day, Red takes a visitor to his beachfront home out to his driveway. "Here, let me show you something," he says. Unlike that day in Iran 55 years before, Red knows exactly where the basketballs are. Klotz pops the trunk of his car. Inside are four red, white and blue Globetrotter basketballs and a standard orange one. "Nothing but basketballs in there. You never know when you'll find a game," he says.

With that, Red Klotz reached in and grabbed one of the balls. He dribbled it down the driveway and past the house next door. His neighbors across the street smiled and waved.

The only sounds were those of the ball bouncing on the concrete, the waves breaking on the shore and Red's quiet laugh.

Curly Neal shares the moment
during Red's jersey retirement
ceremony in Philadelphia.

Red watches as his number is raised to the rafters.

Red acknowledges the crowd.

Acknowledgements

This book could never have been written without the extraordinary support and encouragement of the Klotz family.

Red could have chosen anyone to embark upon this project. He boldly took a chance on a first-time author and spent dozens of hours talking, reminiscing, reading each chapter and editing. He opened up his voluminous collection of articles, scorebooks, programs, letters and video. Red demonstrated incredible patience and steadfast willingness to drop everything to answer an obscure question. Red was always beyond generous with his basketball and political wisdom, and his extraordinary good humor. Thanks, Red, for allowing me to tag along to several Globetrotters/Generals training camps, and to sit on the Generals bench during games, and for introducing me to the great Curly Neal. But mostly, thanks Red, for being a great friend and a great inspiration.

Gloria opened her beautiful home and was unflinchingly honest and when needed, tough. She was the call screener who always said "come on over" or "let me get him for you." She always deflected the praise and heaped it on others. Before any business could be conducted, there was a battery of questions about family and friends. To merely say thank you, Gloria, is not enough.

A special nod also goes to Red's eldest child, Ronee Groff, the family historian. Ronee's calls, encouragement, photos, and post card collection proved key. Thanks to her husband Ron and the rest of her family. Red's other children Chuck, Glenn, Kiki, Casey, Jody and their families were wonderful resources throughout this project. Thanks to all of Red's grandchildren, great grandchildren and their families.

Special thanks to Washington Generals General Manager John Ferrari for his wisdom, guidance, grace under pressure, and inside access. Thanks to the Washington Generals players and coaches. Thanks to the Harlem Globetrotters and the Trotters' Public Relations office and staff for their ongoing cooperation.

Sometimes this project seemed insurmountable, and that is when my friends provided the needed encouragement. A most special thank you, Audrey Baumann. And thanks to your "Pops," John Kemenosh, and your entire family, biological and extended. I love you all.

Also Mike and Judi Blume, Chris and Jayne Unger, Ron and Sue Ferguson, Bill and Diane Kehner, John "Mogo" Stanton, Dennis Raible, Steve Pierson, Scott Woodcock, Scott Scragg, Charlie Leary, Ed Hess, Ken Wilson, Bud Howey, Joe Vogel, Jane Evans Walker, Drew Flack, Bill Illgenfritz and John "Sam" Kellmayer.

Three women are in a class of their own as dear friends and supporters: Ann Edmonds, Theresa Triola and Maryann Skedzielewski. Love you all, and thanks to your families.

Thanks to friends Tom and Ed Bell and their families, Jim Donnelly, Harvey Kesselman, Chris Crowley, Joe LoSasso, Art Davis, Stephen Davis, Eileen Conran-Folks, Regina Kinney, Lonnie Folks, King Farris, Bill Houck, Ken Johnson, Amanda Martin, Paul Chambers, Augusta Baudy-Barrett, and Susan Allen.

Other friends offering needed inspiration: Dave Niedbalski, Susan Allen, Julie Bowen, Mark Lenhoff, Mike Hall, Zoltan Orban, Craig Thomas, Steve Gray, Nick Gatto, Bill Eichelberger, Randy Pennell, Mark Stahly, Jerry Siroff, "Brother Bob" Perlman, Dave Slavin, Joe Richards, Rabbi Gordon Geller, Dan Skedzielewski, Bill Preston, Bill Schmidt, Ray Pidge, Mike Dean, Ken Race, Jack Heath, the late Paul Lyons and the late Larry James.

One of my closest friends, the late Jim Skedzielewski, was an early booster of this project and constant source of humor and support. "What would Skedz do?" is a question I often ask when faced with a tough decision.

My brilliant and beautiful mom, Irene Dickey, provided unlimited love, support, and encouragement. Thanks to my daughter Devon and my sisters Kathy, Linda, and Norah, my neices and nephews and their families. Thanks to my late dad George Kelly, Jr. and my late stepdad Bill Dickey for being the men. I love you all.

Each and every person quoted in the book or cited in the book as a source took time for this project and made efforts for which I will always be grateful. Thanks to Sam Sawyer, Fred "Curly" Neal, Governor Vaughn, Charles "Tex" Harrison, Hubert "Geese" Ausbie, Bobby Hunter, Reds Jordan, Paul Favorite, Chris Ford, Don Casey, Doug Stewart, Benny Purscell Father Tim Hirten, the late Gene Hudgins and the late Maje McDonnell. All of these men gave above and beyond the call of duty. Thanks to everyone else I contacted or spoke to regarding this project.

Thanks to mentors Jack Paolin, Frank Guilianelle, Ron Martin, Harvey Melamed, Wayne Richardson, Bob Viggiano, Tom Engelman, the late Vera King Farris and the late Al Mattern. You all have the right stuff and I hope even a little bit rubbed off.

Thanks to Rob Huberman and ComteQ Publishing of Margate, NJ. Thanks to Temple University and its Urban Archives.

Thanks to the Camden *Courier-Post*, and its staff past and present; The Burlington County (NJ) *Times* and its staff past and present; the *Baltimore Sun*, and the *Press of Atlantic City* and its staff past and present. Thanks to the *Philadelphia Daily News* and the *Philadelphia Inquirer*.

Thanks to WMGM TV in Atlantic City, and to Comcast SportsNet in Philadelphia, especially Brad Nau and Amy Fadool. Thanks to NBA.com and NBA TV. Thanks to Matt Neatock as both a friend and a great videographer and recorder of Red's oral history. Thanks to Bill Horin, "Boo" Pergament, Adam Dvorin, Steve Shusterman, and Alison Ward. You all provided invaluable help and encouragement.

Thanks to Ted Silary, Dave Coskey, Harvey Pollock and Rich Westcott. Thanks to Frank Fitzpatrick, Celeste Whittaker, Elaine Rose, Steve Oskie, Diane D'Amico, Sam Carchidi, Kevin Callahan, FRank Deford, Dr. Jack Ramsay, Stan Hochman, Chuck Betson, Bill Campbell, Martha Esposito, Robert Cabnet, Todd Shaner, Dave Wyche, Rick and Dale Goldstein, George Vecsey, Peter Vecsey, Phil Anastasia, and "Mr. Atlantic City" Pinky Kravitz.

Thanks to the Jerome Avenue pickup game gang, especially Lou DeMeis, Fred Lavner and Cindy Loffel. May all your shots find the bottom of the net.

Thanks to Simcha "Sid" Gersh and the Philadelphia Jewish Basketball League Alumni, to Jerry Decker and to Marshall Brown. Thanks to Kelly Moscowitz.

Thanks to Dan Pratt and the Washington Generals Fan Blog. Your research and help took me down the stretch with this project.

Thanks to everyone else I should have mentioned but forgot.

Tim Kelly, September 2013

Notes on Sources

The author worked in concert with Red Klotz on this project from its inception through completion.

Red reviewed, expanded, corrected and approved the manuscript on a chapter-by-chapter basis. It is difficult and in some cases impossible to corroborate every anecdote and factoid contained herein. Most of Red's contemporaries are no longer with us, and reporting of Globetrotters games is spotty. From Red's earliest days on tour, beginning in 1950 and through the late 60s, many box scores and game stories can still be found. By the mid-70s, when the emphasis shifted more heavily towards the "show" aspects of Globetrottters games, documentation is much harder to come by.

"Does that really matter?" Red would say now and again. "I know it happened. I was there!" Unfailingly patient throughout the vast majority of the project, the author's insistence to search for third party verification sometimes peeved him. "It's not like we're making ridiculous claims," he'd say. "Remember, I lost!"

Not only is Red the primary source of information in this book, his archives were the primary research tool. He is in possession of numerous photos, programs, newspaper articles, videotapes, and letters, all of which proved invaluable as this book was developed.

Gloria Klotz is the other main eyewitness to Red's career from high school through present day. Her memories and insights are reflected throughout the narrative.

Red and Gloria's daughter Ronee Groff, the eldest of their six children, is the unofficial family historian whose memories also played a large role. Ronee has a collection of more than 200 post cards sent from all corners of the planet by Red to the family. The collection also includes cards from Abe Saperstein, Dave Zinkoff and several Globetrotters and Generals players. These post cards were essential in placing times and dates on certain stories contained herein. They also provided an intimate glimpse into life on the road on the early Trotters' tours.

Wherever possible, the author has attributed statements and facts gleaned from the articles, videos and written correspondence within the book's narrative. When reference is made to "a newspaper article" without specific attribution, it is something from Red's collection that has been clipped and has no identifying byline or masthead.

Chapter 1: The U.S. State Department's request of Abe Saperstein to visit Iran is attributed to written correspondence from Red Klotz to Gloria. Details about tour stops and dates and the portable basketball court and goals are from Globetrotters publicity materials.

Chapter 2: Background on Eddie Gottlieb is from Rich Westcott's book *The Mogul*.

Chapter 3: Ted Silary of the Philadelphia Daily News contributed information on the history of the Philadelphia City title game. Ted also contributed information on Sam Cozen's and Ziddie Trautwein's high school coaching records and careers. Individual game scores are from the 1939 South Philadelphia High School yearbook.

Chapter 4:Temple University's Urban Archives contributed to this chapter with articles on James Usilton and Brown Prep.

Chapter 6: Rich Westcott's *The Mogul* contributed to this chapter. Additional information came from *Sphas Sparks*, the game day program of the Philadelphia Sphas.

Chapter 7: The article containing details of Chuck Drizen's death on Iwo Jima is from a clipping of unidentified origin. It is thought to be a Philadelphia paper because of the reference to Frankford avenue without mentioning the city.

Chapter 8: Some of the information about Chuck Connors is from the book *The First Tipoff* by Charley Rosen. *The NBA Encyclopedia* also contributed.

Chapter 9: Information gleaned from *The Mogul*, *The NBA Encyclopedia*, *The First Tipoff* and the Temple University Urban Archives contributed to this chapter.

Chapter 10: Buddy Jeannette quotes are from a *Hoop* magazine story and an NBA.com article. The NBA Encyclopedia and Syracuse University's online sports information contributed to this chapter. Additional information was gleaned from the American Professional Basketball Research website.

Chapter 11: The Cumberland, Maryland city website contributed to this chapter. Factual information on the Cumberland Dukes is gleaned from Programs and news clippings provided by Red Klotz.

Chapter 12: Roster information on the College All Americans is from a collection of programs from the World Series of Basketball. Sugar Ray Robinson information is from Globetrotters' program.

Chapter 13: Tour information contained in this chapter is from Globe-trotters programs. The home movie referenced in the chapter can be seen in *The Team that Changed the World* DVD.

Chapter 14: The books *The First Tipoff* and *The Mogul* contributed to this chapter.

Chapter 15 : Rich Westcott and his book, *The Mogul* contributed to this chapter. Programs from the World Series of Basketball provided some of the information for this chapter.

Chapter 16: Information from *They Cleared the Lane* by Ron Thomas, from NBA.com and from the NBA Encyclopedia contributed to this chapter.

Chapter 17: Information from Globetrotters' publicity materials, the University of Kentucky Athletics Department website, and NBA.com contributed to this chapter.

Chapter 18: NBA.com, YouTube.com, *Wilt, 1962* by Gary Pomernantz, *Wilt* by Wilt Chamberlain and David Shaw, and *A View From Above* by Wilt Chamberlain contributed to this chapter.

Chapter 19: Harlem Globetrotters programs and publicity materials contributed information to this chapter.

Chapter 20: *Spinning the Globe* by Ben Green provided some information contained in this chapter. Other information came from Globe-trotters programs and publicity materials.

Chapter 21: Globetrotters programs contributed to this chapter.

Chapter 22: Globetrotters programs, publicity materials and *Loose Balls* by Terry Pluto provided information in this chapter.

Chapter 23: *Trust Your Next Shot, A Guide to a Life of Joy* by Mead-owlark Lemon, The Weakley County (Tennessee) Press and University of Tennessee Martin website and Sports Information office contributed to this chapter.

Chapter 24: Dan Pratt and the Washington Generals Fan Blog, NBA.com and the NBA Encyclopedia

Chapter 25: Old Dominion Sports Information, NBA.com and *The Press of Atlantic City* contributed.